CHILD CARE:

FACING THE HARD CHOICES

CHILD CARE: FACING THE HARD CHOICES

ALFRED J. KAHN

SHEILA B. KAMERMAN

Columbia University School of Social Work

 *Auburn House Publishing Company*
Dover, Massachusetts

Library of Congress Cataloging in Publication Data

Kahn, Alfred J., 1919–
    Child care.

    Includes index.
    1. Child care services—United States.   2. Child
care services—Government policy—United States.
I. Kamerman, Sheila B.   II. Title.
HQ778.7.U6K34   1987   362.7'0973   86–28710
ISBN 0–86569–164–9

Printed in the United States of America

PREFACE

This book is not intended to help a parent select a child care placement for a child. Nor will it guide a potential provider in launching or operating a program. We have another audience in mind: those public officials, interested citizens, advocates, and academics who frame the policy debate and engage the choices. This is a book about shaping American child care services for the future.

Many desirable things have been occurring in some cities and states. There are large numbers of competent and dedicated child care workers and program directors to be encountered. Some advocates, public officials, and legislators have been imaginative and experimental. Nonetheless, federal government retreats and dismantling in this field have left serious resource shortages and leadership gaps which are not yet overcome.

Thus, at a time of expanded need for child care, there are major lacks and uncertainties. There are calls, on the one side, for planning, leadership, administration, and new resources—and, on the other, for encouraging the voluntary sector and the political-economic marketplace to take on this issue and deal with it. The analyst must ask what can be expected and what will work.

This book explores these issues, reviews what is happening, what the choices are—and, then, suggests a perspective.

We are obviously in the debt of many child care people in both the social welfare and the educational streams—in Washington, in those localities and states which we studied in some detail, and in various professional and scientific organizations. We are especially grateful to those who permitted us to visit, to observe, to hear their opinions, and to make up our own minds. Helen Blank of the Children's Defense Fund, the best-informed of observers, generously shared data from her ongoing monitoring of the states and gave valued advice about an earlier draft of our entire manuscript.

Once again we are in the debt of the Carnegie Corporation, and particularly Barbara Finberg, for funding the research and writing out of belief in knowledge-based policy.

Sheila B. Kamerman worked on the book while in residence at

the Center for Advanced Study in the Behavioral Sciences at Stanford, California, and expresses her appreciation to the Foundation's Fund for Research in Psychiatry for financial support during that year, and to the Center for the very special, all-pervasive support it provided.

Zandra Jones coped with all stages of the manuscript with her usual intelligence, competence, and good spirits.

It will be understood that we alone are responsible for the analysis and conclusions.

A. J. K. AND S. B. K.
COLUMBIA UNIVERSITY
September 1986

CONTENTS

LIST OF TABLES

Chapter 1

CHILD CARE: NUMBERS, TRENDS, AND ISSUES

The child care field in the United States is in the midst of major development and change:

- Care outside of the home by nonrelatives is an increasingly common experience for infants, toddlers, and preschoolers generally.
- The caregiving field has become a large nonprofit and for-profit enterprise.
- There is strong evidence that the demand for child care will continue to grow.
- The national government has resisted any overall policy or program in this domain.
- Reagan administration policies have sought major changes that might be summarized as decentralization, deregulation, and privatization.

This book is about what happened to the child care service field as a consequence of demographic and other societal developments and of the changes in federal policies carried out under the Reagan administration during the first half of the 1980s, and what the implications are for those concerned with these services. More specifically, the focus is on what has occurred or is occurring "on the ground"—in states and in localities—and on lessons for the future.

States and local communities are now the arena for policy and planning in the child care field, just as the federal government was a decade ago. It is in this context that we direct our message to those in communities everywhere and to those who are associated with state and local government and concerned with these issues. More specifically, we address those individuals concerned with

1

increasing the availability of child care services, those who need and want to use them, those desirous of expanding access to these services regardless of parents' ability to pay, those who strive to improve the quality of care provided, and those who quite understandably and appropriately want to get the "best buy" for their public child care dollars.

Child care services, in a sense, are big business in the United States today. The fourth largest expenditure for families with children, after food, housing, and taxes, child care services constitute about a $20 billion industry annually. Yet remarkably little is known about the services, the producers, the financing, and even the consumers of different types of services. Child care is a highly diversified field that includes everything from a publicly owned national chain with more than 1000 centers in 40 states and income of about $200 million in 1985 to a "mom and pop" owned "playschool," a university-based experimental child development center, a public school kindergarten, and the woman down the street who takes care of her neighbor's 2-year-old along with her own new infant.

Participation in a child care program is an increasingly common experience for young children. A growing number of children attend some form of child care, whether or not their mothers are in the labor force, because parents and child development experts increasingly view these programs as important for children's optimal development. Furthermore, almost all children, including most preschool-aged children, are likely to grow up with working mothers and therefore to be cared for in some out-of-home child care arrangement.

Unlike many other major industrialized countries, the United States has no national child care program. In 1971 President Richard M. Nixon rejected efforts to launch an ambitious federal program despite congressional support for it.[1] Nevertheless, throughout the 1970s the numbers and types of child care services experienced continued growth. Federal child care policy encouraged a modest expansion of the supply by providing subsidies to providers of care to children from low-income families. And the federal government encouraged improvement in the quality of services through support of research designed to identify the components of quality and through a requirement (which was never, in fact, implemented) that child care providers receiving federal funds meet at least some minimum standards. In the course of the 1970s child care services made the transition from a protective, treatment, or remedial service for poor children or children in troubled families to a service for average children—for the increasingly large numbers of children from all economic classes whose mothers were in the labor force.

By 1980 it was clear that, despite stagflation, women were continuing to enter and remain in the labor force, and that the child care service field would need to expand further and in different ways to respond to their needs. In addition, new research on how children develop and learn was leading some parents to seek out programs for children that would enhance their development, while others sought to compensate for early deprivation.

The 1980s also brought some very different developments. Beginning in 1981 the Reagan administration launched some major changes in federal policies toward child care. The administration approached this "social service" in the same way it handled all social programs for the non-aged—that is, it emphasized reduction of the role and responsibilities of the federal government in setting child care policy, in providing child care services, in funding child care programs, and in regulating these programs. *Decentralization, privatization,* and *deregulation* became the guiding principles in federal child care policy in the 1980s.

Responsibility for child care policy, increasingly defined as federal in the 1970s, has now shifted to the states. Federally defined minimum standards have been eliminated. And in a variety of ways the market has been encouraged to pick up a larger share of the task of delivering child care services—but not if these services can be supplied by the informal family or neighborhood system.

There is urgent reason to inquire whether all of these developments are responsive to the circumstances and needs of families and their children. Is there enough service? Is it good service? Is access ensured? What is likely to be the situation in coming years? The evolving picture is described in later chapters. We begin here with a look at the supply. How much child care is there? Of what kinds?

Child Care Services: The Supply

In discussing child care services we include family day care homes and group homes; day care centers; public and private nursery schools, prekindergartens, and kindergartens; Head Start programs; part-day and full-day programs; before- and after-school programs. We do not include relative care or occasional baby sitting; nor, although one could argue otherwise, do we include nonrelative care provided within a child's own home. Nor do we address here the important but special issue of child care for children with special needs.

Data on the supply of these services are largely inadequate because of the diversity of programs and auspices, the lack of systematic collection of information at the national level, and the decline in reporting requirements of federal legislation. To obtain a picture of what services and how many child care places or "slots" are available requires piecing together different, sometimes not fully comparable numbers collected by different sources at different times.

The most recent national survey of day care centers was completed by Abt Associates in 1977.[2] The numbers have grown substantially since then, as reported in the following paragraphs. In any case, these data constituted an undercount because they did not include programs under educational auspices, such as nursery schools, prekindergartens, and kindergartens. Such programs were the largest category of child care service for the 3- to 5-year-olds in the mid-1970s, and they have continued to expand during the current decade.

In general, over the last decade the supply of programs serving preschool children aged 3 to 5 has grown significantly. All states now provide kindergarten. Half the states require all their school districts to offer kindergarten, and five states actually mandate kindergarten for all 5-year-olds (depending on when they become 5).[3] No state provides prekindergarten programs for all 4-year-olds, but clearly development is beginning in this direction. Agencies in 15 states and the District of Columbia were funding prekindergarten programs for 4-year-olds in the public schools in 1985 or planned new programs for the 1985–1986 year.[4] Three more states were considering new initiatives in early childhood education. At present, all these public programs for 4-year-olds are directed toward high-risk, vulnerable, or deprived children from either poor families or non–English-speaking families or children otherwise at risk of problems or failure in the primary grades; and most programs are part-day rather than full-day. There is some movement toward more universal coverage, however. Private nursery schools have also expanded significantly over the last decade, just about doubling in enrollment of 3- and 4-year-olds since 1970.

Head Start, the comprehensive early childhood education program for low-income preschool children established during the mid-1960s, continues as the only federally funded child care program with strong popular and congressional support and steadily rising funding. Approximately 1200 regular centers across the country serve children between the ages of 3 and 5, but primarily those 3 to 4 years old. The goal of Head Start is to bridge the gap in early childhood development that is thought to exist between poor children and their economically more advantaged peers, so that they can begin their formal education on a more equal basis. In addition, under the Head Start rubric are another 150 programs, including 15 programs serving the preschoolers of migrant working families, 95 programs for Native Americans, and 30 parent/child centers that provide services to children from infancy to age 3 and to their parents and older siblings.[5]

Day care centers have increased in number dramatically over the last decade. According to the Abt study, approximately 18,300 centers existed in 1977. In contrast, the National Association for the Education of Young Children (NAEYC) and the Children's Defense Fund (CDF) reported a total of 61,079 licensed centers in mid-1985, based on a survey of state licensing offices in July 1985.[6] This is an increase of 234 percent in less than a decade, if the surveys counted the same types of programs. Experts agree that center capacity has at least doubled.

Finally, to complete the picture of what services are available, licensed and registered child care and group homes (family day care homes) increased from the 115,000 reported in the Abt survey to 167,000 according to the NAEYC/CDF study, an increase of 45 percent during the same period. Given that licensed and registered homes are variously estimated to constitute between 10 and 40 percent of all family day care homes, we can assume that there are more than one million such homes, counting both formal and informal care—probably not very different from the supply that existed a decade ago.

Estimating the numbers of places these programs make available requires a similar exercise. As Table 1.1 shows, of the 10.6 million children aged 3 to 5, 5.8 million are enrolled in public and private schools and preschools.[7] We can assume, therefore, that at least this number of places are available in school settings. This figure includes places for more than 90 percent of the 5-year-olds, almost half of the 4-year-olds, and more than a quarter of the 3-year-olds. Head Start has about 450,000 places in programs serving low-income children, overwhelmingly those aged 3 and 4. These children constitute about 6 percent of all 3- and 4-year-olds (and about 18 percent of the estimated 2.5 million poor and deprived children eligible for the program). Approximately 3.3 million slots are provided by the more than 61,000 day care centers located around the country, most for 3- to 4-year-olds and about 10 percent for 5-year-olds.[8] Thus about 2.4 million places exist for 3- to 4-year-

Table 1.1   **Child Care Arrangements in 1984 for Children Aged 3 to 5**
             (numbers in millions)

	In Pre and Primary School[a]		In Day Care Centers[b]	In Family Day Care[c]
	Total Enrolled	Enrolled Full Day		
Total 3–5				
10.6	5.8	2.2	2.7	1.3
Age 5				
3.4	3.2	1.3	d	.3
Age 3–4				
7.2	2.6	.9	2.4	1.0
Age 4				
3.6	1.6	.5	d	d
Age 3				
3.6	1.0	.4	d	d

[a]Unpublished data on preprimary school enrollment and data on primary school enrollment provided by Audrey Pendleton, U.S. Department of Education.
[b]Estimates by authors.
[c]These are all children of working mothers. No basis is available to estimate others. We estimate total family day care supply as a bit over 5 million and find that, covering children to age 13, most of the supply is used by children of working mothers.
[d]The data do not permit a breakdown by single year of age.

olds in day care centers and Head Start and at least another 300,000 for the 5-year-olds.

These data suggest that just about all 5-year-olds are now in a group program, overwhelmingly school-based, for at least some part of the day. Similarly, out of a cohort of 7.2 million 3- to 4-year-olds, approximately two-thirds participate in a group program for at least some part of the day; about half are in a school-based program and half in a day care center. The big problem with the preprimary school places is that many are part-day, and many, especially those for the 3- and 4-year-olds, are likely to be private and thus inaccessible to those very young children in low- and moderate-income families.

No national data are available on child care places for infants and toddlers. Data on group facilities serving these very young children are limited, and data on family day care arrangements, the primary source of out-of-home care for infants and toddlers, are soft at best, as we have just seen. Family day care homes are estimated to provide more than five million places, although the exact number is unknown; many are used before and after school, including preschool and kindergarten, for school-aged children.

Moreover, national data on before- and after-school group programs specifically for school-aged children are also lacking.

Assessing the Demand: The Situation of Children with Working Mothers

Approximately half the children under age 6, including infants and toddlers, have mothers in the work force. Existing consumer studies confirm the picture just presented of child care arrangements.

Infants and toddlers are still cared for extensively by relatives, but this is no longer the dominant form of care.[9] The major form of child care for infants and toddlers with working mothers is family day care, with about 40 percent cared for in this way.[10] Of particular interest is the significant increase in the use of group care between 1977 and 1982 for the babies of full-time working mothers, from 11 to 16 percent in just five years. Moreover, preschoolers aged 3 to 4 are increasingly likely to be in group programs. The consumer perspective underscores the continued importance of family day care, especially for infants and toddlers and as a supplement for children in part-day preprimary and primary school programs. For preschoolers, group care is most important, with almost all 5-year-olds in kindergarten and almost half the 3- and 4-year-olds in need of care in school-based programs, largely part-day and private and the other half in some type of day care center. Relative care continues to be important, especially for infants and toddlers and to supplement school and school-based programs, but it is on the wane for children of all ages.

We look briefly, but in more detail now, at the age-group cohorts: 3- to 5-year-olds, infants and toddlers, and school-aged children. Finally, we address the work force participation of mothers as an ongoing dynamic factor in this field.

Children 3 to 5 Years Old

Fifty-four percent of children aged 3 to 5 had mothers who were in the labor force in 1986, most working full-time. Of these children almost 60 percent, overwhelmingly the 5-year-olds, were enrolled in preprimary (and primary) school programs in 1985 (see Table 1.2). Close to half of the total group enrolled were in full-day (school-day) programs. Neither the enrollment rates for the 5-year-olds (94 percent) nor the proportion in full-day programs (39

Table 1.2   Children Aged 3 to 5 with Working Mothers, March 1985
(numbers in millions)

	In Pre and Primary School[a]		In Day Care Centers[b]	In Family Day Care[c]
	Total Enrolled	Enrolled Full Day		
Total 3–5				
5.4	3.0	1.4	2.7	1.3
Age 5				
1.8	1.5	.7	.3	.3
Age 3–4				
3.7	1.5	.7	2.4	1.0
Age 4				
1.8	.9	.4	d	d
Age 3				
1.8	.6	.3	d	d

[a]Unpublished data on preprimary school enrollment and data on primary school enrollment provided by Audrey Pendleton, U.S. Department of Education.
[b]Estimates by authors.
[c]These are all children of working mothers. No basis is available to estimate others. We estimate total family day care supply as a bit over 5 million and find that, covering children to age 13, most of the supply is used by children of working mothers.
[d]The data do not permit a breakdown by single year of age.

percent) varied by the labor force status of their mothers. Nor did the rates vary by family income or by mothers' education, two powerful factors that often influence the type and amount of child care used.

In effect, preschool for 5-year-olds has become universal. It is the rare child of this age who is not in a preprimary (kindergarten) or primary school program of some sort for at least part of the day. And a growing number are participating in full-day (school) programs. For many of these children the child care requirement now is for care in the hours between the closing of these programs at the end of the school day and the end of the parental work day or to cover the days when schools are closed but mothers' jobs are not.

The pattern for 4-year-olds seems to be in transition. Overall enrollment rates in these programs increase only slightly for this age group with working mothers, to just about half of all 4-year-olds, but full-day, rather than part-time, participation triples if mothers work. Moreover, enrollment rates are dramatically higher for 4-year-olds whose families have incomes over $35,000 annually (67 percent) and even higher for those whose mothers are college graduates (70 percent).

For the 3-year-olds all these factors make an enormous difference in enrollment in these programs: mother's employment status, family income, as well as mother's education. Having a working mother increases the likelihood of a 3-year-old being in a preprimary program by about 55 percent, from 22 percent for those whose mothers are at home to 34 percent for those whose mothers are employed; full-day participation quadruples for those with working mothers. More than half of 3-year-olds whose mothers are college graduates are enrolled (52 percent), as are more than half of those in families with high incomes (54 percent).

Interestingly, ethnicity, but not race, also makes a difference in enrollment patterns. Black and white children participate in very similar proportions, but not Hispanic children. Thus, for example, 52 percent of white children and 51 percent of black children of this age are in preprimary programs, in comparison to only 42 percent of Hispanic children.

In effect, the demand for child care in the 1980s for children aged 3 to 5 is now driven by two factors that are often intertwined: the growth in the labor force participation rates of women with young children and the changed attitudes toward children's patterns of early socialization. After almost doubling in the 1970s, the numbers of 3- to 5-year olds enrolled in preprimary school programs increased by about 14 percent between 1980 and 1984. Since the cohort grew as well, the percentage enrolled remained about the same as in 1980. However, the numbers of day care centers increased also, more than doubling from the mid-1970s to the mid-1980s. These centers now serve 3- to 4-year-olds primarily. They also have been the locus of a large growth in child care supply. It is here we seem to see evidence of the rise in the numbers of proprietary programs, an increasingly large component, perhaps half,of the day care center delivery system.

Infants and Toddlers

Forty-nine percent of the children under age 3, including half of those in two-parent families, had working mothers in 1986, and most of these mothers worked full time. Who cared for these children?

There is no one completely satisfactory source of national information on consumer patterns of child care use. The two major sources, the Census Bureau's Current Population Survey (CPS) and the National Survey of Family Growth (NSFG), do not agree on care arrangement patterns of infants and toddlers. For 1982, the last year for which there are such national data, the CPS found a higher use of relative care than of family day care, whereas the

NSFG found the reverse. Both agree, however, that these are the two major forms of care for very young children, and both acknowledge that group care is growing in use. In effect, relatives and family day care providers constitute the major child care arrangements, each serving about 40 percent of children under 3 with working mothers; there has been only a slight decline in the proportion served in these two types of arrangements since 1977. About 12 percent are in group care and this proportion is growing (Table 1.3).

School-Aged Children

The data on the child care arrangements for school-aged children after school or when schools are closed are very inadequate. Clearly, for the younger children, those aged 6 to 8, relative care and family day care predominate. Family day care for this age group is by far the most important form of out-of-home, nonrelative care, serving more than one-third of these children with working mothers in 1982. Of some interest, the overall pattern of care for school-aged children varies very little regardless if mothers are working.

We conclude our overview of demand with a brief look at the major factor driving these developments, the growth in the labor force participation rates of women with young children.

Mothers in the Work Force

Unquestionably, it is the growth in female labor force participation rates that has been—and still is—driving the developments in the

Table 1.3   Child Care Arrangements in 1982 for Children Under Age 3 with Working Mothers

	CPS		NSFG	
	% Under Age 1	% Ages 1–2	% Under Age 1	% Ages 1–2
Relative care	49.3	40.3	40.4	36.6
Nonrelative care	50.7	59.6	60.6	62.4
In home	9.4	8.5	13.5	10.8
Family day care	33.6	34.9	40.4	37.6
Group program	7.7	16.2	6.7	14.0

SOURCES: Current Population Survey (CPS) and National Survey of Family Growth (NSFG), as reported by Hofferth and Phillips. See Chapter 1, endnote 9. For supply estimates for family day care, see Chapter 7.

child care field (see Tables 1.4, 1.5, 1.6, and 1.7). Other social and cultural factors are also at work, particularly regarding the increased use of preschool programs, but the major catalyst has been the growth in the proportion of women with young children who are in the work force. These rates are expected to remain high; indeed, they are expected to increase still more.

Labor force participation rates for women rose from 43 percent in 1970 to 55 percent in 1986. At the same time, however, labor force participation rates of mothers (women with children under 18) increased from 42 percent to 63 percent, and for married mothers, from 40 percent to 61 percent. More than 70 percent of the mothers of school-aged children are now in the work force.

Table 1.4   Percentage of Mothers with Children Under Age 6, in the Labor Force in March 1980 and March 1986, by Marital Status

	Percentage in the Labor Force	
Marital Status of Mother	*1980*	*1986*
All mothers with children under age 6	47	54
Married mothers, husband present	45	54
Women heading families alone	55	59
All mothers with children under age 3	42	51
Married mothers, husband present	41	51
Women heading families alone	45	49

SOURCE: U.S. Department of Labor, Bureau of Labor Statistics, "Half of Mothers with Children Under 3 Now in Labor Force," *NEWS*, August 20, 1986.

Table 1.5   Labor Force Participation Rates of Wives, Husband Present, by Age of Youngest Child Under 6, March of Selected Years 1970–1986

	Labor Force Participation Rate				
Presence and Age of Child	*1970*	*1975*	*1980*	*1985*	*1986*
Wives, total	40.8	44.5	50.2	54.3	54.6
No children under 18	42.2	44.0	46.0	48.2	48.2
With children under 18	39.8	44.9	54.3	61.0	61.3
With children under 6, total	30.3	36.8	45.3	53.7	53.8
With children under 3, total	25.8	32.6	41.5	50.7	50.9
3 to 5 years total	36.9	42.2	51.7	58.6	58.6
With children age 2 years	30.5	37.1	48.1	54.0	54.3
With children under age 1	24.0	30.8	39.0	49.4	49.8

SOURCE: Adapted from Howard Hayghe, "Rise in Mothers' Labor Force Activity Includes Those with Infants," *Monthly Labor Review*, Vol. 109, No. 2, February 1986. Updated.

Table 1.6   Number and Percentage of Children Under Age 6 by Type of Family and Labor Force Status of Mother, March 1980 and March 1986

	1980		1986	
Labor Force Status of Mothers	Number*	Percentage	Number*	Percentage
Total Children Under 6	17,741	100	19,392	100
Mother in labor force	7,703	43	9,974	51
In married couple families	15,123	100	16,167	100
Mother in labor force	6,385	42	8,241	51
In families maintained by women	2,620	100	3,226	100
Mother in labor force	1,317	50	1,733	54
Total Children Under 3	8,979	100	9,528	100
Mother in labor force	3,597	40	4,680	49
In married couple families	7,871	100	8,166	100
Mother in labor force	3,125	40	4,028	50
In families maintained by women	1,108	100	1,362	100
Mother in labor force	472	43	652	48

SOURCE: U.S. Department of Labor, Bureau of Labor Statistics, "Half of Mothers with Children Under 3 Now in Labor Force," *NEWS*, August 20, 1986.
*Numbers in thousands.

More dramatic, the percentage of married women with children under age 6 and in the labor force increased from 30 percent in 1970 to 54 percent in 1986, and for those with children under age 3, from 22 percent to 51 percent. Indeed, just since 1980 labor force participation rates for married mothers have increased by 13 percent, from 54 to 61 percent: The rates for married women with children under age 6 have increased by almost 20 percent, from 45 percent to 54 percent; and for women with children under 3, the rates have increased by 25 percent, from 41 to 51 percent, in just six years! These trends are startling, necessitating the re-estimatation of earlier projections for female labor force participation in the 1990s. They also revise the conventional picture of the working mother as single, divorced, separated, or never married. Increasingly, the working mother, especially the mother with a preschool-aged child, is a married woman living with her husband.

Dr. Sandra Hofferth, a demographer, recently revised her earlier projections and now estimates that by the mid-1990s two-thirds of women with preschool-aged children and three-quarters with school-aged children will be in the work force. Rates for white

Table 1.7   **Women Who Had a Child in the Last Year and the Percentage Who Were in the Labor Force: 1976 and 1980 to 1985 (numbers in thousands)**

Age of Women and Survey Year	Number of Women	Percent in Labor Force
18 to 44 years old		
1985	3,497	48.4
1984	3,311	46.7
1983	3,625	43.1
1982	3,433	43.9
1981	3,381	41.7
1980	3,247	38.0
1976	2,797	30.9
18 to 29 years old		
1985	2,512	47.9
1984	2,375	44.5
1983	2,682	42.4
1982	2,445	42.5
1981	2,499	40.2
1980	2,476	38.2
1976	2,220	31.8
30 to 44 years old		
1985	984	49.6
1984	936	52.2
1983	942	45.1
1982	888	47.5
1981	881	46.2
1980	770	37.3
1976	577	27.6

SOURCE: June Current Population Surveys of 1976, and 1980 to 1985.

mothers working will be the same as or higher than rates for black mothers, and rates for married mothers will be the same as or higher than those for single mothers. In effect, by the end of the decade, most children from the age of 1 (if not younger) will have working mothers.

While cautioning readers once again that both supply and demand data are currently in some ways unsatisfactory, we offer the following summary of the mid-1986 supply-demand picture from a national perspective. Licensed or registered infant/toddler care remains in short supply in most parts of the country. Relative care remains important but is declining in use. Family day care predominates, with group care becoming more important than previously, especially for toddlers. Parents continue to complain about shortages, and most requests for help in finding care are for this age group. The supply of services for 3- to 5-year olds appears to be quantitatively adequate. However, much of what is available is still only part-day, as parents seek full-day care and as many preschool programs, both full- and part-day, are more expensive than most parents can afford. Few of the preschools are free public services. After-school programs are in short supply and parents appear to have difficulty in locating them, assessing their quality, as well as affording those that seem desirable. Finally, we note that the situation varies significantly across localities.

New Findings, Different Attitudes, and Changing Patterns of Child Socialization

For many years, proponents of expanded child care provision have been faced by critics who claimed that out-of-home care would fundamentally impair children's "attachments" to their mothers, expose them to debilitating infections, or "communalize" their development experiences. These were the terms of the debate in the 1960s and 1970s, having replaced the fears of the 1950s that child care exposure would lead to the abnormal withdrawal and unrelatedness, which John Bowlby and others had found among orphans reared completely in institutional environments after World War II, lacking any connection with parents at all.[11]

The "institutionalism" fears clearly were unfounded, having no established relevance to children living at home. The other concerns, separated from their ideological and advocacy emotionalisms, have merited serious scientific attention. Does child care attendance impair "attachment" or other aspects of normal interpersonal development? Does it exact a price in socialization? Does it expose children to health dangers?

Inevitably, the research commitment is made in a broader social context. The inappropriate citations of the Bowlby research and the strong concern about attachment came in an era in which women were expected to have returned to the home from their World War II labor force excursion; the era of the baby boom and the suburban explosion of family life called for at-home mothers. The strongest of available "evidence" against out-of-home care would be made visible.

Similarly, the accelerated rates of labor force entry of women, including mothers of very young children, and the great pressure to find out-of-home care for children would compel more extensive study of the questions creating doubt. At the same time, alleged advantages of early child care also would be more specifically identified and added to the research agenda, as would evidence as to the efficacy of strategies to increase "opportunity" for minority children, as adopted in the 1960s. Thus investigators would now report on cognitive gains and socialization—and especially on whether the life chances of deprived children were being improved and their long-term costs to society as troubled or troublesome adolescents and adults diminished.

Several other developments that have changed the home environment radically also have had major impact. Not only are both parents out of the home during the day in a majority of families but in addition, families are much smaller. Some children have no siblings at all; many more have only one. Few children are in large families in which the family group is in itself a rich environment for interpersonal socialization. The small family size, and the fact that the children of neighbors increasingly are in two-earner families and thus likely to be in care outside their homes, means that many children cannot readily assemble a play group at home.

Parents have responded to all these changes with increased interest in preschool or day care for their children. During the past decade many parents have become convinced, out of their own experiences and from reading about research, that children can begin to learn in the preschool years. Many public figures have encouraged such learning as desirable to strengthen the future labor force in the international competition. Thus the need for care of children while both parents work, the desire to offer them socialization experiences in the preschool years, and the belief that children can and should begin to learn at earlier ages have combined to create new interest in all kinds of preschool programs and elevated new research questions to the scientific agenda.

Now available are a small library of volumes and an impressive collection of research reports and research reviews on these matters in professional journals. Except among extreme ideologues who are determined somehow to restore the traditional family with an at-home mother, there is also a measure of consensus as to what the results say. Here we offer a summary of major generalizations that inform much of the popular child development literature now read by young parents and, in turn, influencing them:[12]

- Babies and young children can form emotionally important

attachments to several people, including caretakers, which may differ in intensity but not in kind from what is usually experienced with their mother. Separation anxiety is successfully dealt with as these other relationships are carefully and gradually introduced. The development of a relationship with other caretakers does not impair children's relationships with their mother.

- There is no credible evidence that good child care programs are harmful to children's parental attachments, intellectual development, or general growth. ("Good" programs are those that have small groups, high proportions of staff to children, and well-trained caregivers.)

- Children who participate in group child care programs tend to be somewhat different from those who do not. They may show more independence, be more sociable and/or competitive, and be boisterous and aggressive with peers. The response to such findings varies with one's behavioral expectations and preferences for children—in short, one's value system. These tendencies in children who have participated in center programs and preschools may be read by some as a departure from appropriate childhood and by many others as the development of desirable social skills for coping in the current world.

- Well-run day care centers and preschool programs accelerate and improve the cognitive development and socialization of children from deprived backgrounds. The largest impacts are by way of helping needy children catch up. The length of exposure and program quality are associated with extent and duration of impact. Not all gains are sustained. Some enriched programs show long-term effects on such problems as delinquency, school drop-outs, or the need for remedial aid and special help. Families of pupils in Head Start and related programs gain access to useful services and benefits as well. The Perry Preschool Program, which was not typical, was able to report, in a longitudinal study, the association of participation with less use of public assistance, more high school graduation, less teenage pregnancy, higher rates of employment, and positive cost-benefit ratios.

- Children from average, typical backgrounds have not been shown to consistently accelerate their learning or to achieve the other sustained positive gains found in deprived children as a result of preschool experience. Regardless, many parents, educators, and public officials are convinced that schooling should begin before age 6.

- The group exposure in child care speeds up the process whereby children contract the common childhood diseases, but it does not cause negative long-run health consequences. Infant and toddler centers pose some special health hazards, of which infectious hepatitis is the most prominent in centers that do not conform to standard public health practices. (The problems may be more severe for staff than for children.) Such potential problems are readily overcome by good standards, education, and enforcement.

- Since most family day care takes place in an unobserved underground, no overall generalizations about impact are possible. As described in Chapter 7, controlled comparative research in agency- or system-related family day care shows that family day care for very young children may be said to have some advantages and center care other advantages, since the experiences are different for the children involved.

- While not prepared to claim that there is irrefutable research evidence or that experts all agree, Belsky, a widely respected child development researcher, has recently cited grounds for some concern about the placement of infants under one year of age in centers. Proponents of parental leave legislation, which would decrease the pressure to place infants under 4 to 6 months of age in such care, have argued that Belsky's reservations buttress the case for ensuring parents and children enough time to launch their relationships before a child is placed in out-of-home care. This requires both the legal right to a job-protected leave and adequate income replacement.[13]

To summarize, child care has emerged as an increasingly visible issue on the public agenda due to many developments: a high and still growing rate of female labor force participation, with the result that almost two-thirds of all school-aged children and half the preschoolers have working mothers; the likelihood that almost all children will experience growing up with a working mother by the 1990s; the growing conviction that a group experience is good for children; the increase in the supply and diversity of child care services; the continued gap between demand and supply; and the continued debate about the definition, and importance, of quality. These developments underscore the need to assess the child care field's prospects and policies at this time, in particular in the context of the Reagan administration's policies and how they have affected an emerging and poorly conceptualized service domain or "industry," depending on one's perspective.

The End of an Era

Child Care in 1980

By 1980 government-financed studies of the supply of child care services were completed, but only "day care" programs had been included; the large numbers of preschool programs were not surveyed. A variety of research studies also had been carried out to clarify the impacts on children of different modes of care (family day care, center care, Head Start) and different staffing ratios and competence levels. Positive findings on the long-term impacts of preschool education were beginning to emerge.

Parents themselves were paying the bulk of child care fees, somewhat supported by the child care (dependent care) tax credit; this tax credit provided about 4 million families with a subsidy of about $1 billion in 1980.[14] Some portion of costs was paid for by the federal government, a smaller portion by state and local governments, and a still smaller part by private philanthropy.

Public money for child care services came from a variety of sources (see Table 1.8); but educational programs aside, most of the available federal funds came from the income-tested Title XX, the social services title of the Social Security Act. About $600 million, 20 percent of the total Title XX expenditure, was spent on child care in 1980.[15] Of the approximately 12 million children in families with less than median incomes in 1981 and potentially eligible for care, only about 472,000 were served in child care programs. Head Start, the other major public program, was essentially meant as a part-day compensatory program to focus on the 3- to 5-year-olds, but was beginning to serve working parents' needs through all-day programs as well. About $766 million in federal funds was spent on Head Start in FY 1980 for about 350,000 children.[16] Budgeted allowances under Title IV-A of the Social Security Act met the needs of some families receiving Aid to Families with Dependent Children (AFDC). A small amount of child welfare service money (Title IV-B) provided day care in instances of needed child protection. Some day care funding went to mothers in "work incentive" (WIN) job training or placement. Compensatory programs in the schools under the Elementary and Secondary Education Act offered care to some children, and there was supplementary support from the federal food programs.[17] The states matched Title XX on a 1 to 3 basis, and some states and localities added their own funds to day care budgets as well.

There was no clarity as to how the very low Title XX eligibility levels and small-scale reimbursement plans in many states could be improved in the context of the stagflation. Yet the supply of

Table 1.8   Federal Expenditures for Child Care, Fiscal Years 1980 and 1986

	Expenditure in Millions of Dollars	
Programs	1980	1986
Title XX (SSBG)	$600[a]	$ 387[a]
Head Start	$766[b]	$1,040
AFDC Disregard (Title IV-A)	$120[c]	$ 35
Child Care Food Program	$239[a]	$ 501[a]
Title IV-C (WIN)	$115[d]	-0-
ARC (Appalachian Regional Commission) Child Dev.	$11[b]	$ 1
Employer Provided Child Care	-0-	$ 110[e]
Dependent Care Tax Credit	$956[a]	$3,410[a]
Total	$2,807	$5,484
Total Without Tax Credit	$1,851	$2,074[f]

[a]ACYF estimate provided by Patricia Divine Hawkins.
[b]Testimony, Jo Ann Gasper, Deputy Assistant Secretary for Social Services, *Child Care: Beginning A National Initiative* (Washington, D.C.: Government Printing Office, 1984).
[c]E. Duval, et al., "AFDC: Characteristics of Recipients in 1979," *Social Security Bulletin*, Vol. 45, No. 4, 4–19.
[d]Congressional Budget Office (CBO).
[e]CBO, Based on Joint Tax Committee estimates.
[f]Since the inflation rate was 31 percent between 1980 and 1985, according to CBO, this total would have had to be $2,425 to sustain the 1980 direct expenditure level.
NOTE: State and local education and social service expenditure not included in table.

child care clearly was inadequate, and standards obviously were low in many places. The latter story—efforts at federal standard setting—which spans 1968–1981, told elsewhere and in detail, need not be repeated here.[18] What is relevant is that the long process of research, data collection, exposure of proposed regulations to public reaction, and delays had finally culminated in a set of federal day care regulations to be effective on July 1, 1981. The states generally had accepted and implemented health and safety standards. Many had moved far along with regard to nutrition and training rules. The difficult areas of staff-child ratios, group size, and staff qualifications remained to be tackled. According to an Office of Human Development Services report published in late 1981, most providers were in compliance with the proposed federal standards, mainly because they had been anticipated for so long.

The 1981 picture with reference to the auspices of most of the centers receiving Title XX funds and the distribution between centers and family day care homes was as follows:

Type of Facility	Number	% of Total
Centers		
For-profit	2,354	(25)
Nonprofit	5,969	(62)
Public	1,215	(13)
Total	10,773a	
Family day care homes	29,329b	

aSome states provide center totals but not distribution by auspice. The actual total for auspices listed is 9538.
bWe are not told how many are proprietary and how many agency sponsored.

Of children funded by Title XX and in centers, some 6 percent were under age 2, 13 percent were age 2, 65 percent were ages 3 to 6. Age data are not available for children in family day care in 1981.[19]

1981–1986: The Reagan Administration—Cutbacks and Changes

Now as before there is no single source of federal funds for child care services. Funding for services is authorized under a variety of federal laws.

Several dramatic Reagan administration initiatives in 1981 changed the child care environment considerably. The Omnibus Budget Reconciliation Act of 1981 (OBRA) amended Title XX of the Social Security Act to create the Social Services Block Grant, cut Title XX's appropriations by one-fifth, and eliminated the separately funded training program from Title XX. The child care food program, which had helped meet center and family day care meal costs, was drastically cut and only raised several years later. CETA's public service employment, which had helped to staff centers, was ended. The child care allowance under AFDC (Title IV-A) was capped at $160 per month, and other restrictions were placed on allowable work expenses for employed AFDC mothers. In effect, direct federal funding for child care services was sharply reduced, and the requirement of a state-match of 25 percent was eliminated, potentially further decreasing available resources. As can be seen in Table 1.8, federal expenditures for child care services in 1980 were approximately $1.851 billion. Adjusting this for inflation, the 1986 figure would have to be $2.425 billion. Direct federal expenditures for 1986 were $2.074 billion, about a 14.5 percent decline in constant dollars.

On the positive side for middle- and upper-income families, there was a modest 1981 increase in the child care (dependent care) tax credit. This dependent care tax credit has emerged in the 1980s as the largest federal program to help families pay for child care (some states have established a similar tax credit). It allows families to deduct between 20 and 30 percent of child care expenses (up to a maximum of $2400 for one child and $4800 for two or more) from their federal income taxes. The lower the family's income the higher the percentage that can be deducted, but all families who qualify regardless of income can deduct at least 20 percent ($480 for one and $960 for two or more children). In 1983 the credit was estimated to be used by more than 6 million families, nearly half of whom had adjusted gross incomes of under $25,000, at a cost of about $2.1 billion. By 1986 this tax benefit was estimated as costing more than $3 billion. This tax credit benefits only those whose income is above the tax threshold established in the 1980s—not the poor or near poor.

A second federal tax provision subsidizes child care expenses as a fringe benefit. Employers may establish a plan whereby a deduction is made from an employee's salary and the money set aside in a special account to be used to pay for child care or other benefits such as health insurance. Although the employee's money is used, the funds are not included in the employee's taxable income. The taxes saved on these and similar plans are estimated to cost about $110 million in foregone revenues. These plans benefit middle- and upper-income families primarily.

The changes in Title XX ended a requirement for visible, accountable state planning and a filing of reports in Washington. They also ended the reporting of expenditure and service statistics. As a result, no one has a really clear picture of what has occurred and what the impact is; at best, there are estimates.

The new Social Services Block Grant legislation (SSBG) canceled the proposed federal day care regulations and left in place the "applicable standards" of state and local laws. Head Start was protected and continued to grow, but the program could serve only a small portion of the technically eligible children and did not, except for about 10 percent of the participating children, cover a full day of service.[20]

The Children's Defense Fund (CDF), through three rounds of telephone inquiries of the states, has reported on the statewide response to the cuts in Title XX and the related changes in the AFDC program as these affected child care services. Reviewing 1981–1983, CDF reported:[21]

- Thirty-two states provided less Title XX child care in 1983 than in 1981, some cutting more than the federal expenditure cutback.
- In a significant number of states (10) there was a decrease in eligibility for low-income working families.
- Some states (20) made eligibility for child care more difficult for low-income mothers in training.
- Many low-earner AFDC mothers were cut from the rolls by the new policy, and in some states they became ineligible for publicly supported day care.
- Some states imposed fees or raised fees for Title XX day care.
- States were compelled to choose between child care for child protection cases and child care for children of working mothers.
- Many states cut child care staffs (32), lowered standards (33), or decreased training programs (24) in order to conserve funds.
- Some states shifted Title XX child care cases to the AFDC child care disregard (IV-A), a less costly and therefore lower-quality alternative.
- Thirty-three states lowered standards and reduced enforcement staff.

In a 1984 follow-up CDF reported that the majority of states held the line on expenditures for child care from 1983 to 1984, but thereafter some states made further cuts. However, 11 states significantly increased child care funding.[22] By 1985, 30 states had increased their child care funding over 1984. At the same time, however, 35 states were still spending less money for child care services funded through the Title XX SSBG than in 1981. Moreover, 22 states spent less for child care in 1985 than in 1981 even without an adjustment for inflation.[23]

By 1986 no general restoration of funding had occurred, and almost all states were behind the 1980 pace, corrected for cost increases. Many had lowered eligibility ceilings for low-income families. Some states simply left reimbursement to providers very low, thus in effect cutting caregiver wages. Still others reduced training expenditures, standards, and the size of their enforcement staff. Some targeted more of their resources for protective service child care, thereby decreasing what is available to working families. Many state initiatives have since developed, particularly with regard to school-based child care, but there has been no recovery in federal and state child care funding through the social service stream in the country as a whole and serious gaps in coverage continue to be widely reported.

Decentralization, Deregulation, and Privatization: Guiding Principles for the 1980s?

The Reagan administration has stressed decentralization, deregulation, and privatization. In the child care field, the administration's actions have been in support of this ideology. The federal government has largely and deliberately abdicated its leadership role. The combination of cutbacks in funding and the elimination of any requirement for the states to match federal funds led to a significant reduction in the availability of money to support child care services directly. A federal "presence" in child care has disappeared. Except for the Head Start program, there is no federal agency with child care responsibility and no child care staff. Title XX funds are passed through to the states, and policy and program decisions are left to them. Some state governments responded positively to the decline in federal funds for child care by increasing state appropriations, but many did not.

In a review of the impact of the Reagan administration's policies on children generally, one study found that the states tended to pick up on "crisis" services but not the services needed for daily living. Kimmich concludes, "States have had to make hard choices about how to respond to changing federal rules and reduced federal financial participation. Program-specific changes made by states are of three types: changes in eligibility, service coverage, and payments."[24] The usual result has been cutbacks in the services provided, restrictions in eligibility to free or subsidized services, and the establishment of fee charges, which in turn still further restrict access to services or direct service delivery to a different, better-off clientele. Child care is illustrative of all this.

With the transformation of Title XX into the Social Services Block Grant, all constraints on how the funds were to be spent and for whom were eliminated. The federal government completely relinquished its role in assuring minimum standards, at least for programs receiving federal subsidies. The elimination (or bypassing) of the former Federal Interagency Day Care Requirements (FIDCR, also termed HEWDCR) left child care providers subject to state standards only. Administration representatives have gone on record as opposing governmental regulation of any sort at any level for child care. Although most child care services would not have been subject to the FIDCR in any case, the federal standards did present some guidelines for the country as to what minimum standards should be. State standards vary enormously regarding which providers are covered and what specifics are required. Many states leave family day care providers subject to no requirements for licensing or registration. Others omit church-sponsored child care services from such requirements, and still others exclude part-day programs. Given the extensive growth in infant and toddler care, many states have especially inadequate standards for this type of care, most not beginning to comply with the proposed FIDCR standards for such care. Finally, even where regulations are imposed, many states have curtailed their enforcement staff and/or reduced the number of inspections carried out. Obviously, without enforcement, the standards are meaningless.

"Privatization" has been an administration "buzzword." Essentially, it has been used to mean a reduction in the role of the government, including a reduction in funding as well as policy-making. The administration has moved substantially in this direction. It has offered explicit support for the market in delivering services and encouragement, including incentives, for the market to do more. Employers have been singled out as an appropriate source of child care sponsorship, and child care has been defined as a tax-free fringe benefit. The federal subsidies that have been supported have been in the form of tax benefits, part of the administration's general support of lower taxes. Barriers have been reduced or eliminated to for-profit providers entering the market. Administration spokespersons have stressed the adequacy of the child care supply by pointing to the large (and unknown) number of informal family day care providers, emphasizing that if regulations were eliminated this supply would increase.[25]

By the early 1980s greater stress on demand side, parent-consumer subsidies, and the absence of regulatory constraints had provided encouragement for an open market to operate and created increased incentives for proprietary organizations to enter the market. The elimination of reporting requirements and the decline in federal data collection make it difficult to obtain a full and reliable national picture. The long-standing problems of access, affordability, and quality were now exacerbated by greater diversity and fragmented child care service delivery systems, more restricted public subsidies, and less monitoring of quality. At the same time, more parents were seeking good experiences for their young children; more working parents needed decent, affordable child care; more reports were highlighting the value of early preparation for school; and more states were exploring child care as part of an employment strategy for low-income mothers instead of welfare.

By the mid-1980s child care services had been transformed: from a protective service to compensatory education and a support service for poor working women (in the 1960s); to a program to enhance early child development and a support service for middle-class working women (in the 1970s); to an essential component of school reform, a universal program for ensuring the good development of children age 3 and older, and also a necessary—even though debated—service for working parents with children under age 3.

By the mid-1980s the media heard and reported regularly proposals for expanding child care or education by creating and financing public prekindergarten for 3- and 4-year-olds, ensuring all-day kindergarten for the 5-year-old, providing more day care centers or better-quality family day care through more adequate funding, and expanding before- and after-school facilities under one of several possible auspices and funding arrangements. Parental leaves emerged as an issue often discussed as an alternative to infant care services. Extensive publicity about employers and what they might provide or fund led to exaggerated expectations of employers as an alternative to government for financial support. In the middle of all this debate was a clearly visible and substantial expansion in the proprietary child care system.

Some or all of these developments may be seen as inconsistent with one another or as alternative claims on scarce energies and resources. Or should they be considered a repertoire of possibilities, a menu of choices, alternative agendas in a political market? Or is the correct imagery a series of building blocks, available for step-by-step incrementalism? The interested public official, citizen leader, local activist, child care administrator will need to develop a point of view. Those concerned must clarify whether they see all these developments as evidence of slow and steady progress or as the potential, competitive components of a desperately needed mid- and long-term plan, state or federal. Our remaining chapters offer the factual and analytic basis for development of a perspective on these strategic questions and some of the substantive specifics.

What did the child care service delivery system actually look like in the mid-1980s? What was the specific impact of the Reagan administration's policies and of the various concomitant changes carried out by the states? What were the choices faced by states, local governments, and communities, and how did they resolve them? We turn now in Chapters 2 and 3 to a picture of what was going on in local communities and in the states and how some "leadership" locales responded to the decentralization and deregulation challenges. We then turn to an in-depth analysis of privatization and child care. In the remainder of the book we look at the special roles of schools, employers, and family day care in the child care service delivery system. The quality question appears at several points. We conclude with a discussion of the hard choices that will have to be made if the goal is to improve and expand the system and to do so at acceptable costs.

Endnotes

1. "Veto Message—Economic Opportunity Amendments of 1971," Message from the President of the United States, S. Doc. 92–48, 92 Cong. 1 sess. (1971), pp. 4, 5.
2. Relevant studies include:

    Abt Associates, *The National Day Care Study* (Cambridge, Mass.: 1979), 5 vols., and an "Executive Summary" prepared for the Administration for Children, Youth, and Families of the Department of Health, Education, and Welfare, Washington, D.C.

    Abt Associates, *National Day Care Home Study*, 5 vols., and "Executive Summary" (Washington, D.C.: Administration for Children, Youth, and Families, 1980). See also, Eileen W. Lindner et al. *When Churches Mind the Children* (Ypsilanti, Mich.: The High/Scope Press, 1983).
3. Margaret Whaley, "The Status of Kindergarten: A Survey of the States" (Springfield, Ill.: Illinois State Board of Education, January 1985).
4. Carolyn Morado, "Prekindergarten Programs for Four Year Olds: State Involvement in Preschool Education," *Young Children*, Vol. 4, No. 6 (September 1986), 69–71.
5. U.S. House of Representatives, Select Committee on Children, Youth and Families, *Families and Child Care: Improving the Options* (Washington, D.C.: U.S. Government Printing Offices, 1984).
6. National Association for the Education of Young Children (NAEYC), "The Child Care Boom" (Washington, D.C.: 1985).
7. This figure is based on unpublished preprimary school data provided by Audrey Pendelton, Center for Statistics, Department of Education, and on school enrollment data. According to these data, about 5.5 million children are enrolled in preprimary school programs and about 260,000 5-year-olds are in first grade.
8. See the 1981 report on Title XX funded day care centers, estimates from Congressional Research Service. In U.S. Department of Health and Human Services, *Report to Congress: Summary Report of the Assessment of Current State Practices in Title XX Funded Day Care Programs, October 1981* (Washington, D.C.: DHSS Publication No. OHDS–81–30331, January 1982), pp. 53, 54. About 55 percent of the children served were 3- to 4-year-olds and about 10 percent were 5-year-olds; the proportion of 5-year-olds may have declined since then.
9. Sandra L. Hofferth and Deborah Phillips, "Working Mothers and the Care of their Children: 1970 to 1995," Table 10, from the National Survey of Family Growth (1986, publication pending).
10. Ibid.

11. John Bowlby, *Material Care and Mental Health* (Geneva: World Health Organization, 1951); and *Attachment and Loss*, Vols. 1, 2 (New York: Basic Books, 1969, 1973). Also, Rene Spitz, "Hospitalism," *Psychoanalytic Study of the Child, Vol. 1* (New York: International Universities Press, 1945), pp. 53–74.

12. See the Silverstein review in our earlier volume, as listed below along with other major sources. (We are not repeating the several comprehensive literature reviews currently available and earlier work listed by us in our previous volume.)

Jay Belsky and Lawrence D. Steinberg, "The Effects of Day Care," and Mary D. S. Ainsworth, "The Development of Infant-Mother Attachment," as well as several other reports in Jay Belsky, ed., *In the Beginning* (New York: Columbia University Press, 1982).

Jay Belsky and L. Steinberg, "The Effects of Day Care: A Critical Review," *Child Development*, Vol. 49 (1978), 929–949.

Jay Belsky, "Infant Day Care: A Cause for Concern?" *Zero to Three*, Bulletin of the National Center for Clinical Infant Programs, Vol. VI, No. 5 (September 1986), pp. 1–7. There is an as-yet-unpublished strong refutation by Deborah Phillips, Kathleen McCartney, Sandra Scarr, and Carollee Howes.

John R. Berrueta-Clement et al., *Changed Lives: The Effects of the Perry Preschool Program on Youths Through Age 19* (Ypsilanti, Mich.: High/Scope Educational Research Foundation, 1984).

Uri Bronfenbrenner, *The Ecology of Human Development* (Cambridge, Mass.: Harvard University Press, 1979).

Alison Clarke-Stewart, *Day Care* (Cambridge, Mass.: Harvard University Press, 1982). Chapter 5 summarizes research on effects and cites major studies up to that time.

Selma Fraiberg, *Every Child's Birthright: In Defense of Mothering* (New York: Basic Books, 1977).

Adele Harrell, *A Review of Head Start Research Since 1970* (Washington, D.C.: Government Printing Office, 1984).

Adele Harrell, *Preliminary Report: The Effect of the Head Start Program on Children's Cognitive Development* (Washington, D.C.: U.S. Government Printing Office, 1984).

R. H. McKey, L. Condelli, I. Ganson, et al., *The Impact of Head Start on Children, Families and Communities* (Washington, D.C.: CSR Inc., 1985).

R. H. McKey, L. Condelli, I. Ganson et al., *Executive Summary* (Washington, D.C.: CSR Inc., 1985).

Jerome Kagan, *The Nature of the Child* (New York: Basic Books, 1984).

Irving Lazar and the Consortium on Developmental Continuity, *The Persistence of Preschool Effects* (Denver, Colo.: Education Commission for the States, 1977).

Ruth Hubbell McKay et al., *The Impact of Head Start on Children*,

Families, and Communities (Washington, D.C.: Prepared by CRS Incorporated and published for the U.S. Department of Health and Human Services by the U.S. Government Printing Office, 1985).

Michael Rutter, *Material Deprivation Reassessed* (London: Penguin, 1982); "Social-emotional Consequences of Day Care for Preschool Children," in E. F. Zigler and E. G. Gordon, eds., *Day Care: Scientific and Policy Issues* (Dover, Mass.: Auburn House, 1982), pp. 3–32.

Sandra Scarr, *Mother Care/Other Care* (New York: Basic Books, 1984), pp. 33–34.

Lawrence J. Schweinhart and David P. Weikart, "What Do We Know So Far? A Review of the Head Start Synthesis Project," in *Young Children*, Vol. 41, No. 2 (January 1986), 49–55. Also, see author response in Vol. 41, No. 3 (March 1986), 20.

Louise Silverstein, "A Critical Review of Current Research on Infant Day Care," in Sheila B. Kamerman and Alfred J. Kahn, *Child Care, Family Benefits, and Working Parents* (New York: Columbia University Press, 1981), pp. 265–315.

Jeffrey Travers et al., *Research Results of the National Day Care Study*, Vol. II of the Final Report of the National Day Care Study (Cambridge, Mass.: Abt Associates, 1980).

13. See *Parental and Disability Leave*, Report of Joint Hearing before two subcommittees of the Committee on Post Office and Civil Service and two subcommittees of the Committee on Education and Labor, House of Representatives, October 17, 1985 (Washington, D.C.: U.S. Government Printing Office, 1986), especially pp. 21–54.

14. DHHS, Administration on Children, Youth and Families, Memorandum, November 1986.

15. Ibid.

16. Jo Ann Gasper, Deputy Assistant Secretary for Social Services Policy, prepared testimony in *Child Care: Beginning a National Initiative* (Hearing Before the Select Committee on Children, Youth, and Families, House of Representatives, April 4, 1984) (Washington, D.C., U.S. Government Printing Office, 1984), pp. 98–101.

17. For expenditure data and trends in child care at end of 1970s, see Kamerman and Kahn, *Child Care, Family Benefits, and Working Parents*, pp. 185–190.

18. See John R. Nelson, Jr., "The Federal Interagency Day Care Requirements," in Cheryl D. Hayes, ed., *Making Policies for Children: A Study of the Federal Process* (Washington, D.C.: National Academy Press, 1982).

19. *Summary Report of the Assessment of Current State Practices in Title XX Funded Day Care Programs, October 1981*, pp. 53–54.

20. Gasper, *Child Care*.

21. Helen Blank, *Children and Federal Child Care Cuts* (Washington, D.C.: Children's Defense Fund, 1983), pp. 5–7.

22. Helen Blank, *Child Care: The State's Response* (Washington, D.C.: Children's Defense Fund, 1984), pp. 4–11. Also, Helen Blank and Amy Wilkins,

Child Care: Whose Priority? (Washington, D.C.: Children's Defense Fund, 1985). A fourth round of CDF inquiries, reported as we went to press, is summarized in Helen Blank and Amy Wilkins, *State Child Care Fact Book 1986* (Washington, D.C.: Children's Defense Fund, 1986).
23. Blank and Wilkins, *Child Care*.
24. *Madeline H. Kimmich, America's Children: Who Cares?* (Washington, D.C.: The Urban Institute, 1985).
25. Gasper, *Child Care*.

Chapter 2

LOCAL CHILD CARE INITIATIVES

We now examine reports from inventive communities in several parts of the country. Faced by growing needs for child care for the young children of working parents, at a time of federal cutbacks and changed regulations, many communities have attempted to package new solutions. And, while focused on doing what seemed necessary and possible, they also have evolved new local structures for child care operations and leadership. Thus, on the one hand, we offer a review of local developments in child care. At the same time we ask whether the issues of child care planning, leadership, and coordination are now resolved.

As already suggested, the federal government has put its influence on the side of privatization, decentralization, and deregulation in the child care field. The issue is whether Americans have found a way to make such policies work well, produce desired results, and guide future developments.

It should be stressed that this is a picture of the cutting edge, to the extent that it has been identified. Many states and localities did nothing and saw their child care problems increase. In contrast, the inventive communities have tried new solutions and are reputed to be showing the way. They are frequently observed, visited, asked to report, and referred to. It is in the nature of the current era that nobody knows what is representative. All government mechanisms for national reporting, however inadequate, have been dismantled, and new, voluntary efforts are not yet in place. There is some progress in reporting how families cope but not how communities organize and administer.[1]

New structures have developed in several parts of the country to deal with problems of child care financing and delivery and with client access to services. Sometimes they also have concerned themselves with standards, staff training, parent education, and more. Some of what occurred began in the 1970s with the growing gap between demand and supply. Most changes, however, were a response to the changed federal scene between 1981 and 1986 and the varied local and state reactions that were precipitated. Communities needed to cope, and some did. There was no national leadership advancing "solutions" (except for the anti-cut advocates) and no generally employed vehicle for cooperation and exchange. There were no coherent, shared ideologies or theories, except for conviction about the importance of sufficient child care of acceptable quality. In short, the orientation was empirical, pragmatic, trial and error. The issue is: What has been invented and how useful is it?

The responses to be described were reactions to an epidemic of local child care crises, as reported by social service agencies and advocates. Low-income working mothers were left without eligibility for Title XX care, which at best had been able to cover only some of those who qualified. Providers who depended on governmental purchase or subsidy had empty "slots" and few prospects. United Way agencies and private philanthropies were besieged with requests. States were seeking ways of controlling costs and damage. Nobody had a full or accurate picture, but many public officials and citizens were alarmed.

Among the responses that evolved was the "invention" or evolution of new community instruments. Localities that aspired merely to "cope" found, in a few instances, that they had something new to hold onto. A few localities heard about the solutions adopted elsewhere, tried them, and adopted them, with local variations. A few advocates and experts did what they could to pass the word along,[2] and there were many willing listeners. They all were building upon the remnants of the federally inspired local coordination efforts in the day care field from the 1970s (Community Coordinated Child Care, 4-C), initiatives from the women's movement, and other local efforts.[3]

The process of invention continues and, by now, the lead communities are known. It may be the time for stocktaking.[4]

An Overview

What do these community instruments do? The range is considerable, from the "broker" agencies, which in fact take on, by delegation, a large responsibility for public administration, to agencies which fill in, in accord with specific local needs and funding prospects. At the core, a significant number of agencies conduct information and referral, vendor/voucher, and coordination-supportive activities.

We have found local initiatives taking on several related tasks in creative ways, including the following:

- *"Packaging" money* to meet the needs of people who cannot manage on their own in the child care market (drawing upon Title XX, refugee programs, employment programs, programs for the educationally deprived and handicapped, employer subsidies, local and state funds, United Way, and other voluntary funds).
- Developing and/or implementing various forms of state *vendor/voucher programs,* as a substitute for or in addition to the traditional purchase of child care or agency subsidies.[5]
- Taking over public responsibility for determining *income eligibility* of families for income-tested subsidies for child care.
- *Paying agencies and family day care providers* on behalf of governmental programs, voluntary programs, and employers.
- Conducting various types of *staff training and staff certification* activities.
- *Licensing and registering or ,certifying* family day care providers as eligible to care for state-funded children.
- *Operating* family-support services or centers, parent-education programs, toy- and book-lending libraries, and serving to convene and support parent self-help activities.
- Serving as child care *advocates,* lobbyists, public educators.
- *Administering* and meeting visitation and consultation requirements of the federal *child care food program.*
- Carrying out elaborate, comprehensive, or quite limited *information and referral activities* in child care.
- Carrying out *consultation, information, and technical assistance programs for potential providers* of center and family day care services, both proprietary and nonprofit.
- *Operating* centers, family day care homes, and related programs.
- *Organizing systems of family day care providers*—and providing all the related services they require.

None of the programs does all of these things, but most do several. Indeed the newness resides, in part, in the range and connections. Some of the organizations are completely new, and others evolved from earlier, long histories. We refer to such agencies as:

- St. Paul Resources for Child Caring.
- Greater Minneapolis Day Care Association.
- Child Care Resource and Referral, Inc., Rochester, Minnesota.
- Quality Child Care, Mounds, Minnesota, and eight states (now dismantled).
- Central Florida Community Coordinated Child Care.
- Associated Day Care Services of Greater Boston, Massachusetts.
- Child Care Resource Center, Cambridge, Massachusetts.
- Houston Neighborhood Centers, Inc.
- Child Care Dallas.
- Austin Families, Inc.
- Child Inc., Austin, Texas.
- Office of Child Care Services, United Way, Rochester, New York.
- Child Care Resources, Inc., Charlotte, North Carolina, (Mecklenberg County).
- Child Care Inc., New York City.
- Agency for Child Development, New York City (a public agency).
- Corporate Child Development Fund for Texas.
- A large group of county-level programs, including some public schools and some county offices of education, each unique in some ways, affiliated with the California statewide Child Care Resource and Referral Network.

Several other programs belong on this roster, but we have not had the personal experience or evidence to characterize them appropriately. We refer particularly to well-known and visible programs such as:

- The Planning Council, Norfolk, Virginia.
- Community Coordinated Child Care, Madison, Wisconsin.
- Save the Children, Atlanta, Georgia.

The phenomenon may be better understood with more specific reference to particular programs and what they are like. How have they coped with the new challenge to financing and delivery in an era of federal cutbacks and new emphasis on privatization? What are these new instruments like, and how do the strategies they have adopted work? How effective are these programs?

In effect, then, the new child care environment involves a number of new federal policies and preferences, a series of local organizational "inventions," and some significant stirrings within state and city educational systems. Also important are new developments in the schools with regard to prekindergarten classes for 3- and 4-year-olds and after-school programs for school-aged children. (These programs will be discussed separately in Chapter 5.)

There also is a tendency to support child care service consumers directly, whereas previously government has subsidized only the providers. There is considerable promotion of corporate initiatives as an alternative government expenditure (see Chapter 6). There has been dismantling of federal capacity for leadership and even data collection.

We have looked at these new and changed community agencies for several reasons: to learn about their inventions, understand their accomplishments, and consider what can and cannot be expected of them in this changed environment.

The remainder of the chapter highlights developments with the greatest potential impact. Where should they be located in one's vision of the future of child care services?

Our illustrations are quite varied. It may be significant that the initiatives we report are all in states that the Children's Defense Fund found had increased the number of children served since 1981.[6] This fact was not apparent until our work was completed, since our "cases" for study were chosen by tapping the opinions of informed experts as to communities at the cutting edge. We do not know whether the hospitable state environments spawned community exploration or community leaders inspired the states to act. Apparently, both processes have occurred. As seen in Table 2.1, these states differ in standards and expenditures. Moreover, several targeted only the very poorest with social service fee subsidies and others were more generous (Table 2.2).

Some of the program components in these new local agencies are self-evident. Two, in particular, are the anchors for much else and will be elaborated: Resource, or Information, and Referral services (R&R or I&R) and vendor/vouchers. Child care R&R, or I&R, services have been a major development of the 1980s, beginning with and modeled on the California experience, as discussed subsequently. Responding to the diversity and fragmentation of an expanding but decentralized child care service delivery system, this critical and influential development is now being adopted by states and localities throughout the country. Our discussion opens with a brief description of a local I&R in Massachusetts, followed by a more extensive review of a California program and the California "R&R network." We also describe a New York alternative.

Table 2.1 Minimum Standards for Staff–Child Ratios and Reimbursement Rates for States Discussed

	California	Florida	Massachusetts	Minnesota	New York	Texas
Staff–Child Ratios						
Minimum Standards						
Infant	1:4	1:6	1:3	1:4	1:4	1:5
Toddler	1:4	1:8	1:4	1:7	1:4	1:6
Age 2	1:12	1:12	1:10	1:10	1:4	1:11
Age 3	1:12	1:15	1:10	1:10	1:6	1:15
Age 4	1:12	1:20	1:10	1:10	1:7	1:18
Age 5	1:12	1:25	1:15	1:10	1:8	1:22
Provider Reimbursement						
Per Place (1985)						
Center	$17.98/day	$37.50/wk	$13.50/day	set by counties	$85.50/wk (city)	$10.28/day
Family day care	$17.98/day	$37.50/wk	$13.46/day		$55.50/wk (state) (Centers or homes)	$6.40/day

SOURCE: *Child Care: Whose Priority?* (Children's Defense Fund.)
NOTE: The federal standards promulgated in 1981 and, then, dropped were as follows:

Age	Max. Group Size	Staff/Child Ratio
0–2	6	1:3
2	12	1:4
3–6	18	1:9

The current NAEYC voluntary accreditation standards propose varied staff–child ratios based on different group sizes. For purposes of comparison, we note that they call for 1:3 for infants in groups of 6, 8, 10, 12. For toddlers the standards are 1:3, 1:4, 1:5 in groups of 6 and 1:4 in groups of 8.

Table 2.2   Ceiling for Eligibility for Title XX and Related Child Care Fee Subsidies, 1986

State	Maximum Percentage of State Median Income for Eligibility[a]	Maximum Allowable Income for Family of Three[a]
State Discussed		
California	84–100	[b]
Florida	150% of fed. poverty line	$12,708
Massachusetts	70–115	17,292–28,404
Minnesota	75	19,395
New York	106	23,177
Texas	47	11,856
Other States[c]		
Colorado	53.4	14,496
Georgia	55	11,874
Michigan	80	22,260
Mississippi	250% of fed. poverty line	22,125
North Carolina	75	13,652
Utah	54	13,224

SOURCE: Children's Defense Fund.
[a]If two percentages or two income maxima are shown, it means that the family is declared ineligible initially if its income is higher than the lower figure, but (once eligible) may increase its income up to the higher figure before becoming ineligible.
[b]Not reported.
[c]For contrast we took the next state in the data table supplied by the Children's Defense Fund.

We will turn next to vendor/voucher programs, a new development implemented in the 1970s, in which public child care money is used primarily to purchase care for low-income children in private, often for-profit, agencies. The Orlando, Florida, 4-C program is a prototypical example of privatization, where the focus is on subsidizing the parent/consumer rather than the provider and on private delivery of services. Subsequently, we also describe the California vendor/voucher program.

We will then review local initiatives that combine both R&R and vendor/voucher programs, using Minnesota as our "case" here. California, North Carolina, and several other locations have also established this model. The final section of this chapter will sum up lessons from the local level. A more complete perspective on the future of these local initiatives requires that state development also be considered. That is the starting point for Chapter 3.

"Information and Referral," or "Resource and Referral," Services (I&R or R&R)

Special I&R agencies have an almost 20-year history in the United States, emerging first as part of the antipoverty program in the 1960s and then expanding in the 1970s in response to fragmentation in the social service delivery field generally. In some sense, the appearance of this "model" in the child care field is a positive sign because it means that both supply and demand have grown substantially and that many people are seeking help in locating a service. It also can be construed as a concrete demonstration of the difficulties parents have in finding affordable, decent child care in a fragmented delivery system. Child care R&Rs, as they are most often called, are now expanding rapidly throughout the country in many localities, in a few states with state support, and as an employer-sponsored service initiated by IBM. Here we focus on developments that were at the forefront. We begin with a "model" local service in Cambridge, Massachusetts. We describe next a local program that is part of a statewide "network" in California. Our third illustration is a public I&R in New York, with some private parallels.

Cambridge, Massachusetts, Child Care Resource Center

The Child Care Resource Center (CCRS), important for its regional and national influence, is one of the original agencies in the project that launched the new I&R movement.[7] (Although not described here, Associated Day Care Services of Greater Boston has played a similar innovative role.) While its main office is in Cambridge, CCRS serves metropolitan Boston. Most of its funding is from the several public agencies served, but it also receives foundation and other private money and volunteer time. A local child care information and referral service, CCRS is organized into four teams: (1) I&R, (2) technical assistance (to potential and current providers), (3) services to corporations, and (4) a vendor/ voucher program. The team activities are obviously interrelated; for example, corporations are offered I&R as well as the technical assistance service. Since the I&R service is the vehicle through which the agency meets its consumer public and thus dominates all activity, all team members rotate on the telephone.

In early 1984 the agency was handling 8000 to 9000 parent calls, in addition to provider inquiries, yearly, up from 1500 four years before. People were learning about the center through word of mouth, public service announcements on the radio, and the yellow pages. The agency was at its maximum capacity, given available funds.

Some two-thirds to three-quarters of callers were parents of infants and toddlers, underscoring their problem in obtaining services. Parents of the birth- to 6-months group and of the 12- to 18-months group were having particularly great difficulty finding care. Almost all callers to this service are working parents, represent all income groups, and seek all-day care. Some want centers, some family day care. The experience in this agency is that for children under 15 months of age the preference for a family arrangement over centers runs 60 to 40 percent. For toddlers it is 60 to 40 percent in favor of centers. Parents preferring "sitters" or family day care arrangements apparently believe it ensures more nurturance, whereas the day care center is seen as offering more structured "play" and the nursery school as featuring "education."

One is impressed with the fact that the phone I&R inquiry is a rich 30- to 45-minute contact, not at all casual—as also was the case in some of the stronger I&R we observed in other states. The interview combines information and consumer education with counseling. The telephones are covered, day and night, by professionals or community people spanning the ethnic range of the inquiring population. Only licensed or registered facilities are listed, except for after-school programs, which have no licensing requirements.

The I&R service tends to suggest some four or five possibilities to the inquirer, drawing upon a data bank, which was updated twice a year by mail until the IBM program provided computers in 1985. The parent calls back if the first list is insufficient. To assess the workings of the system, an agency callback follow-up with a "rolling" sample is used.

The telephone call is also used to screen for potential eligibility for financial aid. The actual certification review is carried out at the center to which inquiries may be referred (or, if in the employment-training program known as ET the client's eligibility for vouchers is determined elsewhere). Currently, the voucher device is used in the ET program on a significant scale, and the CCRS agency is one of a number in the state which have their area's voucher contracts. This makes them the payout agency; state reimbursement is swift and the local centers and family day care providers are paid quickly. This voucher initiative in the state is off to a good start, in contrast to an earlier endeavor, based in the social services department, administered in CCRS among other centers, and both unpopular with providers and inconclusive in its research evaluation. What is especially important is the fact that a parent who arrives at the agency is referred to a voucher management section and receives a more extensive counseling, placement, and referral service in support of the work/training/educaiton program for welfare clients.

While thus expanding in response to the state's initiatives for public assistance clients, CCRS has increased its corporate I&R contracting in 1985 and 1986 and offers special attention to the contract-company employees. Others are now charged service fees if they are not poor.

The experiences of CCRS reveal the advantages and limitations of this model at the local level. When we visited we noted that the agency staff could report their experiences, offer suggestions, and advocate. They could administer or accept vouchers, but they could not determine the rise or fall of state budgets. They could give good I&R services and help providers, but they could not themselves deal directly with the quality of staffing, equitable salaries, or the types of service available at state reimbursement rates. They could service corporate child care initiatives and encourage them in every way possible. But a good, local I&R cannot solve the child care problems alone. As we shall see, Massachusetts also was to benefit from a 1986 state-level initiative as it upgraded its child care program.

Would a statewide network of R&Rs make a larger impact? We turn to California to see a local R&R initiative that is part of a statewide system.

California: Statewide R&R

California has the largest child care budget of any state in the country and has been the site of several innovations in the child care field. California's is a statewide story, the details saved for Chapter 3. For now we note that California has an ongoing statewide child care system, dating back to World War II and based in the public schools until the early 1970s. The system now includes a group of energetic, creative county programs that mix advocacy with information and referral and also, in many instances, a vendor/voucher program as well as a host of supplementary efforts. We will describe the information and referral (or resource and referral or "R&R") services and then discuss the vendor/voucher program.

In the latter part of the 1970s, as part of a larger effort to diversify and expand the child care service system in California,

Governor Brown provided modest pilot funding to launch a series of resource and referral efforts. The initial $900,000 went to 11 programs, no two alike, with the San Francisco "Switchboard" and "BANANAS" in Oakland particularly visible. In response to advocates' enthusiasm, funding was increased several times. By 1980 there were 55 information and referral agencies statewide, each guaranteed a minimum of $57,500 annually, a few funded in the $75,000–$100,000 range, and three receiving over $250,000.

In 1985, California became the first state with statewide R&R coverage, when some 67 R&R programs were funded.[8] Some of these agencies are essentially specialized information services attached to schools or traditional social agencies. Others are in organizations conducting a wide variety of child care–related services as well as R&R. Other states have watched these developments and sought to follow suit.

Each R&R program has added unique components to a core program that often includes information and referral/resource and referral services, a vendor/voucher program (labeled "alternative payment," or "AP"), community education and advocacy, and technical assistance to providers. Some programs administer the federal child care food program, as organizers of family day care "systems." Others have developed private foundation-funded projects. A good number have training grants. Several provide supportive services to families. A number have initiated corporate child care programs. Several are county-funded and perform services on behalf of the county. Here we concentrate on R&R.

BANANAS: A Leader in the California CCR&R Network

The phrase "resource and referral" connotes a joining of the more traditional "information and referral" functions with resource development and provider support. This was the activity in which the San Francisco Child Care Switchboard and BANANAS pioneered and excelled before state backing began in 1976.

Covering half of Alameda county and serving the low-income and the university communities in the area between Oakland and Berkeley, BANANAS, Child Care Information and Referral Service, is a feminist collective that was organized in the early 1970s. Recognized as effective and innovative, it contributed some of the ideas and energies that shaped the 1976 AP and R&R plans.

BANANAS serves working parents who need help in finding care arrangements. Some need help in meeting the costs. Many want assistance in judging and finding quality care and in dealing with their children's developmental problems.

BANANAS is staffed by 10 members of the cooperative plus approximately 10 part-time or full-time employees. About two-thirds of the budget ($665,000 when we visited) is funded by the state subsidies for R&R and AP: information and vendor/voucher services. The permitted overhead of 21 percent for "administration" pays for many of the parent service and support activities. Special grants from foundations, local governments, or corporations fund special projects.

In 1985 BANANAS was serving about 3500 callers monthly and they were pressed. While not the largest item on the agency's budget (that place belongs to the vendor/voucher program), the R&R is the visible activity by which BANANAS is known. It is also the agency's "ear" to the community and the basis for detecting and responding to new needs. What they do not "hear on the phone," they are not sure about.

The telephones are covered from 10 A.M. to 4 P.M. four days a week, from 10 A.M. to 1 P.M. on Fridays, and from 5 to 7 P.M. on Tuesday evenings. Clients get the information number in the yellow pages (where BANANAS is listed under both "child care" and "emergency"), at the front of the white pages (on the page of "essential numbers"), through word of mouth, or through the media. The phones are handled in shifts by well-trained experts. Bilingual staff, available part-time, handle inquiries in English, Spanish, and Chinese. The caller is asked the reason for the call, what is wanted, and what is preferred. Callers are told some of the options that may not be known. Potential eligibility for AP is explored and information provided. Then, the person covering the phone goes to the master file, finds the right geographic area (related to home, work, or transportation route), and offers a number of options that fit the request. Often, personnel mail a packet of handouts about child care, including their publication on "choosing child care." They make it very clear that a license does not guarantee quality and that visits to several family day care homes or centers are desirable.

Provider names are obtained from the state licensing/registration printouts; new providers are asked by mail if they want to be part of the listing. Every two or three months providers are phoned to update the files; if no contact is made, a postcard and then a callback will request whether the provider still wants to be listed.

If there is a charge of abuse or neglect, the provider is removed from the file until the matter is settled. Three complaints of the same sort, but not involving abuse or neglect, also remove a name from the file.

The referral activity makes the agency a strategic place for potential providers to inquire about need. The experience with parents unable to find needed resources and responsibility for AP administration gives the agency strong motivation to help potential providers. In recognition of the general need to develop family day care resources, especially for children under age 2, BANANAS, like a number of other R&R programs, has attempted to encourage providers and simplify the meeting of state requirements.

BANANAS' work, and the attraction of AP clients, has contributed to bringing some family day care out from underground. The issues remain complex, however. Some high-quality, high-fee suburban family day care does not bother with licensing, only to avoid the "bureaucratic hassle." Recently, BANANAS has published a helpful packet that guides providers in obtaining a center license as well.

The R&R activity is a very productive mix of a local access services and mixed public and private funding that is responsive to local community needs—and a resource development/technical assistance activity targeted at supply. The latter could be private or governmental. It encompasses some participation as well in the governmental licensing mandate.

BANANAS has a track record of successful program exploration and innovation. From 1972 to 1982 it piloted a family day care registration project as an alternative to the more onerous licensing that was said to discourage providers. At any given moment, it has several foundation, corporate, or local government grants to carry out special projects and services related to the overall mission. At the time of our visit, the following were among their current or recent projects:

- A program that stimulates interaction of school-aged children and the elderly in five districts with a nursing home population.
- A program to fight housing discrimination against families with children.
- Assessment of possible Oakland city responses to new child care needs expected to emerge as the result of economic development plans in one area (work with employers, a committee, a parent-preference poll, and so forth).
- A "shares" program for women who cannot afford the full cost of in-home care but are interested in sharing a caretaker, with

the children cared for in one or the other home. Two or three families share. BANANAS serves a clearance function, bringing potential cooperators together. "Sharing" constituted their most active infant care file in the summer of 1985.
- A "warm line," or telephone number, that can be called for advice about a child's eating, sleeping, or other behavior. About 1000 calls a year are handled by a nurse who staffs this program.

Unlike many of the new child care leadership agencies, BA-NANAS does not administer the child care food programs in its area because there already are two or three "systems" in the community (see Chapter 7).

BANANAS, like all R&R agencies in the region, is a member of the San Francisco-based Child Care Resource and Referral Network. The CCRR network, described earlier, offers a splendid illustration of both advocacy and public education from an R&R base, even though neither its leadership nor anyone else in the state would describe it as "the full answer to the child care problem."

New York's Public Alternative

The recognition that R&R is a strategic service does not solve all questions of community planning and design. In New York City, the Agency for Child Development (ACD) is the subunit of the city's Human Resources Administration that negotiates contracts with over 380 nonprofit centers and a small group of family day care homes, enrolling over 40,000 children, and also administers a Head Start program for 10,000 children in about 140 centers. It is the public lead agency for child care and has many related functions. Responding to the interest in the child care activities of private business, ACD launched a corporate initiative in 1983. For present purposes what is relevant is that this initiative included plans for an elaborate computer system covering child care information. Corporations could have computer terminals of their own and serve their own employees.

In an expensive undertaking jointly financed by the state and city, ACD has spent several years on surveys and system design. Whether the program will take off, however, is not yet clear. Some wondered whether companies would want terminals. Others argued that a terminal without a qualified, trained person to run it on behalf of specific families' needs is not a useful resource. Certainly, the service will offer a valuable computerized "vacancy control" system with reference to ACD's own responsibility when it becomes operational in 1987, after a few years, replacing a simple information file. One cannot predict whether it also will yet become a successful "loss leader," attracting corporations. Much of that initiative has not advanced for reasons not immediately relevant.

Concurrently, Child Care, Inc., a private nonprofit agency and in many ways like new I&Rs elsewhere in the country in its service innovation and advocacy, has grown and become part of the IBM network. Other information services are offered by the older Day Care Council, a provider association. A cooperative 13-unit voluntary I&R network in the metropolitan area has found that here, too, I&R may anchor much else that occurs in the field. The ACD program would apparently be independent of this network, despite the fact that all elements are largely publicly funded out of one program and governmental unit or another. New York has not yet faced the obvious issue about roles and coordination that arise.

Vendor/Voucher Programs

Voucher and vendor/voucher programs emerged in the 1970s as an instrument for expanding consumer choice and for permitting more flexibility and efficiency in the use of public funds. These programs are part of a general trend toward subsidizing consumers rather than providers and toward buttressing demand rather than supply. Here we illustrate how this instrument has been used in the child care field and how it has "taken hold." Orlando, Florida's program, which grew by trial and error, has become a model for many localities around the country, in part because of its remarkable director. The California program is more "theory-based" and constitutes an interesting alternative. Of some interest, in California, R&R and AP (California's vendor/voucher program) developed in tandem. Yet California is known nationally for its R&R services, whereas Florida, where the initiative was much more haphazard, is known for its vendor/voucher program. We describe the Florida program first, then California's.

Community Coordinated Child Care for Central Florida, Inc.

This extraordinarily influential program, led by Mrs. Pheobe Carpenter, its administrator, is known locally as "4-C" (a survival name from a federally initiated "community coordinated child care" effort of the 1970s). The program covers the central Florida counties of Orange, Seminole, and Osceola. Orange is a center of corporate development and intensive growth, best known to the country for Orlando, Disneyland, and Epcot. Seminole is a bed-room community, and Osceola is largely rural-agricultural. The three-county area is about 50 miles long in a north-south direction and about 30 miles east-west. The program operates out of nine offices, several of them covered by traveling staff on a part-time basis. The "model" has since spread to several other Florida counties and has influenced developments in a number of other states, including North Carolina and Texas.

The 4-C program was not planned or invented; it developed. Mrs. Carpenter, an active community volunteer, took over a church-based child care center and ran it for four years after its director resigned. When, in the early 1970s, federal social service funds became available through the state on the basis of a local match, she urged a local official to respond because of the evidence of need for care. The local 4-C was created for this purpose. The United Way, but not the county government, was willing to participate. The funding mission came first; the more usual 4-C coordination efforts came later.

For a while the program was a "crisis," shoe-string operation, but it nonetheless produced a local match, multiplied with federal funds, and kept some very poor centers alive. But subsidizing centers under state and federal rules was complicated. The funded centers were in black residential areas, but poor white children also needed care. Some users in areas with funded centers were not poor and should have been able to manage on their own. The new idea gradually developed: Why not fund financially eligible families in need of care instead of centers? Let the parents decide where to go. Some families would be entitled to full subsidy, and some part. Moreover, families could then drop out of centers not worth the fee, and such centers would close for loss of a "captive" clientele.

The Florida 4-C group was not part of any debate about subsidy of demand rather than of supply and had not followed voucher experiments in other fields. Nor, a we shall see, did they invent a pure voucher. Nonetheless, they made a transition during 1973–1974 and went from a 27-center provider group to one overseeing 100 centers. They no longer fund centers but rather selectively "purchase" some slots (trying to control the proportion) in a large number of centers. Providers are helped by up-front money.

Another unique component is a quality rating scheme developed by the 4-C agency. The agency contracts with over 100 centers, not about use of a specific amount of care, but about agreed rates and procedures. The 4-C rates all centers on a rather simple quality scale. After it signs its annual contract with the state, indicating what the state will pay for Title XX clients, the 4-C advertises for bids. The agencies announce weekly rates. Then a 4-C committee examines a chart in which point scales are interrelated with weekly fees and draws a line to indicate which are the approved agencies. A "rejected" agency may make the cut by raising its quality score or lowering its price. (The vast majority of agencies continue from year to year.) The potential client has access to the charts. When a child is placed with a center, its rate on the chart becomes the fee. The parents know a center's going rate and what they are expected to pay personally out of their earnings, but they do not actually know what 4-C pays since it may have negotiated a lower rate than that paid by the nonsubsidized families (but the difference will not be large, given the additional 4-C USDA food supplement).

Since Florida requires continuing education for child care staffs, 4-C conducts courses and also contracts with a vocational school and a technical college for degree and paraprofessional in-service training. The 4-C group runs a child care transportation program. It has added a toy library for providers and offers other needed technical assistance, especially for the simple "mom and pop" proprietary operations. A variety of activities, especially an annual fair and a speakers bureau, contribute to a public education program. It conducts a modest social service program and a health service in support of providers, and in relation to its own eligibility work.

Now funds are channeled through 4-C from sources other than Title XX (Social Services Block Grant): child welfare, work training, United Way, refugee programs, some local employers. Despite a substantial effort, much publicity, and considerable conviction about the matter, the last is modest in a program serving over 4000 families a year with about 3000 in child care at one time.

The program fits the local ethic: Public funds do not undercut proprietary operators; all providers may compete for subsidized clients. An effort is made to keep publicly subsidized clients to a minority in any one center; 60 percent of centers, including the proprietary as well as the nonprofit, in the counties covered are serving some of the 4-C children. They include preschool programs and nursery schools as well as day care centers. (Florida has similar licensing requirements for both the social welfare and the educational child care services, and both types tend to offer all-day coverage.)

It should be stressed (Table 2.1) that licensing requirements and

[handwritten margin note: Public Funds that do not hurt local initiative]

prevalent standards are both low from a national perspective, as are subsidy levels. Only the very poor qualify, and then only to help a work or training activity. People are soon ineligible in Florida if their earnings go up a bit, and there is little private philanthropy or employer money to fill the gap. Inevitably, given the low ceilings for full eligibility and the limited funds for supplementation, over 90 percent of those served are very low-earner, single-parent families, about 20 percent of them receiving some public assistance.

The state can operate under this pattern because of a policy for purchase of child care services that specifies that it works through central agencies and agencies administering family day care networks. It does not wish to deal with individual providers, and it insists on a local 12.5 percent match. Families and children must meet the department's income eligibility rules. The number of day care units purchased in an area will depend on availability and cost of service and availability of a local match as well as state and local funds. The purchased service must be licensed and meet applicable state standards. The central agency (in this case, the 4-C) may select among bidders if necessary by applying a quality standard (the practice developed in Orlando).

The program described here has organized the day care market, inspired new providers to enter, and clearly made a contribution to upgrading quality and training. It has developed an efficient centralized system for paying subsidies to providers on the basis of verified attendance records. It has recently encouraged a modest amount of employer subsidy. The public education and user education components are also significant. Nonetheless, one should not overstate: Only the lowest-income workers are helped for the most part, quality is improved but low by national standards, and there is little rigorous evaluation of programs and personnel. There are few supply and demand data and no long-term plans. Families become ineligible as their incomes rise a bit because of modest salary increases. Funds remain in short supply, and there are waiting lists for subsidized care.[9]

California's Alternative Payment (AP) Program

In contrast to the Florida program, the California vendor/voucher program, labeled an "Alternative Payment" (AP) program, was designed deliberately and with full knowledge of the concept of a "voucher." (It was not called a "voucher" program after 1980 for several reasons, including the fact that the term perhaps was politically unacceptable, given an earlier intense battle about education vouchers.) California child care advocates had been fighting what they saw as the rigidity of the existing school system child care, a licensing system that closed out community groups, and a lack of funding for family day care. They were concerned, too, about the lack of infant care in the context of a rapidly growing demand. They wanted to loosen up the delivery system. The AP funds provided by the state as part of overall 1976 expansion initiatives go to subsidize care for low-income children through a vendor/voucher program.

BANANAS, the R&R agency described earlier, also has an AP program. BANANAS devotes its AP program to infant care because that is how it has defined its local need. The funding provided by the state (and constituting almost half its budget) allows BANANAS to subsidize about 100 children at one time. Since a child is eligible only until age 2, there is considerable turnover and a long waiting list. The state eligibility schedule, which follows the Title XX pattern, allows eligibility with incomes (scaled to family size) below 84 percent of the state median (unlike the Texas and Florida ceilings, pitched low, to accommodate more limited expenditures). Alameda County has a large low-income population, and a majority of families are eligible. A family's income may rise to 100 percent of the median without a forfeit of eligibility. We recall that Florida, lacking such sliding scale provision, creates major problems for parents who receive modest wage increases.

The family usually phones to apply and is placed on the waiting list. Sometimes the family day care mother calls and says that the child is in care and that the family needs financial help. Given the income ceilings, over 90 percent of those eligible (as almost everywhere in vendor/voucher programs) are single-parent families. When reached on the waiting list, the AP applicant comes into the office for eligibility determination and verification (usually a payroll slip will suffice). AP families must use licensed caregivers only and must have their children immunized. The parent makes the final choice of caregiver. Sometimes the child already is in care. Otherwise, the parent is given a list of possible places in the preferred area, is supplied with literature about choosing care, and discusses the process with a counselor.

Once the parent has indicated a choice, a BANANAS staff person goes out with a contract for the provider's signature. In effect it is a three-way contract: BANANAS and the parent also sign. This clearly is a vendor program, with the provider paid directly by BANANAS up to the allowable daily subsidy. (Only San Diego uses AP for a large voucher program in California.) Given the high infant care fees in the area, the state allowance leaves many parents with a substantial burden of supplementation.

The parent returns to BANANAS for recertification every three months and more often if in a work training program. As the child approaches age 2, parents receive lists of providers and centers available to older children.

Administration of the AP program thus places the agency in the eligibility-determination and vendor payment roles, often carried by government, while counseling, educating, and supporting parents using the program.

Combining R&R and Vendor/Voucher Programs: Minneapolis and St. Paul

California, as we have seen, exemplifies a state in which the new local child care "instruments" developed against a backdrop of state child care structure in the Department of Education, going back to 1943. The Twin Cities, by contrast, now are served by dynamic, local child care service and advocacy agencies, which came first.

Minnesota, particularly the Twin Cities, has a long tradition of high-quality child care and better coverage than most of the country. At various times over the past 25 years, Minneapolis or St. Paul has been the location of important experiments, innovation, and advocacy. Several representatives from these communities have been major actors on the national scene. In Rochester, the nationally visible Child Care Resource and Referral, Inc., founded in 1972 as one of the new-style R&R agencies, also has a rural constituency. It has been more involved with the schools than its Twin Cities counterparts.

The Twin Cities are the hubs of Hennepin and Ramsey counties respectively. They are the bases for the Greater Minneapolis Day Care Association (GMDCA) and the Resources for Child Caring, two lively and effective organizations under strong executive directors that often collaborate. Much of their specific programmatic activity is similar to several California counties and to Florida, but some differences exist.

The Greater Minneapolis Day Care Association evolved out of a late 1960s-type of model cities community development agency. It gained respect and visibility in the early 1970s as a 4-C agency, cooperating with federal efforts to expand child care and Head Start and with considerable parent participation. It still retains the area structure inherited from that period and its local staff combines community organizing and advocacy with technical assistance to local child care centers.

Resources for Child Caring is relatively new. As Ramsey County sought to cope with the problems faced by the child care field following the federal Title XX funding cuts and a series of policy changes, its 4-C agency, which still existed, came together in 1982 with a training and resource program known as Toys 'n Things and with both a Family Day Care Association and an Early Childhood Director Association to establish the new entity.

Just as the Hennepin program reflects its community development heritage in flavor and perspective on some issues, so does Ramsey retain within itself all the previous structures and give support to family care provider and center director concerns and interests as well. Nonetheless, in essential core activities they are very similar.

Each offers an information and referral program. Ramsey was handling 750 to 800 calls a month when visited, Hennepin under 700. The latter operates in a context of other I&Rs, plus some ongoing United Way information service; there was local United Way resistance to funding such services by individualized agencies. The county welfare agency was providing minimal funding because it did not value the expensive monthly updating of the database and the elaborate efforts to provide the inquiring parent with a list of potential providers and specific details about what they offer. The I&R was computerized in 1981, has a rich database, and can be quite individually responsive. As described for California, responsible I&R work requires a strong educational and counseling program. Many of the inquirers are first-time parents. Hennepin has recently begun to meet some of its costs by billing parents who are served and are not income-eligible for subsidy, but collection is low key. They also have begun to contract for special I&R services for the employees of locally based companies, a program that met 25 percent of the budget at the time of our last contact.

The St. Paul operation shares the latter two patterns, having started billing users somewhat later, but its computer operation was not yet operative at this writing. It, too, has been imaginative in analyzing its experience. It does not attempt to update its database as frequently.

The two agencies also have parallel voucher programs, known in Minnesota as the "sliding fee program." The program began in 1976. With the state Title XX eligibility cutoff set above 60 percent of the state median income, this voucher program was intended (on a sliding scale, reflecting income) to supplement those working-poor parents in need of child care and ineligible for Title XX financial aid. The expectation was that people with incomes between 60 and 90 percent of the state median would be reached. Shortage of funds, however, has defeated this objective, and much of the money has supplemented day care costs for AFDC parents at work or in training whose costs were not being met (because social service funds are used in their counties for other purposes or the limited $160 per month "disregard" for child expenses in budgeting an AFDC mother's earnings proves inadequate). Some of the money has aided the working-poor parents with incomes between 50 and 70 percent of the state median. (A rise to a 75 percent ceiling was voted in 1986.) Almost all recipients are the families of single mothers. Nonetheless, the sliding fee program constitutes Minnesota's vouchers, and both agencies are among those who deliver them, much as do the California AP agencies. In 1984–1985 the total state funding increased from $3 to $10 million, and participation by all counties was mandated. Parent choice is emphasized.

The information and referral services provide printouts or lists of available places, information about them, and a pamphlet containing advice about how to select. The parent contribution is income-scaled, and the subsidy ceiling specified. Here, as elsewhere, parents choose centers or family day care, and here the latter has become more important in the picture, especially for infants and toddlers, than when government subsidized only supply since center contracts were easier for government departments to manage.

By way of context it should be noted that Hennepin County converted its day care program to a vendor/voucher arrangement as of January 1982. Clients eligible as AFDC recipients or as income-eligible under the remnants of the Title XX program (social service block grant) are reviewed for eligibility status in county offices, find their own center or family day care space, and have their fees paid. The sliding fee scale program, administered by the Greater Minneapolis Day Care Association, assists those above the eligibility ceiling. A similar responsibility is carried in St. Paul by Resources for Child Caring.

The Greater Minneapolis Day Care Association pulls together modest funds from the job training program (JTPA), the community development block grant, the social services state grant, and state appropriations for this purpose. The waiting lists have been long, and the program remains small, nonetheless, despite expansion based on the substantial state budgetary increase voted in 1985. The county welfare departments expend considerably more funds directly for welfare recipients and those eligible under the Title XX program (social services block grant) and the Title IV-A "disregard." What is of interest here, as in St. Paul, is that financial eligibility, traditionally a governmental function, also is determined by the agency and recertified after six months. We saw similar delegation in Florida and California, as we shall in Texas.

Not that the GMDCA staff would convert the entire endeavor to a subsidy of consumers. Their experience is that some inner-city centers that cannot attract voucher or cash payment by parents from surrounding areas would not survive without some direct subsidies still provided by county social services and community development block grants. This significant policy issue is arising in a number of places, but there is no broad discussion of it as yet, as there is no general agreement as to how a diverse funding stream should be meshed.

Resources for Child Caring is no less dedicated to the sliding fee program, and its packaging and delivery are similar. By contrast, much of Minnesota did not take part in the effort until 1984, when there was an increase of available funds from $1.3 million to $3 million. With the substantial expansion in the sliding fee budget voted in 1985 (a $7 million increase) came mandating. The issue will arise as to how counties outside the Twin Cities and Rochester, covering almost half the state's population, will implement the program, since they have no local R&R agencies.

The Ramsey County agency also administers the federal child care food program by serving as a "system agency," and its operating budget is helped by the overhead funds. This follows naturally from its incorporation of the family day care association. It ran a successful family day care recruitment program in 1985, convincing 346 providers to become licensed, in response to an attractive advertising campaign, encouragement of word-of-mouth publicity, corporate distribution of flyers, and the incentives of an equipment loan program, access to I&R listing and training, and the advantages of the food program. (See Chapter 7 regarding the importance of such supports.)

Hennepin has a separate county day care association that joins centers and family day care providers, offers a variety of services such as insurance to members, and operates a training program and a toy library as well as a competitive information and referral program. This organization is the administrator of the federal day care food program. Since the administrative overhead has aided a significant number of the agencies described in the several states, it is no surprise that the administration budget remains a problem for GMDCA.

The agencies have in recent years shared two major program activities. First, they have joined with one another and the Rochester R&R agency in creating an effective statewide advocacy instrument which has had visible impact on state funding and policies in recent years. In its latest form, with foundation backing, the advocacy network is helping to launch child care coalitions elsewhere in the state as well. Second, they have together explored the corporate child care issue (Parents in the Workplace), trying a number of things with some small successes but no major impact on child care supply. As will be seen later, their experience is not atypical: These new "instruments" conduct educational activities for companies, raise awareness of the growing need for child care services, sometimes sell them specialized "information and referral," and occasionally administer modest fringe benefit vouchers on their behalf.

As we checked the activities and preoccupations of these two agencies over a two-year period, we were struck during our visits with the validity of the observation by the St. Paul director, David Allen, to the effect that there is no "center" in state government for all this activity. "Sliding fees," licensing, and block grants are each in a different unit of government. Child care is looked at as a "function of other activities, such as job training or getting people off welfare." Minnesota's considerable initiatives in education were not conceptualized as part of the child care issue at all, apart from a modest latch key effort, and were considered by still different state and community people. For all their dedication, sophistication, and effective local operations, these two county agencies lack an overall model or design for child care coverage. They still watch for and respond to project initiatives by the governor and make their statewide contribution by lobbying the legislature and the different administrative agencies. Then, in their own counties, they initiate or partake in whatever advocacy or planning is possible.

A Note on Other Activities

We have focused on vendor/voucher and R&R as the operating core of these important, active, effective local agencies. We also have mentioned the fact that some of them have organized "systems" of family day care providers around the federal food program—seeing this as a way to increase and diversify supply and to get help with their own administrative costs. More on this in Chapter 7.

Almost all these local agencies also have histories of great aspiration and expectation with regard to employer-sponsored child care. As we suggest in Chapter 6, the hope for a significant scale of direct employer subsidy or operation proved unrealistic for the most part, but the R&R support by employers based in the nationally initiated IBM network is valuable. Employer R&R contracts have expanded, if modestly, in many communities.

A more complete roster of local initiatives has already been provided. Here we wish to highlight yet another contribution. An R&R service that gives inquiring parents a printout of centers or family day care homes that meet their specifications soon also concerns itself with parent preparedness as consumers. Almost all the R&R agencies prepare and distribute their own "how to choose child care" brochures. Some follow up. Many conduct parenting seminars on their premises, for employers, or elsewhere in the community.

Some go further. We illustrate from another of the California R&R agencies, Resources for Family Development, in Livermore. This organization's parent education and support efforts, based at a special location about a mile from the main office and known as Parent's Place, are particularly noteworthy. Most of the AP recipients are working single mothers. Many others who call for R&R information are at the point of transition involving divorce or separation or some family crisis. The centrally located Parents Place, in a refurbished old building, is staffed by a young mother who recently had her second child. She is interested in parents and in child development and is obviously relaxed, sensitive, and supportive. Mothers may come with their children to the "living room," and the children may play. There is a small parent library and a small toy library. A mother may come for respite, relaxed conversation, or for information. A family day care provider may find books, toys, or guidance. The Parents Place is also used for lectures, support groups, and meetings. Materials are disseminated.

The child care field has sought a family support model for many years and has invented several in the context of Head Start. The support services tied to R&R programs here and elsewhere offer intriguing possibilities. Interestingly, they are all encompassed within the R&R budget and some of the administrative overhead from the other programs, as is a social service component.

Lessons from the Local Level

Clearly, central questions about the financing and delivery of child care are as yet unresolved, but there has been a major increment to the field's fund of knowledge and technology.

I&R Programs

I&R or R&R developments have been most impressive and clearly do meet a significant need. They have shown the way to organize child care access. While only one state, California, currently funds a statewide coverage R&R service, several others are subsidizing significant amounts of service, and the state commitments are growing rapidly. Massachusetts has made a commitment and a large start; it will offer statewide coverage in 1987. New York has passed legislation but not voted funds; plans for a system are being developed.

The private corporate sector has recognized the effectiveness of these initiatives. IBM now provides a national I&R service for its employees by contracting with existing services or creating capacity where it did not exist. Forty centers took on significant IBM loads where the corporation has large numbers of employees; the remainder do less, but the program has influenced more than 200 cities. IBM provided personal computers to help the systems achieve necessary capacity and developed a computer program for the function. Other companies contracted for local I&R services before IBM, on a small scale, and now the process has begun to grow considerably. In some instances local I&R services are providing contracting companies with enriched services and special quality assurance, as well as special staff and telephone lines. Thus they become a universal access service, dealing with company employees, fee-paying consumers, and low-income users who are eligible for public subsidy or are at least not to be charged for this community service. Some, like Child Care Dallas, offer different levels of service (listing either convenient providers or providers known to have vacancies), depending on the nature and immediacy of the need, and they vary their charges accordingly (but expect only token payment by low-income users).

Tied to what has obviously become a valued service in many communities—and is the major child care commitment of hundreds of corporations—is often a resource development function as well (R&R). Needs may be pinpointed for potential providers, and people interested in launching child care centers or family day care homes may be recruited or given information, technical assistance, licensing or registration help, and other supports, depending on the place.

Many of the I&R services undertake extensive consumer education and counseling in the course of the process, perhaps even helping parents clarify precisely what they want and working hard at the "match." Others do less or very little, whether out of resource scarcity; belief in the autonomy of the consumer, who is to be given a printout and information pamphlet only; or because they regard it as inappropriate to favor some listed providers over others.

A few of these new agencies, recognizing that their publicly subsidized clients are mostly single mothers who work, also offer extensive educational and group programs and various supportive services in the parent centers and book-toy libraries that they operate. The child care service proves to be a place where a truly preventive program may originate, not defining the families as "cases" having difficulties.

Clearly, then, the I&R development, not quite new, is an important invention of these local agencies for this time. It would appear to have a firm place in any future pluralistic delivery system, particularly for infant-toddler and after-school programs. Its importance for preschoolers will depend on how central the public prekindergartens eventually become for the 3-, 4-, and 5-year-olds. The I&R operation or something like it is critical to the vendor/voucher and sliding fee programs that are currently also expanding around the country.

Vendor/Voucher Programs

Under the banner of "consumer choice" several variations of such programs have either channeled public social service funds alone or packaged them with occasional employer fringe benefit supplements or philanthropic and United Way contributions. The parent selects a service and pays an income-related fee (unless eligible for full subsidy), and the agency pays a weekly supplement at an agreed rate after attendance is verified. Potential providers must be licensed/registered to be listed or may be helped to qualify during the process. The agency may or may not impose higher quality standards than the laws dictate and may or may not use the relationship as leverage for technical assistance, practical aid, and agency program monitoring.

One result of these vendor/voucher programs, including California's "alternative payments," has been a considerable increase in the use of family day care in jurisdictions in which most public child care funds had been channeled to day care centers. This trend would appear to reflect some parental preferences with regard to infants and the youngest toddlers in many places, an inadequate supply of center care for very young children, the lower fees for family day care in most places, or some combination of all of these.

Another effect in some places has been a broadening of the roster of centers serving publicly financed users. Again, in the past, "purchase of service" contracts tended to be concentrated on centers in specified geographic areas, often set up with public help. Now, as parents choose, the favored centers reflect far greater diversity in orientation, program, and location. Many places include proprietary programs and specialized schools among current providers. In some cities fees for after-school programs may also be handled by the voucher system. In others, voucher programs have enabled families to escape from segregated or "poor only" centers.

To date no definitive evidence exists that vouchers achieve the greater economy-efficiency and quality effects announced by their most ardent proponents (see Chapter 4), but no rigorous, controlled experiments have been conducted. Clearly, vouchers are popular with those who administer or support them and can operate successfully. Their contributions to choice are obvious. From the point of view of government budget-watchers, they offer a simple mechanism to expand and withdraw commitments. This is a much simpler matter than writing a contract to purchase a specific proportion of a center's places. Moreover, the capital investment is left entirely to the provider, who must then attract "business."

Why some opposition? Some believe that an "intake" expert can best pick the center and setting a child most "needs." Others feel that parents who set out to find care too often settle for the quick, the easy, the convenient, or the superficial appearance. They challenge the evidence that the choices made are subsequently regarded by their makers as more satisfactory than under the older system.

The major opposition comes from providers accustomed to purchase of service contracts, particularly those in now partially deserted inner-city areas that are without guaranteed constituencies unless they are created by the allocation of places. A few have had to close down, and others have operated marginally where full or partial voucher plans were instituted. Other providers have opposed vouchers lest they too would or could be bypassed if vouchers were to spread. In at least one state, an operating voucher plan was killed because of such opposition, only to be revived by another unit in state government.

If public funds are to assist the working poor to purchase child care, there is need for "sliding fee" systems for those parents not eligible for full subsidy. Some states do base initial eligibility on a low-income cutoff (as a percentage of median income) but then

Dis-Bump children off

have a taper to a much higher level, allowing a child to remain in care as family income goes up. Less generous or less affluent states have sudden cutoffs, "bumping" children to low-quality unsubsidized care because parental earnings have risen a bit.

These programs either take the form of a partial subsidy of a voucher, as described earlier, or of the per diem fee under the older "purchase of service" contracts. Since what are in most places called "vouchers" are in fact vendor/voucher contracts, the parent perceives little difference between this system and the older plan once the child is in care. The real difference occurs initially: Is the child assigned to an existing place by the agency, or does the parent find the place, agree on the arrangements, and inform the agency? This difference is what carries the alleged advantage and the controversy.

Again we would conclude that insofar as pluralism is valued and the market expanded, the vendor/voucher plan remains an attractive way to channel public funds and to package public and private money while protecting some desired qualities and even speeding up payments to providers. Vouchers would become less significant if there were expansion of universal services through the schools—in particular, if there were full school-day preschools and after-school programs. Vouchers work best in a context of state licensing/registration or other quality protection, tapered subsidy scales, and good I&R services.

Organizing Family Day Care

We shall discuss elsewhere (Chapter 7) the question of whether family day care does or does not have a long-run future. Will there be a labor force if it does not everywhere become quite expensive? If it does, must it not become more specialized? For present purposes it would appear that family day care is the child care arrangement of choice—or the only financially feasible option—for many parents of very young children. Much of it operates in the underground, unregulated and unknown. The public has a stake in turning it into a visible and reliable service. Some local agencies, taking advantage of the federal child care food program and its requirements, have organized family day care "systems" and served the public well in so doing.

Here we cannot claim that there is no other instrument that might accomplish these results. We report in Chapter 7 on the now disbanded Quality Child Care, which was operating in Minnesota and seven other states, as an alternative model. In many places state or county family day care associations have also become sponsors; in others, various other nonprofit agencies have assumed the role. Nonetheless, one must be impressed with the good fit among a "resource and referral" service, which identifies need and helps launch sponsors; a vendor/voucher system, which must in some way monitor them and concern itself with their quality; and the role of an administrator of the food program. The extra funds help the providers. The administrative overhead can be critical for the agency. The inspection visits mandated by the food program can be cast in the context of a larger role. The nutrition education and consultation become part of a technical assistance process.

We have seen these opportunities available to family day care "systems" very well used; it is important to upgrade family day care in this and other ways if it is to be employed on so large a scale. Especially encouraging is the growing provider sophistication about business practices, tax opportunities, cooperative supply and equipment purchasing, and so forth. These providers have been helped with health and liability insurance. They are given access to toy, equipment, and book libraries. In a few instances, too, they are provided with access to centers so that their charges may have group experience and they, respite. At its best the approach has even managed some interchange among them, mutual support, training, and upgrading. If family day care is to be encouraged so that it will emerge from the underground, this is not a bad beginning, but more will be needed.

Advocacy and Planning

Here the lesson is a mixed one. These new-style agencies tend to be militant advocates, often at the state level, where the funds are to be found. Child care needs increased and improved advocacy, and these agencies have impressive records of success. Nonetheless, we also must note the inevitable self-interest and opportunism. In addition to working to restore Title XX cuts through state appropriations, these groups have concentrated on state money for vendor/voucher programs, I&R, and training activities. Several have performed valuable service in seeking to strengthen the state's capacity to monitor licensed and registered facilities. Others have successfully promoted family day care registration as a less onerous alternative to licensing which, they claimed, discouraged providers from making themselves visible, yet did nothing to protect quality.

From time to time, as well, these local service agencies have played important public educational roles—as when they reacted to the child abuse scandals in child care in 1984 and 1985. They are trusted and listened to as experts by the general public and public officials and have successfully channeled the concerns in some communities in constructive directions.

Where there are city, state, or voluntary sector task forces to look ahead in child care, these groups play their part. Such activities usefully highlight needs and may provide new vehicles for cooperation. Since they tend to include competing interests, the blue ribbon panels and mayoral forces do not ordinarily and easily make significant contributions to policy or specific plans. An exception is California, where several local groups have created successful action coalitions with local industry to plan new facilities and upgrade services.

Here we arrive at outer boundaries. None of this valuable activity, we have seen, encompasses the major needed policy development and planning for a city or a state. There are preschool and after-school initiatives that come from public officials and legislatures. There are competing claims as to roles, or even competing claims on space and capital funds. There are alternative conceptions as to public responsibilities. These new local groups do not carry the answers; they become experts or advocates in battles for turf, self-interest, or alternative conceptions of the public interest. In looking at them alone one cannot tell how such matters will be resolved or by whom. To expect this would be unreasonable.

Endnotes

1. As evidence of the diminished federal reporting capacity we cite U.S. Department of Health and Human Services, *State by State Summaries of Child Day Care Services Funded by the Social Services Block Grant in FY 1984* (Washington, D.C.: 1985). Compare with Helen Blank, *Children and Federal Child Care Cuts* (Washington, D.C.: Children's Defense Fund, 1983), pp. 5–7; and Helen Blank, *Child Care: The State's Response* (Washington, D.C.: Children's Defense Fund, 1984), pp. 4–11. Also see, Helen Blank and Amy Wilkins, *Child Care: Whose Priority?* (Washington, D.C.: Children's Defense Fund, 1985).

   Slow progress continues to be made in Census Bureau and Department of Education reporting on care for children of working mothers and on preschool enrollment trends.

2. Gwen Morgan of Wheelock College convened two conferences in 1982 and 1983 that provided an important occasion for exchanges. See her unpublished, "New Models for Community Child Day Care Systems" (Boston, Mass. Wheelock College, 1983, processed). Morgan's take-off was a 1978–1980 collaboration of the U.S. Department of Health, Education and Welfare and

the Ford Foundation and focused on information and referral. See endnote 7, below.

3. Gwen Morgan, "New Models for Community Child Day Care Systems." We are indebted to the Wheelock conference and materials, which offered early and helpful access to the emerging "networks."

4. Each of these cities or states continues its process of response. While no report remains current for very long, our interest here is in understanding these organizations as community instruments, not in evaluating organizations, cities, or states.

5. A pure "voucher" program for child care would operate like food stamps. Eligible parents would receive "stamps" equal to some dollar amount and purchase child care wherever they wished. A vendor/voucher limits parents' choice to "approved" (licensed or registered) providers; most importantly, payment is made by the responsible agency directly to the provider, once the parent qualifies for the subsidy and makes a choice among approved providers. In effect, the vendor is paid on a per-child basis through this system. The parent either pays in part and the agency pays the remainder or the parent pays nothing.

6. Blank and Wilkins, *Child Care; Whose Priority?* p. 9.

7. In 1978–1980 the Ford Foundation and the Administration, for Children, Youth and Families of the then Department of Health, Education, and Welfare jointly funded Project Connections. This was an exploration of the developing child care information and referral services and "movement." There has been no overall report. See Joseph J. O'Hara et al., *Project Connections, Phase I Results: A National Profile of Information and Referral Services* (Cambridge, Mass.: American Institute for Research in the Behavioral Sciences, 1980).

8. By now many of these are also included in the IBM-initiated computer network Work/Family Directions.

9. Florida is a state with more child care service in 1985 than in 1981. The state improved things in 1985 by raising eligibility ceilings so that a mother with one child could earn $10,700, where she previously had become ineligible at $7099. A $10 million budget allocation would serve 10,000 more children in FY 1986, according to the Children's Defense Fund's 1985 phone survey, *Child Care: Whose Priority?* p. 11. The state made significant budgetary additions for 1987 as well.

Chapter 3

STATE CHILD CARE ACTIONS

The local activity described has been energetic, inventive, and important to children and their families. Few of the local leaders are satisfied, however. They have often been effective "fire-fighters" and have put some important pieces of delivery system structure into place. But they continue to face serious resource and supply problems and see major uncertainties about the future configuration of services. Several touch only a small part of the child care delivery system.

As problems arise, local leaders respond. As opportunities appear, they move. For most of them the state is a target for resources or policy, but seldom a source of inspiration or leadership. For many, there is no "state" presence, as such, but only a "social service department," an "education department," or an "employment program." Unless somewhere, locally or at the state level, a fuller strategy emerges, we shall continue as we are, coping but not shaping an adequate U.S. child care response in most places.

Local initiatives have had more backing from state resources, leadership, and structure in some states than in others. We begin by highlighting the price paid in a number of Texas cities because of the lack of a more supportive state presence. We have chosen Texas for this illustration, but a dozen other states might have served the purpose. Many of these states did not increase commitments as much as Texas did early in the 1980s. By way of contrast, and as part of our probe of the necessary state roles, we then offer an overview of California, which has a 45-year history of incremental state policy building. Massachusetts, in a different mode, appeared by mid-1986 to be moving deliberately and systematically on a broad policy and action front.

Texas

Texas has long been in the minimalist government tradition. Now, ranking third in population after California and New York and no longer poor, Texas reflects its economic explosion of the last decade and its rapid cultural and political shifts. It may properly be characterized as "torn between faith in the free market and a desire for government safety nets."[1] The oil price squeeze of the mid-1980s has created financial pressures and a new debate about state policies; there has been some tendency to undo some of the program improvements and funding gains of the early 1980s, but our case story antedates the 1986 state budget "crisis."

There was no Texas state money in child care before the late 1970s except for small funds voted for child care to support rehabilitation. The opportunity then created under Title IV-A and, later, Title XX of the Social Security Act to draw upon federal dollars at the rate of 3 to 1 was met by allowing local nonprofit groups to multiply their own funds by putting up a "match." Poor areas and most rural areas had little or nothing; big cities found many takers. The public social service agency was little more than a vehicle for channeling federal money. "An industry was created on the basis of donated dollars which were matched," in the view of one observer. Then, an association of city child care groups began to lobby for state money, too, and for increases from time to time. They also called for standards, state policy, and uniformity. The state responded positively during the oil boom prosperity and began to share costs significantly in 1982. By 1984 over one-third of the state child care budget was state funded. Then, as its economy slumped in the mid-1980s, Texas froze its commitment. By 1986 the state had reverted to an earlier pattern: No state money would be added to the Social Services Block Grant. Cities were constitutionally forbidden from funding child care out of city taxes, but a number of cities assigned some federal dollars out of Community Development Block Grants.

As has been the case elsewhere, the state has gone from direct subsidy of a limited number of providers (purchase of service) to a bidding system that has brought new agencies and participants, including minority groups, into the system while protecting the old as well. The state agency (Texas Department of Human Services) advertises for bids (on a per day rate per age group or per day for a melded group). The agency with a contract then becomes a state agent and processes applicants among those self-referred, referred, or recruited. Since 1981 state matches have not been required for federal Social Services Block Grant funds, but federal funding declined and the state child care financial picture recovered only gradually (and temporarily) through state budget increases from 1982 to 1984, local community funding, and some private support. Local leveraging of state money (mostly federal social services money) and business/private sector leveraging of public money became the prevalent pattern, modified somewhat by geographic equity and political considerations. Only recently have more objective formulas been introduced (percent of population on AFDC, numbers of protective cases, and so on).

The limited federal money and the state add-ons concentrate on income-eligible families connected with AFDC and involved in work training, job searches, or a transition—for a time-limited period. The eligibility ceilings are among the lowest in the country. Agencies that want to continue to service low-income users must raise their own funds, combine them with United Way money, and collect those fees low-income clients are considered able to pay. Almost all public subsidy goes to children in single-parent families. There are still some provider agreements (rather than vendor/voucher plans), mostly with proprietary groups in poorly served, remote areas where a small number of places are needed; then, the state conducts the financial eligibility study.

Large agencies that take on the broker roles often combine use of spaces in their own child care centers and family day care homes with making agreements with providers to serve eligible clients who have been processed in the "intake" service that these agencies operate. Then there can be resemblance to the Florida, California, or Minnesota voucher/vendor arrangements.

How these policies, traditions, and practices combine in localities with different histories and institutional structures may be observed in specific communities. We have chosen cities and agencies that have had energetic and able leadership and have enjoyed some success. It is important that the limits of the locality in a minimalist state also be understood. It must be emphasized that the Texas DHS is highly decentralized and that Texas has, in fact, 13 versions of state policy.

Houston

Neighborhood Centers, Inc. Houston's Neighborhood Centers, Inc. (NCI) was established in 1907. It took its present shape in 1968 when an association of neighborhood centers joined with the city's day care association. For almost 20 years after 1968, the agency followed a common pattern: Under entrepreneurial leadership it developed an enormous range of services, reflecting the antipoverty war, the community mental health development, and the many categorical social service initiatives funded by federal, state, and local grants. It remained a private, nonprofit agency, leveraged public money with United Way and private philanthropy as necessary, but in effect was and is heavily dependent upon public funds and the direction of public policy. By the mid-1980s it was making forays into profit-making ventures to meet heavy financial pressures, in the spirit of the new "privatization." At the time of our visits the agency was "spending" and/or passing through some $3 million for child care, of which $2 million was public money and $700,000 was from the United Way. This child care activity was "embedded" in a large multiservice agency operating a group of community centers with broad programs and including eight day care centers, which it continued to operate directly.

Neighborhood Centers is one of four "broker" agencies handling child care in Houston, two on behalf of the state and two on behalf of the city. The concept, in short, is only partially implemented and quite untidy. And, unlike Florida's 4-C, the agency operates its own centers and refers to them first, as appropriate. Client "choosing" is emphasized in areas not served by the agency itself or for people seeking family day care. The State Department of Human Resources makes referrals for care for protective cases, the first priority, and for child care connected to work training. A well-qualified intake staff determines income eligibility (acting as a surrogate for the public agency) and offers help to the parent seeking child care space. Much of this work is done on the telephone. Gross income is determined and parents are told whether they have a right to child care assistance. There is much less stress here than in the California, Florida, or Minnesota services described earlier on educating the parent as to quality issues or providing a "menu" of appropriate possibilities. Programs are not rated on quality. In any case, having found and confirmed a place, the eligible parent does come in for income verification since the family's part of the fee is set as a percentage of income. The broker system serves only very low income families.

Of the cases eventually accepted for service by this Houston vendor/voucher program, some 25 percent are protective cases, 10 percent are work-trainee families, and over 60 percent are AFDC, food-stamp, and other income eligibles. Help is limited to the training or job search time or until earnings of those employed bring them above the very low eligibility ceiling. The money is needed to give someone else on the subsidy waiting list similar transition help. Well-qualified staff pick up difficult situations when the parent comes in for the paperwork. Sometimes a referral for help or an exploration of another problem becomes far more important than the child care arrangement.

The approach to broker operations should be seen as resulting from a state initiative informed by the Florida experience and intended to spread available funding to a more geographically dispersed low-income population; and it has succeeded in doing this. In a locale with large representation of for-profit child care chains and "mom and pop" private, for-profit centers (comprising some 70 to 80 percent of all Houston centers), the new pattern allows considerable use of the "for profits," except to the extent that the agency refers to its own centers first.

The state's contracted-fee maxima are low, and centers that care about quality are in a tremendous bind. At the time of our visits Neighborhood Center's unit rate was $10.40 per day, including administration costs of implementing the program. The state, after issuing its RFP (request for proposals), had contracted at $6.40 per day for family day care and $10.28 for centers. The prevailing rates in the Houston area were between $45 and $50 per week for preschool children and a little more for infants. The agency judgment was that quality care for preschoolers at the time had to cost between $75 and $80 per week. The typical center with 50 children, what they regarded as an "ideal" size (elsewhere in the state people talked of 70), clearly was not cost effective. The proprietary chains that seemed to be making a profit were enrolling 100 to 150 children. But everywhere staff-to-child ratios were low, groups were large, caretaker qualifications were very poor— and the salaries and fringe benefits were inadequate by any standard. Staff turnover was high.

The eligible parent is charged according to the state DHS income-related fee scale, quite independently of provider costs. The parent's portion of the fee is paid directly to the child care agency. Every two weeks the provider submits an attendance form to NCI and within two weeks is paid directly. Under the old state purchase-of-care pattern, the usual wait was two months or more. Here, as in all the vendor/voucher cities, this is an enormous improvement for the small centers with no cash reserves.

NCI has contracts with 150 outside centers serving 600 publicly subsidized children as it implements its broker role. It also administers a high-quality family day care system.

What do parents do who do not qualify at the very strict income levels or under the time limits? Unless able to draw upon the agency's very limited United Way budget, the working poor who have risen a bit over the salary eligibility level or escaped from

AFDC must turn to unsupervised family day care arrangements, paying $35 weekly in low-income areas and $45 to $50 elsewhere. Many keep their children with these "private sitters" (family day care homes) until they are 3 or 4 years old. Middle-class parents, recently unemployed, are helped with private funds for brief periods until reemployed, as are others in temporary financial difficulty or crisis.

Drawing as it can on the state and the United Way, NCI has not ignored the national interest in the corporate sector. Its explorations yielded what is an almost universal conclusion: Perhaps corporations will help strengthen I&R and educational activities or undertake some special projects. However, given a weak labor market, corporations have no reason to expend their resources on subsidizing child care. On-site care and special fringe benefits will develop only in unusual circumstances.

The Houston developments do not suggest arrival at a new, stable operating pattern or leadership structure. The contracts and broker arrangements do not function badly, on their own terms and given limited administrative capacity in state DHS. But a state plan that "bumps" low-income earners at a low level and leaves them to the vagaries of insufficient United Way or other philanthropic funding for a subsequent sliding fee arrangement is not enough. Most of the working poor get questionable black market child care. Nor can the more affluent count on state protection of quality and other standards. While also dissatisfied with standards and its lack of capacity to enforce them, the state DHS will not be able to do better with current budget allocations, limited staffing for enforcement, the levels they must set for payments, or the eligibility ceilings they can allow.

Thus the most difficult of issues remain. How can a local agency like NCI influence the organization of supply in a market dominated by for-profit agencies? How can a local agency like NCI use its leverage in organizing demand if it serves the poorest users, for the most part, and only briefly at that? How is quality to be improved at this price level and under prevalent philosophies and state budgets? In fact, is there a solution to be found in an environment in which most groups of women in the labor market earn very little, can therefore pay very little for child care, and so must be served by similarly underpaid caretakers? Clearly, the circle must be broken in a more definitive fashion. The NCI people understand this and are asking probing questions.

Committee for Private Sector Initiatives. While NCI made no progress with the corporate sector, the Houston Committee for Private Sector Initiatives was established in 1982 with the mayor's support. It launched several needed, but very small, projects. It provided start-up grants of $5000 to eight after-school programs in school buildings, funded training of personnel in a number of agencies, and attempted to organize support groups of registered family day care providers, who are neither regulated nor monitored by the state. In 1984 the committee established Child Care Resource and Referral in cooperation with the public library. This program is developing core R&R activities and related parent education and is attempting specifically to use its resources to serve employees of a large group of supporting companies. It is the local IBM contract agency as well.

Austin

Just as Houston's major agency has been supplemented with an independent R&R initiative that is oriented to the corporate sector, there has been a similar development in Austin.

Child Inc. Austin's Child Inc. is a continuation and adaptation of program forms created by the Great Society: Head Start, Model Cities, and other neighborhood and participatory programs. Child Inc. describes itself as a child and parent development program serving 1300 prekindergarten children in Austin and Travis counties through a diversity of educational, nutritional, health, and social service programs. In industry it would be considered a conglomerate since, at the time visited, it was the local Head Start agency, served as the central administrative auspice for 17 homes serving 35 or 40 children in family day care, operated 13 day care centers (expanding to 17), and offered special programs for handicapped children. It also carried out state eligibility-determination functions.

In addition to accepting state and local social service, health, and educational contracts, Child Inc. responds to federal grant possibilities and is sometimes successful. The agency works with a community college on paraprofessional training for Head Start teachers; it administers a visiting teacher program for 200 children. Its director, James Strickland, is a nationally known and visible child care leader and activist.

Child Inc., in short, is the modern social service agency; it *is* what is funded. The system here, as in many other cities throughout the country, is an ever-changing mosaic of categorical initiatives plus a few general funding and block grant resources, spending public funds through whatever agencies have written successful grant proposals or responses to RFPs or have lobbied and politicked successfully. Child Inc. is thus the largest private, publicly funded delivery agency for child care in Austin.

Child Inc. is. a program that respects parents, children, and population diversity and does what it can with what it has. Despite tradition and practice elsewhere, all child care programs, even Head Start, are open all day here to serve working parents. (But Head Start is funded for a nine-month school year and summers are a problem.) Innovative training of professionals, using Head Start approaches adapted to adults, is employed to create a competent if low-paid caretaking corps. Many of the program initiatives of this imaginative agency are impressive and important, yet its director knows that something more is needed by way of policy, planning, funding, and governmental administration. Many child care needs are not met locally, and there is much below-standard care.

Austin Families, Inc. Begun in 1976 as an advocacy effort in child care, Austin Families, Inc. sought to target employers and create a voucher program. As a first step, a rudimentary I&R service was attached to the agency. For present purposes, the initial history of shoe-string funding, volunteering, and small grants need not be reviewed.

Orlando was visited, other experience was tapped, a series of trial-and-error forays were made, and by 1983 the agency outlined a concept of "building blocks": information and referral (on the California pattern); vouchers (to be publicly and employer funded); assisting employers (to meet employee needs in other ways, too); quality upgrading (of family day care). However, in a departure from the Florida quality control, any licensed or registered provider could be used without an effort at rating.

Austin Families is clearly only a supplementary program. Child Inc. has the bulk of the Title XX load (which, nonetheless, meets only a small part of the local child care need). Austin Families, when visited, was receiving marginal grants under Title XX and work-training and refugee grants and was seeking foundation money and private contributions as well. Funding was small-scale; the information service was surviving largely on overhead. Little employer support was obtained, and employer interest was low.

Until 1985 all that could be said about Austin Families, Inc. was that it had a vision and enthusiasm but limited funds or impact. Private employers were neither interested nor responsive; the only employer contract it obtained was one covering female bus drivers for the local public school district. By early 1986 the report was "more solid funding" and a "better position" generally. The agency had become the local contractor for the national I&R network for IBM employees, and the contract included a computer and a software program. Four other local companies had "bought into" the system. A city and county contract enabled the I&R to serve the public generally. Three companies were making voucher money available in a modest program for their employees. The local school district had continued the contract for its employees. Moreover, Austin Families had organized a conference locally for employers; subsequently, several purchased groups of "slots" for their employees in child care centers, and one developed an on-site child care facility.

In the face of the state funding freeze and a low support level, Austin Families, Inc. continued to see itself in a supplementary role. Others, especially Child Inc., served as state "brokers" for families eligible for Title XX day care support or for Head Start. This agency served those just over the Title XX level and able to pay modest fees or others covered by a short-lived work-training contract. The I&R and related services would continue to focus on these groups and on employees of companies with contracts.

This adaptation of the new Florida-California model is operating on the perimeters of the child care problem. Austin Families is not a major actor; Child Inc. is the main service source. Austin Families' limited ad hoc grants from employers or categorical training programs are not a substitute for adequate resources in a state that spends limited funds through a broker (vendor/voucher) strategy. In this decentralized state the available instruments yield neither adequate information nor coherent strategy, and the introduction of new agents, however promising, does not suffice.

Dallas

Although new R&R agencies have the IBM contracts in Houston and Austin, this function and related corporate initiatives went to a very old agency in Dallas. Child Care Dallas had its origins in a free nursery established by German immigrant philanthropists in 1900 to serve the children of mothers working in the cotton mill. Part of a social agency, it had shrunk but still had four centers by 1940. Growth resumed during the Great Society.

In 1971, when the state offered local child care agencies the opportunity to get three federal dollars for each one they had, Child Care Dallas became the Dallas sponsor agency. In 1981, when the Reagan administration cuts came, funds decreased $800,000 a year. United Way and private philanthropy have been unusually responsive here, and the agency has taken advantage of other federal funding opportunities. It continued significant growth and development until the extreme financial crunch of the mid-1980s.

Child Care Dallas has attempted to sustain the best of the social agency traditions. The agency emphasizes professionalism, quality, and assessment of results. At the same time, its responses to the new initiatives (I&R, corporate child care, vendor/voucher programs, and accreditation) shed light on the emerging issues and the limitations of local initiatives. When visited, the program included the following activities:

- Direct operation of eight neighborhood-based child care centers (about 560 children).
- Placement of about 200 children in 50 family day care homes in an agency-operated network.
- Administration of a state-funded "broker" program (vendor/voucher) for up to 300 children (some of whom are placed in the agency's centers and family day care homes).
- A federally funded corporate initiative program (to 1985) and modest follow-up activity.
- An IBM-funded information and referral service, in which some other companies have joined.
- A variety of research and staff development initiatives.
- Some advocacy activity at the local and state levels.

In mid-1984 about 80 percent of the children were government subsidized and about 20 percent were covered by the United Way. The client fees for children in the corporate program were being paid by parents, but a significant portion of actual program costs were met by the federal government.

The operation is given perspective when one counterposes its total of 1100 children, the agency's maximum direct service load, against the report that in 1984 Dallas had a licensed capacity of over 36,000 for center day care in 405 centers, as well as almost 12,000 children in nursery school. Much of the city's child care capacity is in proprietary chains and "mom and pop" operations of relatively low standard.

The eight centers stress quality. Qualified administrative staff are responsible for the "business" side (half-time for each center) so that directors may focus personally on the child caring program. The agency's program director is a leader in child development theory and guides programs and ongoing child assessment. A demanding "child progress audit" form, adopted from work done at the Bank Street College of Education, is filled out regularly by staff specialists who monitor the centers. The agency cooperated with

the National Association for the Education of Young Children
(NAEYC) in the development of voluntary accreditation procedures and has been urging the adoption of voluntary NAEYC
accrediting through the community. Late in 1986, five of its
centers were among the first to be accredited in the new program.
Staff are higher paid and have better fringe benefits than the
prevailing local patterns; thus turnover is lower. Staff strengths are
shared with others through a variety of training offerings.

When mothers' earnings go above the low state cutoff level for
eligibility of 47 percent of the state median income (the rate when
we visited), the agency uses United Way money and a sliding scale
to keep children in care. Once a child is in care, there is continuity
until kindergarten, whatever the income change and the public
eligibility. The experience reported for Florida and much of Texas
suggests just how valuable this commitment can be. The alternative "bumping and dumping" phenomenon has become a major
U.S. child care problem of the 1980s. The substantial United Way
support—beyond what is typical elsewhere—is the result of ongoing day-to-day work by the executive director, Madeline Mandell.
The community is kept informed and involved.

The per child cost of this quality effort, in centers limited to 72
children, was over $70 weekly, with the average parent paying $7
daily in 1984, at a time that state daily reimbursement in its broker
program was $10.28 daily in centers. By 1985 the agency was
reporting average daily care costs of $15.79 for its 1109 "spaces."

The agency is not able to contemplate any expansion of centers.
Here, as elsewhere, construction of new center facilities by not-
for-profit agencies has proven to be financially impossible (in mid-
1985 the cost was $1 million for a center for 72 children: four
groups with 18 children in each room and two teachers). Only
corporate chains with access to venture capital have been managing. The alternatives are the families who use their homes for
family day care or who undertake renovations and "add ons" for
small centers.

The agency's family day care homes program is described as
"cost effective," which means that per child costs are one-third or
one-half less than those of centers. (The 1985 state reimbursement
was $6.40 daily.) This situation is, of course, a common one
nationally and is part of what is behind the emphasis on family day
care in recent years. However, there also is some conviction here
that infant and toddler care is best assigned to family day care
homes. Moreover, there is some evidence of parental preference
along these lines.

The problem is, of course, one of quality. Most family day care in the city is unregistered, unlicensed, unvisited—and some of it is known to be very questionable. Here, too, though less successful, Child Care Dallas is working at the task of selecting family day care providers and offering strong support. A heroic effort is needed to upgrade competence and to equip and improve the homes. Success is modest at best. For example, Child Care pays providers to attend training meetings on Saturdays, but can afford only four meetings a year. Despite quite low standards, only one in five family day care applicants can be accepted.

The broker program, known as Parent's Choice, emphasizes the advantages of a voucher: A parent can elect family day care or center care and choose the particular facility. This is the major state DHR contract with the agency and is not unlike others in the state already described. It is the only broker contract in the county. In keeping with the agency's standards, it does not work with unlicensed centers or unregistered homes, but because registration has meant little in Texas, the agency inspects homes to ensure that mandatory standards are met. Homes that have been recruited by potential clients or by DHR caseworkers will be visited by agency staff and helped to register.

Like R&R and vendor/voucher agencies elsewhere, Child Care Dallas has become a resource for potential providers. In the ongoing relationships with centers and family day care homes receiving state payments through the agency, the Child Care Dallas staff does what it can to offer technical consultation so as to raise standards.

In return for fulfilling the broker service, the agency receives $1.40 per child per day from DHR daily rates. Duties include certifying client eligibility and priority under state regulations and giving the provider written certification that the child is eligible and within the agency's broker quota (a 300-child maximum).

The program has major problems. A mother seeking work is eligible only for 30 days, and her child is then dropped if she has been unsuccessful. Here, they have no United Way money to supplement. And the earning limits are tight.

Child Care Dallas' Corporate Initiative Program is a cautionary tale more than justifying the agency's statement before the Select Committee on Children of the U.S. House of Representatives on May 2, 1984: "It would be very unrealistic to assume that employers are going to play an immediate or major role in resolving the child care crisis." (See Chapter 6.) In 1982 the agency received a federal grant "to develop and demonstrate an employer-assisted family day care home system as a new approach to solving the severe shortage of quality care for infants and toddlers." The assumption was that this program could be implemented more rapidly and with less capital investment than a center program and that family day care was responsive to employee preferences. Although the agency announced success ("the program works"), its documentation requires very close reading. The agency approached 31 employers that "fit the profile of potential participants"—had a work force that seemed to need the service—but they would not consider the program. Twenty-one others "considered" but were not responsive; they bowed out. Six companies cooperated—but in a program in which they shared no costs at all.

As this nationally publicized "success" reached its end, only one of the companies continued its program and made a modest investment. The agency faced the inevitable discovery that it could not justify two separate family day care programs. Like the rest of the country, it saw I&R as a more promising corporate initiative. Without a problem in recruitment of mothers of young children as employees, businesses have little reason to take on on-site operations or any heavy investment in provision of services.

Just as Child Care Dallas had the same experience with corporate child care as did many of the new-style agencies in California, Florida, and Minnesota, so did it discover the validity of the I&R approach initiated elsewhere. I&R began in 1984, when the agency joined the IBM national network and computerized; high volume and other evidence pointed to a useful program. By mid-1985 seven other corporations had written I&R contracts for their employees. Others were added during 1986. Clearly, the I&R function fits nicely into a traditional agency program and broadens its constituency and usefulness. The larger number of subscribers helps meet agency costs.

Employers are provided with dedicated phone connections for their own use and unlimited free access to service by their employees. (Others who call upon the R&R service are charged either $25 for a provider listing in the required area or $55 for a list of verified vacancies. Low-income users are charged $4.)

True to its tradition of quality service, the agency has been regularly monitoring and assessing the progress of the children in its care. Professionally led and with a good component of well-qualified top staff, it had adopted excellent tools for child assessment and also entered into research agreements, but there are as yet no reports of allegedly positive results available for review in research journals.

On the advocacy level, in addition to its work on behalf of state budgets, the agency has concentrated on efforts to raise standards. It has urged the state as well to add to its licensing-inspection staff and to increase inspection visits and enforcement generally. Its program director chaired a city task force which concluded in 1984 that if there is no state upgrading, the city itself should undertake licensing and enforcement. The report urged local citizen educational and staff training efforts, efforts to increase funds available, and encouragement for voluntary accreditation by NAEYC.

We conclude this review by noting that Child Care Dallas continues in the best voluntary child welfare and child care tradition and, in an environment in which funding is a major problem, has not compromised quality for quantity. Nonetheless, Child Care Dallas touches only a small part of what occurs by way of child care service in its area, perhaps 2 percent of the Dallas children in licensed day care and nursery schools in 1984.

The Texas Schools

We conclude this section by noting that none of these agencies, except Houston's Committee for the Private Sector Initiative (providing very modest start-up funds for after-school programs), has encompassed the education-based component of the state's child care effort. Child Inc. in Austin is a Head Start agency, of course. But there has been a Texas statewide effort to bring schooling to the 4-year-olds in recent years, and some implementation began in 1986. Houston's school district has launched a variety of pilots covering "extended day" schools; year-round schools; school-company cooperation to permit children to share vans with parents en route to work, to attend school near the plant, and to return home with their parents; and other explorations. The Houston school district now provides free building space to non-profit organizations willing to undertake school-based child care programs and able to meet the costs.

Neither the agencies described nor the state Department of Human Services has a mandate to think about all of child care. They are operating within the social welfare context only. State government's education initiatives are in another domain and perhaps even reflect a larger readiness for a state leadership role.

California Moves

California has the largest program and the highest state budget for child care services in the country. Its history is continuous since 1943. Nonetheless, given labor force patterns, increased single parenthood, and changing cultural attitudes about the desirability of group experience and education for children of preschool age, there are constant calls for expansion, many vigorous initiatives, and some debates about priorities.

We discuss in Chapter 5 California's unique history of education-based child care. California was and remains the lead state in its responses, anchored in state initiatives and financial support, to the need for child care provision. Its large preschool program along the Head Start model is unmatched, and its resource and referral and alternative payments programs have been of considerable nationwide influence. When the state developed new initiatives in this field in the late 1970s, it left the education programs in place and turned to the locally based social service agencies for the new departures. In a sense California was out of phase. In much of the country people see the preschool initiatives as bypassing or energizing the more traditional social service system. Here, some of the R&R activism has attracted some of the small school districts, too.

School-Age Care

The big, new issue for California was school-aged child care, and its 1984–1985 actions are instructive.[2] The first grants were made early in 1986. In a political compromise between Democratic legislators and a Republican governor, the state passed laws involving a large program of "extended day care services" along with a major work-training program (GAIN) for welfare recipients that ensures their school-aged children access to child care. An extended quotation from the Children's Defense Fund account provides detail:[3]

> *The state has created a new school-aged child care program. It will provide $8 million to localities for operating expenses the first year and $16 million, annually, thereafter. Participating localities must provide a dollar for dollar match, which will bring the total operating budget to $32 million. The match may be raised by enrolling enough middle-income families, paying full tuition, to equal the amount received from the state, or by operating local fund-raising drives. If these methods are unfeasible, the locality can apply for a waiver based on demographic data. The state has also authorized a total of $36.5 million in start-up costs for latchkey programs, $14 million for all low-income school-age child care programs and $22.5 million specifically for capital outlays for the children of people participating in the state's workfare program. The state has allocated $10.6 million in operating costs or up to $2100 per child for school-age care for the children of former AFDC recipients enrolled in training programs and job search.*

There are strong requirements for community involvement in the planning and for education–social welfare coordination, but child care for GAIN is under local welfare departments, while the remainder of the effort, as all other non-AFDC child care in California, is under the department of Education (DE). County welfare officials have much flexibility in serving GAIN clients, but some observers worry about a possibly expanding two-tier system. For the rest of the program, DE-administered program rules will ensure a social-class mix of children, but funding formulas will protect poor areas. To save transportation costs, programs at or near school sites are to be favored, but schools will be encouraged to contract with private providers. Except for children in need of protective care, and who will have priority, eligibility will be limited to children with parents who must be away from home because of work or training. Families will pay on an income-related sliding fee scale.

Most impressive is the spelling out of program components in a fashion that permits diversity: Local districts will be able to select cultural, recreational, or educational emphases and build their staffing plans accordingly. The superintendent of public institutions may encourage diversity by waiving day care regulation for good cause when inappropriate to the circumstances or program design.

In short, California appears to be following its decade-long pattern: a child care initiative concerned with after-school programs but not necessarily limited to the schools at all. But the GAIN rules could separate one group of children from the rest.

Other California Developments

Other statewide developments in 1985 and 1986 are of interest, supplementing the R&R and AP report in Chapter 2. The San Francisco-based Child Care Resource and Referral (CCRR) network is a major actor. With R&R, then AP and individual projects as a base, these groups, such as BANANAS, the Switchboard, and seven or eight others, have done much to energize California child care in the past decade.

These new developments may be understood against the backdrop of the ongoing CCRR network advocacy role. With its executive officer Patty Siegel (also the chair of the Governor's Advisory Committee on Child Development Programs from 1982–1984), the CCRR group has lobbied actively with regard to child care funding, advocated for specific policies, and kept child care issues visible. It has launched studies and projects. Its quarterly bulletin has been circulated nationally, and CCRR is central to the creation of a new national organization for R&R groups.

Once a series of foundation start-up grants were exhausted, and for lack of a significant funding source for its own administrative and coordination tasks, apart from limited member dues, the CCRR took on several demonstration and training activities. Inevitably, in recent years these have been concentrated on child abuse, especially in child care centers.

The more recent initiatives began with a child care information kit produced as a cooperative venture by the Bay Area R&R agencies. The kit is a cooperative form of information sharing on child care supply, demand, and demographic context. It has substantial educational content: a glossary, consumer and provider vignettes, and information about the R&R network. It provides a context of trends, issues, and public opinion.

The kit was, in the view of the network, an "instant success." Circulation was significant, and two corporations provided funds for reprinting. Moreover, several R&R agencies outside of the Bay Area adapted the format and "plugged in" their own data. A number requested consultation. A useful tool for planning of a sort and advocacy had evolved.

Then, the Bank America Foundation helped set up a "supply" development project for six pilot sites, drawing upon the CCRR network headquarters for administration and project direction and placing local staff on site. Public and private groups have been mobilized for this effort, which includes, at present writing, state government (the largest contributor), at least six major corporations, two county governments, and one city government. The project is focused on understanding gaps in child care supply and ways to help specific to the locality. Expanding the supply of licensed family day care providers is a particular goal. In three communities there are "needs assessments" under way, which are expected to yield predictable results and to help create community support. A "developer's kit" was prepared to help builders of large complexes and local government think about work force needs in new areas. The Child Care Law Center contributed guidance with regard to zoning laws. The funding permits the production of a diversity of training materials.

In short, corporations and their resources have been mobilized in a somewhat more systematic way to join local government in development of an improved child care supply. Because large capital funds are not available, the principals have placed their emphasis more on family day care and pre- and after-school programs than on new centers; there has been a small amount of funding for equipment for after-school programs. This development is not quite a planning structure, but it does move corporations in a new direction. Although they have not chosen to help their low-paid employee-mothers directly, these corporations are no longer concentrated only on information and referral and employee-education efforts. Several other R&Rs in other cities are following the lead.

Late in 1985, there was a new development: A local San Francisco law, sponsored by Supervisor Nancy Walker and passed with the mayor's backing, requires that developers of new downtown skyscrapers must provide either space or money ($1 per square feet) for child care centers. Concord has followed, and other communities are considering the issue. Will this change the capital funding picture? Downtown child care space was considered necessary to cope with waiting lists. At the same time, several new after-school initiatives have been proposed by members of the board of supervisors. Child care is being escalated as a municipal political issue in several communities. Of equal interest, as noted, the state legislature moved on after-school care for school-aged children during its 1985 session.

Perhaps California has "grown" a design: The R&Rs are the child care core, with a strong subsidized center sector and a strong for-profit sector, both of which now depend on R&Rs. The latter are advocates, educators, and sources of seed money and contribute to staff development. Nonprofit, center-based contractors and school districts divide the program money almost equally. Some of the school districts resemble the new community agencies we have described and are operating local R&Rs and developing innovative programs for special needs groups. The AP programs, which buy service for poor children, also turn to the private sector and thus bridge the systems. Since California's new school-aged child care law requires school districts to serve fee-paying families as well as the poor, the R&Rs play a central role there, too.

Inevitably, of course, questions arise: Does this suffice? Will it all come together? Can a state with strong, creative local agencies like the ones described plus the ongoing program of school district and nonprofit center subsidy, a work-training initiative by the governor, and an interested legislature move ahead soundly and adequately in this field? Do periodic, imaginative initiatives that move from local R&R and AP to corporate projects to school-aged care and to work program supports—all while the core program continues on a large scale, comparatively, but still not large enough—eventually add up to the sound, quantitatively adequate, and continuing program that is needed? Is this now the needed

design, the model for states? Has the needed state-level policy
emerged from independent and competitive initiatives in a political marketplace? Is more needed? If so, what? We do not pretend
to know that the U.S. political scene will sustain more coherence,
but we do turn to the alternative Massachusetts scenario.

A State Takes Action: Massachusetts

As we have seen, even the most exemplary and successful of local
initiatives depend on state resources and cooperation. Moreover,
the sum total of what localities do leaves out many issues, including
the question of standards. Finally, there are developments in
education that may impact on child care and are not in the purview
of most of the most inventive of the new-type local child care
organizations. What is the relationship between the privatization,
decentralization, and deregulation that we have observed and the
total requirements of a child care initiative? Massachusetts has
moved as much in developing a statewide strategy as any state thus
far.

Massachusetts has encouraged some local initiatives similar to
those in Florida, California, and elsewhere. We already discussed
one such agency, the Child Care Resource Center headquartered
in Cambridge. Indeed, Gwen Morgan at Wheelock College in
Boston has been a major facilitator, initially through the I&R
"Project Connections" (federal government and Ford Foundation
funded);[4] then by convening a series of conferences where those
experimenting with local initiatives could exchange experience;
and, finally, by contracting to develop, implement, and administer
Work/Family Directions, a national I&R system that began with a
large IBM contract, encourages other companies to buy in, and has
proven to be a major stimulus to the new-type local agencies
already described. (The leadership is shared with Fran Rodgers.)

Nonetheless, we shall now focus somewhat differently. Massachusetts, in recent years, has been searching for vehicles and a
mode of action ensuring a somewhat more than typical degree of
coordination and integration in child care strategy. It is highly
unlikely that the current pattern is fixed; nor does it answer all
obvious questions. The discussion therefore contributes—as do the
"local initiative" cases discussed earlier—to the clarification of the
agenda for the remainder of this volume. The state leadership
debate is about division of roles, conceptions, and resources.

It is clear from the history and the picture of developments
already presented that many departments in a typical state have

some stake in or responsibility for child care services: the public assistance agency, the social services unit, the education department, the child or youth or family office (if separate from the above), the unit concerned with women's issues, the economic development agency, the mental health agency, the health department, the building or community development department. Beyond this, there may be some arrangements for attention to such issues in the legislature and in the governor's office, varying with the particular administration. If a special effort is made to plan, coordinate, or develop public support, there may also be created state-level blue ribbon panels, task forces, or advisory groups.

What has characterized the past decade is fluctuation of interest, and/or competition, and/or shifting of responsibility among such units, as states have coped with different funding opportunities and shifting priorities. The following themes have been evident:

- Care for children of very low income working mothers or mothers in training.
- Protective care for endangered children.
- A compensatory experience for deprived children.
- Development of programs to help mothers leave AFDC or to create child care employment opportunities for such mothers.
- The guarantee of child care as a component of new work-training or "workfare" initiatives in welfare departments administering AFDC.
- The encouragement of child care expansion as a component of city or state economic development strategies.
- Upgrading education by beginning with preschoolers.

Many of these preoccupations occur simultaneously, and an initiative may be interpreted in several ways. Given the nature of the public funding patterns, the local agencies in the several states have been dominated most recently by the work-training and protective commitments, while also attempting to encourage corporate action by stressing the economic development rationale. State initiatives tend to respond to acute funding shortages or fascination with new instruments (the voucher or I&R) but seldom "put it all together." Whereas panels and task forces write broad programs, follow-up is usually categorical. Our conclusion, based on our assessment of local efforts, is that there are impressive and important local initiatives in service delivery but a serious lack of scale, scope, and coherence. This lack clearly requires remedy through more adequate state response. Massachusetts suggests possibilities.

Massachusetts arrived at its present statewide approach only gradually, after several approximations, and after two governors clarified their major preoccupations and preferred ways of working. In effect, three successive statewide "reports" or proposed plans exemplify the process. The first two will have brief mention since it is the third which was part of the current statewide action.

First, the day care field offered its perspective in a report by Gwen Morgan, *Caring About Children in Massachusetts: Feasible Day Care Policy for the 1980s*.[5] The report grew out of a conference; reflected the I&R, voucher, and corporate initiatives which Morgan and others were encouraging nationally; retained a strong concern for quality; and called for increased resources. It needed to become a departmental or gubernatorial program before it could move. Next came the substantial effort by the state's Department of Social Service (DSS), the Title XX agency charged by the legislature in 1982 with developing a "comprehensive plan for *day care* services . . ." (emphasis supplied) and submitting it early in 1983. The department was then also under mandate to evaluate the voucher plan, as described earlier.

The report of DSS, *A Comprehensive Child Care Delivery System: A Working Plan*,[6] was offered as building on the Morgan effort. Its list of child care objectives included most of the possibilities presented in the above listing. A commitment was stated to affordability, availability, access, and quality. Its main delivery proposal called for a network of "child resource agencies" outside of the government network and carrying out the functions we have described for the new types of local initiative agencies: I&R, packaging of funding, educating parents in selection of child care, encouraging employer financial participation, and aiding providers through technical assistance and training. California and Florida were specifically mentioned as models. A management information system would be built into this network to facilitate the tracking of supply and demand and contribute to planning efforts. At the state governmental level, a policy planning unit would be created to work across departments; there also would be a statewide advisory group, a general upgrading of state administrative capacity, and policy as well as resource improvements through sliding fee, voucher, training, tax credit, and related reforms.

Placing this report in the context of the then prevailing division of responsibilities in the state is useful. Since DSS contracted with providers and had been mandated earlier to experiment with vouchers, it was the obvious center of day care activity and had appropriately been charged with the overview. It had a commissioner and staff committed to social services and had been actively involved in restructuring service delivery generally in a state that had organizationally separated the administration of cash assistance from the service programs.

However, the state also has an Office for Children with a regulatory and licensing role for child welfare programs, including day care. Its program also encompasses an advocacy activity, staffed to focus on individual needs of children, and a statewide network of staffed "councils," through which citizens may seek to make a contribution to the legislative debate. The statute that established the office also assigned it a broad coordinating role and potential veto on proposed day care spending proposals, but these roles had not been implemented.

The DSS report had called for an increase in the monitoring and licensing staff of the Office of Children. The office, with considerable community backing, saw the plan as "creative, stimulating, controversial." Like others, it complained that the report was written by DSS without adequate comment and review by "consumer and provider communities" and called for a six-month comment period. The report itself endorsed a similar process.

The first of the above two reports was delivered to a state administration whose governor was not sympathetic. The second found a new and very much interested governor and an active interest group debate. The state economy was doing well, and child care was needed. The governor's employment training initiative for welfare recipients also required strong child care service support. Although two reports were on file and the action they had proposed could have been considered at once, they were not the new administration's reports and did not begin with its concerns. Early in 1984 Governor Michael S. Dukakis created his own Governor's Day Care Partnership project to be chaired by a state senator and the governor's adviser on women's issues. Four working groups were set up at once: government, the private sector, local government and school system, and higher education. The Partnership was to submit a report by September 1984, answering these questions:

- How should future day care policy be determined?
- What is the best model for delivery of services?
- Who should be eligible for state-subsidized services?
- How can the state encourage other sectors— employers, labor, local government, school systems, higher education—to invest in day care services? The emphasis on employers was clearly to differentiate this from other reviews.

The Partnership combined staff work and expert consultation with a substantial statewide forum activity. Its members began by

reviewing highlights and proposals from the two earlier reports
and submitted a final report to the governor in 1984. This docu-
ment, *Final Report of the Governor's Day Care Partnership*,[7]
became the launching pad for an impressive series of legislative
and administrative steps. In their cover note the co-chairs stated
that they had developed "a comprehensive child care policy . . .
[by approaching day care] not only as a key human service but also
as an integral piece of employment policy and economic development." The state could take the leadership in establishing this
policy as a priority, in improving quality and in stimulating other
sectors, but the state could not do it alone.

Now the necessary combinations of executive leadership, legislative support, and interest group coalitions had come together in
an economic and resource environment that would enable action.
Traditional social welfare day care providers were to be helped to
expand and improve quality, the state's ET (employment training)
program would be serviced, the governor's interest in a larger
employer role pushed, and the new I&R delivery component
created on a statewide basis. The schools would also be encouraged
to participate but not permitted to close out consumers, community agencies, or day care centers. Priority would be given to poor
children.

The *Final Report* was organized around the goals of resource
development, quality, affordability, and policy coordination/imple-
mentation. Beginning with a commitment to recognize the diversity of family needs and protect parental choice, the report argued
that each community should have all options available: infant/
toddler centers, preschools and school-aged day care centers,
work-site care, in-home care, family day care homes and systems,
extended day programs in schools, emergency services. Every
option should be designed to meet a child's developmental needs.

Resource development was highlighted, especially creation of a
statewide R&R network within three years and covering the
responsibilities recommended in the two earlier reports. This
network would be developed and coordinated by the Office for
Children, contracting with existing agencies or new community
groups, or itself operating the service out of its area offices if
necessary. Many observers in the state leadership see creation of
this network as potentially the most lasting and important of the
report's results. Other resource development plans proposed
cover initiation of employer-sponsored projects, state programs for
its own employees, and encouragement of school-aged programs in
the education department.

To improve quality, the report recommended increasing reimbursement rates paid to providers to permit increased salaries in

centers and family day care. The new R&R agencies would be helped to develop training activities for providers in their localities. Expansion of services would feature "systems" of family day care providers, thus allowing improved quality control. The Office for Children would be more adequately funded so that it might discharge its licensing responsibilities, simplify procedures, and create a reliable registration arrangement for family day care. A variety of proposals about continuity, reform of federal tax credits, reorganization of the sliding fee scales, and state tax relief were developed under the affordability topic.

Finally, to plan, implement, and monitor, the report proposed that the governor's Office of Human Resources "function as the focal point for the development and coordination of overall day care policy," that the governor establish a day care cabinet including the major executive branch departments concerned, and that he also appoint an advisory committee with a "broad constituency." The idea of one statewide operating day care agency was rejected. The report also proposed an annual day care plan and budget to be prepared by the cabinet, reviewed by the advisory committee, and submitted to the governor. The governor's Office of Human Resources would have a lead role in planning, staffing the cabinet, coordinating resource development, coordinating implementation, federal liaison, and evaluation.

The report appeared in print in January 1985. The governor's Office of Human Resources has in fact become the lead agency. Much had been started by early 1986; by late 1986 the implementation was well along:

- A significant increase in day care funding through the social service system, to expand the sliding fee scale, increase provider reimbursement, and strengthen the licensing-monitoring capacity of the Office of Children, particularly as a way to expand family day care for infants and bring that school-aged care which is not school-run effectively into the regulation system. The state budget for 1985–87 raised day care worker salaries 32 percent (at a state cost of $8 million), expanded subsidized child care slots in the state by 26 percent to 26,000 children in all categories and including 8000 served through vouchers in the state education/training work program known as ET.
- A commitment to full statewide R&R coverage through a network of 12 nonprofit contract agencies was being rapidly implemented. Seven R&Rs were operating and a "request for proposals" for the remainder had been issued. There were good state models. A fee-for-service pattern was established,

and each agency was expected to raise some money locally and to seek contracts for R&R service with private sector firms as well. The annual cost for the network would be $2 million.

- The enactment of a pilot grant program allowing the Board of Education to enable local school committees to develop innovative early childhood programs for 3- and 4-year-olds, enhanced kindergartens, and creative combinations of early childhood education and child care. The legislation authorized expenditure at a $20 million level. For the first year the appropriation was $10.2 million. The fiscal 1987 budget is $18.7 million. The legislation requires that at least three-quarters of the funds go to low-income sites. Local applications must be supported by local early childhood advisory councils representative of community racial and ethnic diversity. The program is to be administered by an early childhood office; guided by a broadly representative state advisory committee; prepared to develop program standards (these standards must be equal to or may exceed those developed by the Office for Children for the social welfare system) and offer technical assistance to local boards; and expected to create a preschool program with heavy components of Head Start, social service, child care, and community agency participation (see Chapter 5). There may be contracting with either public or private agencies to operate services.
- A corporate child care program established in the Office of Economic Affairs to assist and encourage employers to act. Below-market rate loans were available to stimulate employer establishment of on-site centers. Some 63 employers were offering on-site care and it was said to be very popular, especially with parents of infants and toddlers who liked having their children nearby.
- Although the social service department had dropped a voucher experiment in 1985 with no obvious success and provider opposition, it was administering the important and popular ET voucher initiative of the welfare department. Traditional programs also were expanding and said to be improving, given the infusion of new money. Licensing and inspection were being emphasized, unlike the trend in some other states; for example, there were home inspection visits before any new family day care licenses were issued.

The result of all this was a 50 percent increase in funds over two years, reflected in the reported increases in subsidized children, provider reimbursement and salaries, and the launching of a new statewide delivery system through the R&R network. A policy planning and implementation instrument was in place. Child care had become a visible public policy matter.

The political history of this reform is not yet written but one notes that the child care advocates had joined with providers and unions of day care workers to achieve both an increase in coverage and better provider reimbursement. Together they had contained a school-based initiative, so as to protect favored standards and ensure a role for community groups and the day care system. For this reason the program offered grants, for which a locality had to qualify, rather than a new school reimbursement formula. Everybody in the "industry" could back the access and technical support system created with the launching of the statewide R&R network. The trade unions could endorse the package because it provided for salary increases and for staff to bring the child care issue to unions and also promised protection of standards.

Industry and the public at large were attracted to the use of child care to support state economic development plans and to provide work for welfare recipients. A new loan fund for start-up money and several new corporate initiatives encouraged everybody. The Office for Children, with its grass roots constituency, had an important new program (R&R), while its licensing/regulation staff was to grow!

Massachusetts had made some choices, and some actors were eclipsed, but clearly there was direction, structure, financial investment, significant expansion, some policy, and some commitment. Localities had both new support and operational context as they responded to acknowledged child care needs. A state role was developing. One could not yet tell whether the changes were relatively permanent (in the sense that any established state government or policy change is regarded as ongoing even though it is likely to evolve). However, the continuity of state administration after the November 1986 election suggested that the development would continue. The time had come to shift from a time-limited two-year governor's initiative to an ongoing function of state government. Plans were being completed to move the leadership and coordination function from the governor's office to the Executive Office of Human Services, which would set up a pattern of formal "integrating meetings" with the commissioner of education.

Learning from Local Initiatives and State Actions

We set out to understand the new community instruments at the local level, developed in response to the funding cutbacks and shifts of the 1980s, and the new demands put on the child care delivery system by social change. What emerged suggests dedication, creativity, and a conviction about the significance of the need. It justifies admiration and praise. Some of the lessons are ongoing and should be made explicit.

At the same time, the exploration yields a picture of a field in rapid change, of major policy issues unresolved, of critical programming choices unsettled. Communities and states have child care activities but not full programs. Child care for America's children, for many infants and toddlers, for most preschoolers, appears, despite its long history, as an institution only beginning to take its mature form. And until some very difficult questions are resolved and choices made, these often interesting and perhaps inspired local inventions will continue to have their feet planted in midair, reacting (albeit often creatively) to constantly shifting winds. They may even occasionally affect the directions taken, but without being certain just who will have the initiative the next time around.

We do not wish to be misunderstood. Living institutions and systems serving the public are never fully fixed. Change is inherent and inevitable. But transition is quite different from not being certain about the societal view of one's tasks, sanctions, resources, accountability, and institutional relationships. It is these aspects that should be given something more than transitional form as a new social institution or institutions are created.

In this context the limitations of the new or reshaped local agencies become apparent, as we discussed at the close of the last chapter. They have become creative, inventive, dedicated players on an undefined field. Yet, the next moves must come from a higher policy level or levels—or from unmistakable public choices—if further progress is to be made. Our several local cases and description of the Texas situation have illustrated the possibilities and raised questions: Can and should city or state agencies be created that will make some of the parameter-setting decisions about policies, instruments, responsibilities? What should be the roles and relationships of the educational and social welfare systems? Of employers? We shall return to a more detailed discussion of these issues shortly. For now, we turn to our major question, Can child care policy emerge from current local and state initiatives, and, if it can, what kind of policy would it be?

What exists in child care at the local and state levels may, in one vocabulary, be described as the outcome of decades of incremental policy making with little intergovernmental or interfield coordination. The initiatives were often provided by the creation of new federal funding streams. The pattern persists, but now the federal impetus comes from cutback strategies and there are some state commitments.

An alternative formulation would say that we now have, in states and cities, a disorganized political and economic market. Responding to a growing need for child care, states follow diverse strategies, helping suppliers directly at one time, users at another. Responding to the social welfare community on some occasions, to the educational system and its supporters at others, funds are voted, programs launched, regulations developed, or departments staffed. The pattern yields both the limited Texas responses and the impressive California statewide coverage—whatever the unresolved issues and resource gaps in the latter.

In general, naturally, the resulting supply is inadequate, quality uneven, access difficult or inefficient, and impact for different population groups inequitable. The new community organizations we have described represent local inventiveness in trying to repair some of the imperfections and failures in this political-economic marketplace. Their accomplishments do not solve the large problems that remain; their reach is not sufficiently broad, and they are hardly in a position to cope with major issues of finance and delivery.

As one looks ahead, it is necessary to begin with some assumptions about future state action or inaction, the larger questions and resource issues being beyond the capacities of local governments. Will the same anarchic environment persist in the child care field in most states over the next decade, whether out of choice or necessity, or will some effort be made to apply knowledge and to organize intelligence and public influence so as to deliberately deploy resources and shape developments in accord with some public purpose? In short, is there to be some public planning and coordination?

It may be assumed that until more leadership states demonstrate that there are to be large gains from the latter process, and clarify just what state roles work best, most will persist as they now are. The order of the day for child care advocates, as for educators, is to organize for state-level lobbying. The types of agencies about which we have written will work to create statewide coalitions (see Minnesota) and to help other communities develop similar instruments. For, what we have seen is a good response to enable localities to cope under very unsatisfactory circumstances. The effectiveness of the development would be enhanced by statewide cooperation and lobbying. State government could contribute by offering administrative supports for I&R and voucher operations and improving licensing-registration machinery and monitoring. National, if voluntary, standard setting and lobbying could help.

But even if no more than this occurs, it behooves the leadership of these local activities to develop a point of view about some of the issues listed subsequently as they pick their targets and make their proposals. For if they have no philosophy and policy about schools and social welfare agencies—about purchase of service, public delivery, employer subsidies or vouchers—beyond what their next operating budget requires, their actions will not add up. The current complex hodge-podge and its inequities and inefficiencies will persist.

We assume that some states will choose an alternative scenario. They will recognize that child care is not a sometime thing. It affects much of the population at some time, if only a small part of the population at one time. State governments need some vision of who will provide what service, for whom, where, and who will pay. They need to locate responsibility for leadership and administration within state government and to clarify how the legislature and governor will remain appropriately involved. After all, they have institutionalized their arrangements for fire and police protection, road building, education, and mental health.

We have looked at recent Massachusetts developments, not because we regard all issues as settled there or all the choices made as necessarily sound. Rather, here is one possible state approach: Core issues are defined, policy options stated, new structures created, local initiative encouraged, diversity guaranteed, and action begun. Both local communities and the corporate sector have a reference point and supports for what they now do. California has been shown as more incremental but eventually touching many bases. Efforts have begun to achieve a major state initiative in New York.

States inclined to move in the direction of larger responsibility will need to attend to "stakes" and "turf" relating to education, social services, income maintenance, economic development, health, and mental health. The process will not be easy. There will be some inclination to appoint commissions or task forces that will outline "needs," announce goals, but not resolve any difficult issues. This occurs regularly, in many places. The alternative may look like yet another blue ribbon citizen panel, legislative inquiry, or governor's committee, but it will pursue a more difficult agenda. Key policy issues will be articulated, choices reviewed, decisions made. Perhaps the process will begin with a series of forums, then with data collection, and finally be assigned to a legislative or gubernatorial drafting group.

The result will not necessarily be a neat plan, a fully integrated operation. That is one possibility. What the result should provide is a vision of what the state's pattern of child care will be and how it expects that concept to be brought to reality and then administratively supported. There are real choices.

The listing of several critical agenda items, which follows, is intended to suggest the types of issues a state may face in the course of such a process. What are the parameter-setting questions facing child care today? The reader will already have put them in similar form.

Conclusions

We have offered an appreciation of inventive local groups that have served their consumer clients well in the anarchic economic and political marketplaces prevailing for much needed child care. We also have noted that deregulation and devolution to the locality, no matter how inspired the initiatives, will not solve all problems. State resources and leadership are essential, the necessary precondition. Now we list some of the issues that emerge as important on any state policy-development and action agenda:

- The future roles of the social welfare and educational systems in the delivery of child development services.
- The role of employment-related or -sponsored child care services.
- The approach to family day care.
- The choice between or the balance of supply and demand strategies.
- The development of a database for planning.
- The protection of child care quality.

In the following chapters we elaborate three topics (education and social welfare, employer-sponsored child care, and family day care). We introduce other issues in context, including the questions of quality and of a future federal role. We begin, however, with Chapter 4, which looks at the results of privatization initiatives in day care since 1981, as much a Reagan administration strategy as decentralization and deregulation. Here we include specific attention to discussion of the choice between supply and demand strategies. In each chapter we continue to return to the question of whether a laissez faire economic and political marketplace will do as an alternative to public policy making, support, or leadership.

Endnotes

1. Michael Barone and Grant Ujifusa, *The Almanac of American Politics, 1986* (Washington, D.C.: *National Journal,* 1985), p. 1273.
2. Helen Blank and Amy Wilkins, *Child Care: Whose Priority?* (Washington,

D.C.: Children's Defense Fund, 1985), pp. 69–72. Also, "California: New SACC Funding," *SACC Newsletter* (School-Age Child Care Project, Wellesley College), Vol 3, No. 2 (January 1986), 1, 3. Also see California's Senate Bill 303 for 1985, amending Section 822.7 of the Education Code.

3. Blank and Wilkins, *Child Care: Whose Priority?* p. 70. For detail on assignment of GAIN school-age child care to county welfare authorities, see Helen Blank and Amy Wilkins, *State Child Care Fact Book 1986* (Washington, D.C.: Children's Defense Fund, 1986), pp. 26–27.

4. Project Connections is described in endnote 7, Chapter 2.

5. Gwen Morgan, *Caring About Children in Massachusetts: Feasible Day Care Policy for the 1980s* (Boston: Wheelock College, 1982).

6. Massachusetts Department of Social Services, *A Comprehensive Child Day Care Delivery System: A Working Plan* (Boston: The Department of Social Services, 1983).

7. Commonwealth of Massachusetts, *Final Report of the Governor's Day Care Partnership Project* (Boston: Executive Department, 1985).

Chapter 4

CHILD CARE AND PRIVATIZATION

Child care is essential for working parents to meet their responsibilities. In order to help families have flexibility and to be able to determine the setting and type of care for their children, we are working to encourage greater private sector involvement in child care, we have supported modifications to the dependent care deduction and we have proposed that nonprofit dependent care facilities be classified as tax-exempt organizations. . . . The President's Private Sector Task Force has been actively involved in promoting employer supported day care.[1]

At present the Federal Government is shifting away from giving direct support and subsidies to day care centers and toward an emphasis on tax credits for parents and tax incentives for employers. This trend is likely to continue.[2]

Earlier chapters focused largely on the local delivery system response to the policy changes of the Reagan years and on a variety of related state initiatives. A second aspect of this development requires systematic attention as well. Just as the Reagan administration has featured the desirability of decentralization and deregulation, so has it emphasized privatization. In various ways it has defined child care as an issue not for government but for the corporate sector, for voluntary effort, for parents themselves. Thus, the story of recent American child care requires that we examine some of the developments touched upon in the earlier chapters, and other elements as well, from the perspective of privatization as a policy.

We have explored elsewhere and in some detail the conceptual and political underpinnings of the recent privatization discussion.[3] For present purposes we highlight the emphasis of privatization proponents on the alleged unresponsiveness and rigidity of big government, the allegedly greater economy and efficiency of the market, and the claims that private nonprofit and religious groups can be more responsive to ethnic and racial diversity. These and other beliefs have been employed within the Reagan administration to justify a general withdrawal from program leadership or technical assistance in child care, a call to private industry to take the lead, and discouragement of the notion that this is a major area of government responsibility—except for compensatory and remedial programs like Head Start.

The child care field is one of the main areas of social policy privatization in the current era and is here reviewed as such. What does experience teach us about privatization? What does it suggest about the future of child care policy and programming? The chapter offers a general overview and assessment. Chapter 6 is devoted to a more detailed look at employers and child care.

Child care services in many ways constitute the prototypical illustration of "privatization" as an explicit policy of the Reagan administration. The child care industry has always been a "mixed economy," in that privately funded and operated programs have always coexisted with totally public programs. But now the situation is different. The Reagan administration has reduced direct federal expenditures for child care services; stressed a policy of subsidizing demand rather than supply (creating an incentive for parents-consumers to purchase care in the open market); encouraged private sector providers to produce and deliver services; eliminated the federal role in setting minimum standards for federally funded child care; and stressed the value of informal rather than formal care.

The specific questions addressed in this chapter are, How effective has the administration been in carrying out its policies? and What have been the consequences?

The Impact of the Reagan Administration Policies: Child Care in 1985

Assessment of the impact of the Reagan administration's efforts at "privatizing" child care services is complicated by three separate developments. First is the absence of any recent consumer or supply survey, leading to imprecision in estimates regarding the number of child care places available and the numbers of children in different types of services (see Chapter 1). Second are the consequences of turning Title XX into a social services block grant. As a result, the requirements concerning how Title XX funds are

spent were eliminated, as were most of the reporting requirements imposed on the states and the publication of regular reports
by the federal government on social services expenditures, users,
and services. Third has been the continued growth in female labor
force participation rates, in particular, among married women with
very young children (see Table 1.5). The Reagan years experienced
a dramatic continuation of a trend begun in the 1970s: the growing
convergence in labor force participation rates between single and
married mothers. What is more startling, however, is that the
surge in the rates for married women with very young children
(those under age 3) has now resulted in a situation in which
married women with children of this age are even more likely to be
in the labor force than their nonmarried sisters. The visible
demand for child care services, therefore, is coming increasingly
from married women, from families with two wage earners, and
thus from middle-class parents. In effect, therefore, the demand
for child care services, already high in 1980, increased substantially thereafter. The growth in the demand for infant care has been
particularly large. To note one astonishing development that
underscores growth: 33 percent of married women with children
under age 1 were in the labor force in 1979, while 51 percent were
in 1986, more than a 50 percent increase.

Consumer Choice and Sovereignty

"Demand" subsidies is the term used to describe the financial
assistance provided the purchaser or consumer of services, in
contrast to the "supply" subsidies that are given service producers
or providers. In the case of child care, demand subsidies include
the dependent care tax credit and the work allowance (an earnings
disregard) permitted under AFDC, both provided by the federal
government, as well as the child care vouchers a few employers
provide to their parent-employees.

Permitting parental choice, and responding to parent-consumer
preferences, is one outcome stressed by those who favor demand
subsidies and private sector delivery of child care services. The
traditional alternative way of serving the poor was to subsidize or
reimburse those who supply services. Do these new demand
strategies result in a wider range of child care options for parents?

Demand subsidies have clearly increased under the Reagan
administration. The Dependent Care Tax Credit, usually referred
to as the Child Care Tax Credit, in place earlier, is the one child
care policy that has expanded significantly during the Reagan years
and is currently the largest single federal source of financial

support for child care. Under the tax code, a credit is available to families with children under 15 who incur child care expenses when both spouses work full time or when one spouse works full time and the other works part time or is a student. Divorced or separated parents who have custody of children, and single parents may also claim the credit. (It is also available to adults in a similar situation who have physically dependent [handicapped] spouses and/or parents who require constant care and incur expenses for their care.)

Under prior law, the credit was limited to 20 percent of dependent care costs incurred, up to a maximum of $2000 for one dependent and $4000 for two or more dependents. In 1982 the credit was increased to 30 percent for taxpayers with incomes of $10,000 or less, with the credit reduced by one percentage point for each $2000 of income between $10,000 and $28,000. The limits on eligible expenses were increased to $2400 for one dependent and $4800 for two or more. Expenses for services provided outside the home in facilities that care for more than six individuals (other than individuals who reside at the facility) may be counted for purposes of the tax credit only if the facility complies with all applicable state and local laws and regulations. In effect, working parents could take a maximum tax credit of between $480 and $720, depending on income, for the care of one child and a credit of between $960 and $1440 for the care of two or more.

According to the Department of Health and Human Services' (DHHS) Administration on Children, Youth and Families (ACYF), the amount spent under the Dependent (child) Care Tax Credit was about $1 billion in FY 81. The total for 1985–1986 was estimated at over $3 billion, representing the source of actual increased public child care expenditure (see Table 1.8).

Of the 4.6 million families claiming the Dependent Care Tax Credit in 1981, the majority of families (64 percent) were above the median income level. Only 7 percent had incomes below $10,000. One witness at a hearing held by the Select Committee on Children, Youth, and Families explained:[4]

> *This program, which subsidizes the child care and other dependent care costs of families, does not, in its current form, benefit lower-income families, and it provides limited support to lower-middle-income families. Even with refundability (a provision which would return to families that portion of their earned credit which their tax liability will not offset), the credit is not the best approach to assisting low-income families.*

Child care advocates lobbied successfully in 1983 to get the federal dependent care tax credit added to the short income tax form (1040A) so that it might better serve low- and moderate-income taxpayers. This objective was achieved, and a public education campaign was successful. In 1983 there were 6.4 million claims for the dependent care credit, largely for child care. An increase of 1.4 million claims for the credit occurred in 1982 to 1983, and those with adjusted gross income under $20,000 represented one-half the increase, according to a memorandum from the National Women's Law Center in Washington (January 1986), based on data compiled by the Internal Revenue Services. Forty-nine percent of $2.1 billion in tax benefits claimed through the credit for 1983 went to taxpayers with adjusted gross incomes under $25,000 (in fact, 22 percent went to those with adjusted gross incomes under $15,000). Sixty-two percent of all claims were by people with annual gross incomes under $30,000.

There are no data on how parents spend this subsidy, but it can be spent on far more varied forms of child care than can a grant given directly to child care providers. Thus, family day care, in-home care, and various forms of out-of-home group care (centers, nursery schools, prekindergartens, kindergartens) all qualify as child care providers for children under age 6, as do summer camps and various after-school activities for school-aged children. Parental costs are also offset by modest tax credits or deductions in 27 states, generally keyed to the federal tax credit and enacted in the late 1970s.

At the same time, several states, faced with a curtailment of SSBG funds, reduced the proportion of these funds spent on child care and turned instead to use of the AFDC disregard. The AFDC child care disregard is a work expense allowance to pay child care expenses of AFDC recipients so that they can find and continue employment. It can be deducted from earnings before assessing income for the purpose of calculating the recipient's AFDC grant. In 1980 the child care disregard paid for $120 million in child care costs. In 1981 this child care expense allowance was limited by law to a maximum of $160 per child per month. In 1986 child care payments under the disregard, as seen in Table 1.8, amounted to $35 million.

Still, a third demand subsidy involves the tax benefits related to employer-sponsored or -supported child care (see Chapter 6). Recent tax provisions have been designed to stimulate employers to provide or pay for child care for their employees. The Internal Revenue Code now explicitly excludes from an employee's gross income any payments by an employer for dependent care assistance if the assistance is provided under a plan which meets certain conditions (Section 129 of the Internal Revenue Code).

Another related subsidy provided through the tax system is a salary reduction plan whereby the employee and the employer agree that the employer will lower the taxable income to the employee and set aside the difference between that amount and what would have been the employee's salary for spending on child care (or certain other benefits, such as medical care). In effect, the employee spends pretax "cheaper" dollars for child care, and the employer has a lower wage base on which to pay social security and unemployment insurance taxes. Both sides benefit. In 1986, about $110 million in foregone taxes were estimated to be "spent" to pay for these various forms of employer-sponsored child care.

Finally, several states changed the way they paid for child care services by shifting from direct public delivery (publicly operated programs) and direct purchase of service contracts with providers to using these funds for purchasing "care" on a per-child basis or other types of vendor/voucher programs.

Thus, for example, we have described how initially in a three-county area of Florida (and later through much of the state) all Title XX (now SSBG) child care funds are channeled into one agency that determines eligibility, rates providers, sets reimbursement rates, and pays for individual "slots" or places once parents choose the provider (see Chapter 2). Except for rating providers, Mecklenberg County in North Carolina follows a similar pattern. It is not the provider who is given a grant under this system, but rather the payment follows the child; in some sense, this is similar to the way that Medicaid and Medicare work. Parents choose a program from a list of approved (licensed) providers, and if the parents qualify for Title XX funds, the provider is reimbursed by the county.

As we have seen, other states have designed their own vendor/voucher programs, but the major strategy is the same: to have the public dollars follow the child to whichever provider the parent prefers, usually limited only to the choice of a licensed caregiver, but obviously limited also to one whose fee is covered by what the agency will reimburse.

This program, of course, is very different from the earlier mode of setting up public programs or subsidizing private nonprofit providers to operate a child care service that would be free or heavily subsidized for those children whose parents qualified for the service.

Although the overall approach is similar across the states, the actual devices used may vary. They may involve the following system:

- Giving the consumer authorization to purchase child care and paying or reimbursing the provider either through a public agency or a special private agency given funds to pay for care or given control over how they are spent (vendor/voucher).
- Giving the consumer a "voucher" to purchase the service directly.
- Permitting the consumer to pay cash for the service (Title IV-A [AFDC] disregard).

One result of this extensive growth in demand subsidies, and the shift from supply to demand subsidies generally, has been a significant increase in the mix of services available generally, and in the diversity of services used by those in receipt of public subsidies, in particular. The heads of several proprietary chains have indicated that the child care tax credit was a special boon to their companies since it provided an indirect public subsidy to providers who were largely unable or unwilling to serve children from low-income families and who would never have qualified for Title XX funds under proposed standards or been eligible under policies in many states.

Consumers who qualify for Title XX child care now have a far wider range of options, in most states, than under the earlier system in which they could enroll their children only in specific centers. Similarly, the California Alternative Payment Program, with state funds subsidizing a vendor/voucher program, has made it possible for public child care dollars to be used to pay for family day care for the first time and to expand the supply and variety of infant care services, a service in very short supply earlier. Other states had similar developments.

Clearly, the diversity of services available has increased. For many parents, this means that they have a wider range of options in choosing child care. For middle-class parents, in particular, the range of choices is greater *and* they are assured of at least some modest subsidy regardless of the type of care used.

On the other hand, for very low income parents the picture is at best a mixed one. Some among those who qualify for Title XX funds now are able to place their children in a center of their choice. Most directly subsidized centers under the prior pattern tended to be in low-income neighborhoods and were therefore larely attended by minority children. Parents may now have more opportunity to choose an integrated center if they wish, or they may be able to choose family day care if they prefer.

At the same time, however, for many poor and near-poor

families, the shift to a demand subsidy and the simultaneous decline in Title XX funds means a reduction in available options. Their problem is the far more restricted eligibility for Title XX child care and the lower eligibility levels set by states coping with inadequate budgets. States allow Social Services Block Grant child care support only to women actually working or in training (and often restrict the time period for the latter, sometimes for the former). A good number of states give help only to the poorest, with the result that in most places over 90 percent of the eligibles for state-subsidized child care are single mothers with very low salaries (apart from protective services cases, refugee programs, and limited programs for the handicapped). Some states do not have sliding scales and drop a mother as soon as a small salary increase puts her income above the threshold. Parents who once preferred center care or preschool programs now find themselves in a situation in which they may no longer qualify for any subsidized care at all and thus are left to use whatever care they can themselves afford, often poor quality, informal family day care. Or, even for those who still qualify, the prevailing reimbursement rate may not permit their child's enrollment in a high-quality program. The $160 maximum under the AFDC work expense child care allowance will certainly not pay for decent quality group care in almost any state; and AFDC parents are clearly not in a position to supplement that amount further.

On balance? The diversity of services has increased, and some parents have more options. Middle- and upper-class parents have the widest range of choices, and all now receive some public subsidy to help pay for these services. Some poor and moderate-income families have a larger range of choices than before, but most cannot afford, and therefore cannot use, the options that exist; and many, especially the poorest, face fewer options than before.

Part of the diversity, too, comes from the growth in public preschool programs, a recent development that has occurred on the state and local levels in response to factors other than the administration's policies. Further development of such public school-based programs clearly would expand access to group programs. Some minority groups and organizations object to this development as less responsive to children's and their parents' needs than the more traditional social welfare day care and Head Start systems are said to be.[5] In short, they prefer more of the privatization of the late 1960s and early 1970s (the use of community organizations), and in that sense they are inadvertently supportive of the Reagan thrust, which favors such providers, but also the proprietaries.[6]

The Supply

Economists tell us that if consumers have greater purchasing power, effective demand increases and the market responds by expanding supply. Economists also tell us that if regulations are reduced, the numbers of providers as well as the numbers of services available will increase.[7] These expectations are repeated by those who favor privatization. The Reagan administration expanded consumer (demand) subsidies and eliminated federal regulations. Did the supply of child care services increase as a consequence?

According to the Children's Defense Fund (CDF), 23 states were serving *fewer* children in 1986 than in 1981 with federal social services and child welfare funds.[8] Despite the increase in female labor force participation rates, 5 more states were still serving the same number of children and only 15 states increased the number of children served. Traditionally, however, the child care statistics deal with services in the social welfare stream (Title XX, IV-B, WIN, Head Start, and so on) only; data on other child care services are not reported. We note here that an NAEYC/CDF survey reported a 234 percent increase in the numbers of centers between the mid-1970s and the mid-1980s. Many, of course, were not funded through Title XX or the SSBG.

At least half the states have been paying growing attention in the 1980s to public kindergarten and preschool programs for 4-year-olds (see Chapter 5). Five states have mandated kindergarten for all 5-year olds, and some states have moved toward full-day kindergarten (6 or 6½ hours), comparable to a full school day. Still others have established small part-day programs for 4-year-olds, especially the poor or otherwise deprived. There is a parallel increase in schools providing before- and after-school programs.[9]

The large proprietary child care chains have grown substantially during these years, either by expanding internally or by purchasing other chain operations. Thus, for example, at the end of 1980 Kinder-Care, the largest commercial child care service chain, was operating about 510 centers serving 53,000 children, while in 1985 it was operating 1040 centers serving more than 100,000 children.[10] Children's World, the third largest chain and one of those described by others in the industry as a "high-quality child care operation," was operating 84 centers in 7 states in 1980, while by 1986 the company was operating 248 centers in 13 states.[11]

An "experiment" in moving toward demand subsidies began earlier, in the late 1970s, in California, as discussed in Chapter 2. This "Alternative Payment Program" was conceived initially as a cost-effective method of increasing the supply of child care services in the state and expanding the variety of program sponsors offering subsidized care. A major impetus in supporting the initiative was to increase the supply of infant care. California data suggest the device has been effective, in particular in providing a direct public subsidy for family day care for the first time for working parents and in increasing the numbers of providers who now offer infant care.

Nationally, there also is a significant volume of activity involving regulated and unregulated family care funded by social services block grants, sliding fees, and various other kinds of vender/voucher programs. There is no way to estimate the effect this has had on supply.

Finally, in advancing a policy of encouraging private sector initiatives, the Reagan administration created various incentives for employers to sponsor child care services for their employees. A 1978 national survey, updated in 1981, found 19 day care centers sponsored by industry at or near the workplace, 7 sponsored by labor unions, 14 by government agencies, and 75 by hospitals. In addition, 200 centers were sponsored by the military.[12] Other subsequent surveys, none carried out very systematically or with any rigor, estimated a continuing pattern of increased employer involvement.[13]

Dr. Dana Friedman, a researcher at The Conference Board and a nationally known expert on employer-sponsored child care, estimated that about 2500 out of the more than 6 million employers in the country offered some form of child care "sponsorship" in 1986.[14] Once again, hospitals dominate the on-site providers: 400 hospitals offer such programs. In contrast, only about 120 firms have on- or near-site programs. The major types of child care help offered by the small number of employers doing anything are as follows:

- Paying for information and referral services for their employees (500).
- Obtaining discounts, in particular from large commercial chains, for employees using the chains' service (300).
- Setting up flexible spending accounts or salary reduction plans

covering child care, often with no financial contributions from the employer but using employees' pretax dollars (80–100).

Although the increase in employers' interest has been substantial over the last five years, the actual numbers of employers involved is still minuscule; the actual increase this development has contributed to the total number of child care places is still less. We leave for a subsequent chapter our analysis of these developments and their potential for contributing to the supply of child care services in the future.

On balance, has the supply of services increased? Probably. Have the Reagan administration policies led to this increase? It is unclear.

Eliminating federal regulations undoubtedly led some large commercial chains to expand into states with standards that are low enough to ensure the operator a profit (and in the case of high-quality operators, high enough to let them be competitive). Increased use of demand subsidies may have led to some growth in supply but may also have just made family day care more visible in some places (a good thing but not necessarily leading to an increase in the numbers providing such care) and/or led to some shifting around in the market rather than any real growth, as children were moved from centers to family day care when their families lost eligibility for Title XX services.

Finally, as a result of the rise in female labor force participation rates of married women with very young children, there has been increased pressure for more services while the social service funding streams failed to grow and even the tax credits did not offer adequate resources. This is one of several factors in the growing move toward public school involvement in creating preschools for the 3- to 4-year-olds and full-day kindergarten for the 5-year-olds.[15] This development clearly suggests that the existing supply of services for 3- to 5-year-olds is either inadequate or not of the quality parents prefer or not at a price they can afford. In any case, this state-level expansion of public-school-based programs is a development that has emerged independent of any Reagan administration policy; as a decentralized development, largely financed by state and local funds, it has not been acknowledged by the administration as important or worth encouraging.

To conclude this section, we note that the Reagan Administration's child care spokeswoman insisted in mid-1986 that there is no evidence indicating a shortage of places because there is an unknown and indeterminate amount of informal care available that is as good or better than professional care.

Equity and the Distributional Impact

Those who oppose the decline in publicly operated and publicly sponsored nonprofit programs and the concomitant growth in the private for-profit delivery system argue that these developments have left middle- and upper-income families better off and low- and moderate-income families worse off. Are they correct?

Direct federal funding for child care services has declined over the past five years, in particular when one adjusts expenditures to take account of inflation and increased demand. According to CDF, the leading child advocacy organization in the country, controlling for inflation, Title XX child care dollars (both federal and state) are now about 75 percent of what they would have been in 1982 if OBRA 1981 had not been passed and if Title XX had not been turned into a block grant. Head Start funding has been increased modestly, child care food money has been increased but actually now pays for fewer meals.

At the same time, however, tax benefits for child care have more than doubled: from $956 million in 1980 to more than $2.1 billion for 1983 and an estimated $3.4 billion in 1986. The subsidies for employer-sponsored child care increase this figure still more.

The total federal expenditures on child care increased during these years, but almost all of the increase is expended through the tax system. In 1986, over 60 percent of federal child care support was through the Dependent Care tax credit (Table 1.8). Almost all the real growth is through these indirect subsidies, and many such subsidies are not available to the working poor (fewer will be once the 1986 tax reforms take effect). Some of this has occurred because the administration wanted to reduce direct federal social expenditures and some because it has favored lower taxes.

Families who qualify for Title XX child care services are likely to have very low or quite moderate incomes. Even generous income eligibility criteria, 60 percent of median income, for example (far higher than in many states today), would limit receipt of these services to families with incomes under $14,500 in 1981 and not very much higher in 1985. Indeed, in some states, a single parent earning $10 a week more than minimum wage would not qualify for Title XX child care. Moreover, as indicated, more than 90 percent of the families who do qualify are single-parent, mother-only families, and overwhelmingly low income. (And Head Start, by definition, is required to serve poor families; 90 percent of the children enrolled must be from families with income below the poverty level.)

Finally, the demand subsidy under the AFDC child care "disregard," the work expense allowance, was capped in 1981 at an amount lower than the prevailing fees for group care throughout the country. According to a Massachusetts report on the impact of these changes, within six months after AFDC benefits were terminated, 40 percent of a population sample changed their day care arrangements for at least their youngest child above 2. The main reason for the change was the financial burden created by having to pay full costs of child care. Within 18 months of AFDC termination, formal day care arrangements shifted largely to less formal and less costly arrangements, and the percentage of children left with older siblings or alone increased substantially. Many people moved to arrangements that involved no costs at all. A good number reported that the new situation affected their employment status in the sense that work had to be missed, they were frequently late for work, they had to reduce work hours, or, in the instance of 10 percent, they had to quit their jobs. Many did not take advantage of the sliding fees available either because they did not know about the possibilities or could not manage the amount of money involved. The report placed special stress on the shift from 2 percent to 16 percent of the sample leaving children unsupervised. The "disregard" continues to decline in importance.[16]

The large commercial chains estimate a 20 percent vacancy rate in their centers but claim that this rate is not due to an oversupply but rather the inability of low-income parents to afford the fees. Similarly, where there are reports of nonprofit centers closing, the reasons the providers offer are the same: inadequate direct public financing, the inability of low- and moderate-income parents to afford the fees, and the inability to stay in business and charge fees that these and other families in their communities can pay. Providers in Texas and North Carolina, in New York and California, talk about the gap between what their costs are and what the parents in their communities can afford.

Still another problem has emerged from this move toward the market by encouraging demand rather than use of supply subsidies. Most private for-profit providers, the large commercial chains for example, will not locate their services in low-income neighborhoods. Time and again senior executives of these firms explain their marketing strategies by stressing careful siting. A major highway, a location between a middle-class residential area and a commerical area, a community with high female labor force participation rates, and husband/wife families with two earners and incomes more than 50 percent above median family income are what they seek.

One Texas child care agency director pointed out to us that Texas has continued to provide both demand and supply subsidies because the state and the cities recognize that private providers will not enter low-income and/or minority communities. If these communities are to be served, a public or publicly subsidized center must be established; otherwise, these parents will have no options at all.

Demand subsidies in child care, as in Medicaid and Medicare, assume that an adequate supply of services exist. Unlike Medicaid and Medicare, however, the child care demand subsidies are neither an entitlement program nor open ended as to cost. The decline in direct funding has led to fewer low-income children being served within the organized service system, and in some instances to the unavailability of services, while service options and subsidies have increased for the middle class. The shift to a policy of indirect expenditure from one of direct expenditure has occurred at the expense of those who benefited most from the direct expenditure: the low- and modest-income families.

Quality of Care

One of the most significant developments in the Reagan administration affecting the quality of child care services was the elimination of the Federal Interagency Day Care Requirements (FIDCR). These minimum standards for federally funded child-care programs were established in 1980 after more than a decade of debate and research and were due to be implemented October 1, 1981. Before that date, OBRA 1981 was passed and Title XX was turned into the SSBG, in effect eliminating federal standards along with all other requirements imposed by Title XX.

According to an OHDS report published in 1981, most states at that time were in compliance or close to it;[17] many private providers who received no federal funds were upgrading their standards nevertheless because the FIDCR were emerging as the preferred norm. Within three years of the elimination of the FIDCR (now referred to as the "HEWDCR" for the "Department of Health, Education and Welfare Day Care Requirements"), the national picture, as reported by CDF, is very different.

CDF reports that by 1984, 33 states had lowered their child care standards for Title XX programs.[18] At the same time, an indeterminate number of states had reduced the numbers of their inspectors and/or inspections of service programs and followed a far less rigorous approach to enforcement than previously. And some states changed their policy of licensing family day care homes to one requiring only that providers register and list themselves as meeting standards.

Beginning in 1984 a rash of incidents of sexual abuse of children were alleged to have occurred in child care centers around the country, and reports and allegations continue. Despite a variety of claims, it is not known whether the problem is in fact a large one and—if so—whether the decline in monitoring and the lowering of standards is directly responsible.

Some critics of state licensing and registration requirements insist that not only do they fail to achieve their basic objective (to ensure minimum health and safety standards for children), but they lead instead to an increase in the costs of service, "driving providers underground and limiting the number of children who can benefit."[19] A report critical of regulation continues: "Unnecessary regulations are stifling the supply of day care at a time when the need has never been greater and shows every sign of continuing to surge."[20] In developing a rationale for eliminating even state-level standards, the report mixes legitimate complaints about stringent zoning requirements with standards related to staff–child ratios and staff qualifications, distorts and misinterprets findings of the Abt evaluation study, and ignores the real supply shortages (infant care) and the real issues (affordability) when discussing supply. Its overall message is clear: Private approaches to regulation should be supported rather than statutory requirements, and deregulation is the primary need.

To compensate for the absence of adequate, uniform, minimum standards, consumer-parent assessment of quality is being stressed increasingly as the preferred approach.

Beginning in the 1970s, but increasing in the 1980s, a few states, and many organizations, established child care information (or resource) and referral services, offering parents information about all types of child care including fees, available space, and so forth.[21] In addition, almost all issue or publish guidelines for parents to help them choose among the diversity of programs available. They identify the characteristics associated with good quality and offer help to parents trying to decide which program is best for their child. Some do this briefly; others offer extensive counseling.

Although parents seem more aware of the importance to their child of a good experience, it is not known how many parents can and do assess differential quality correctly as a consequence of the educational or counseling resource expansion.[22]

At least one effort has been made at rating providers on the basis of quality and costs. But even that effort must be assessed in a context in which the quality of care available seemed to range in our view from "dreadful" to "barely acceptable," with no providers offering what child development professionals would consider exemplary care.

As part of the ongoing debate about what is happening to the quality of child care services, some have expressed concern about the growth since 1980 in the numbers and percentage of for-profit child care providers, in particular, the large commercial child care chains. They are convinced that proprietary child care lends itself to the same types of scandals as proprietary nursing homes, and that profiting from child care will inevitably lead to cost cutting and a decline in quality.

The current estimate is that about half the licensed day care centers (those licensed under health and welfare regulations, not education) in the states are under for-profit auspices. How does the quality of care they offer compare with that given by the nonprofit agencies? Our own very limited assessment of the for-profit and nonprofit services reveals no consistent, uniform pattern. Good quality programs are as likely to be found among the for-profits as among the nonprofits, and vice versa. The for-profits do not include the model, experimental programs with very high staff–child ratios and highly trained and well-paid professional staff; but apart from these special programs, which are very limited in numbers in any case, the whole gamut is covered. Thus, visiting Children's World centers in Colorado and Palo Alto Preschools in Arizona, we found well-equipped, well-staffed programs, with happy, healthy, and spontaneous youngsters, much interchange between children and staff, and a generally positive atmosphere. And we also saw both for-profit and nonprofit programs in several regions of the country with sparse equipment, limited space, few and untrained staff, and children sitting around watching TV in darkened rooms.

There has been no rigorous research comparing the quality of programs under for-profit and nonprofit auspices. One statewide study in Connecticut is near completion, and preliminary findings have been made available.[23] This study found that there are no differences between nonprofit and for-profit centers in average group size, but staff–child ratios are higher in nonprofit centers since they have more volunteers. The nonprofits report more special equipment, rank higher on caregivers' behavior in relation to children (and caregiver–child interactions), have more racially and ethnically diverse child groups, and serve more low-income children. On the other hand, the for-profit centers in Connecticut offer more hours of service per week than the nonprofits and tend to be open for a greater part of the calendar year.

Finally, in assessing the differences between the proprietaries and the public, or publicly subsidized nonprofit, centers, we note a few unresolved issues: In many communities around the country, the for-profits are fighting against the growth of public (free) preschool programs, accusing them of constituting "unfair competition" and "stealing our bread and butter business—the 3- and 4-year-olds, just as they have already taken over the 5-year-olds."[24] They consider it unfair for public policy to have left them a service vacuum to fill and now to threaten their large capital investments and livelihoods by creating school-based, tax-financed competition. These same providers reject the notion of concentrating their service on the younger group, those under 3 years old, because infant and toddler care is "too expensive"; it is only viable at present because it is "subsidized" by the higher-than-cost fees charged for the 3- to 4-year-olds.

On balance? There appears to be some decline in the quality of the services available to low-income families; there seems to be a very wide range in the quality of care available to and used by parents who purchase care in the marketplace. Whether parents are unable to judge quality differentials, or are unable to pay for higher quality care even when they can identify it, or are unwilling to pay for such care, even if they can afford it and can identify it, is unclear. What we can tell is that poor parents are often limited in what they can obtain; and much of this is very poor quality. Some affluent parents use excellent care and some use poor quality care, and it is unclear whether they know the difference. Whether or not the auspice is profit-making does not seem to correlate with the quality of care provided; parents never even ask whether a center is operated for profit. It is often difficult for them to know the difference if they deal with "mom and pop" operations or family day care. At best, the picture is cloudy and the evidence mixed.

Efficiency

The conventional wisdom is that the private sector is more efficient than the public. A repeated statement of those encouraging privatization of child care services has been that substituting demand for supply subsidies and permitting parents to buy what they want in the market, substituting private providers for public, and eliminating regulations would inexorably lead to an increased supply of services, at lower cost. We have already dealt with the issue of supply. Here we turn to the question of cost. Is child care provided by the private sector cheaper than that provided by government?

North Carolina, one of the leading states in the quantity of child care services available, had a county-operated day care system in the 1970s that included a large number of high-quality centers serving poor children. As the demand for care increased, more families qualified for subsidized care. As the state picked up more Title XX funds, the county governments purchased in the private sector slots for children for whom spaces were unavailable in the county-operated centers. However, these slots were reimbursed at far lower levels than the cost of care in the public centers. In addition, the costs in the public centers continued to rise. These centers were considered to be the highest quality centers in the state. At the same time, however, there was growing resentment expressed by parents whose income was quite modest but not low enough to qualify for Title XX care, and whose children were enrolled in far lower quality private centers.

In the late 1970s the state legislature set up a study commission to analyze and review the costs of day care in the state. The commission criticized the county operation and recommended that the state fund the counties only at the same level per child care place as the counties were reimbursing the private providers. In Mecklenburg County, the United Way set up a task force to review the recommendations of the commission and to assess how the county should proceed. The task force's analysis made it clear that the county would be getting substantially less money from the state and would have to fund the centers themselves if they were to be operated.

The main impact of the commission's report and the subsequent follow-up activities were that almost throughout the state the counties gave over their public centers to nonprofit organizations to operate. (This and similar processes led to the virtual disappearance of publicly operated child care in the United States outside of the educational system.) In effect, by 1981 almost the whole day care delivery system in North Carolina became privatized. In Mecklenburg, the United Way recommended the establishment of a new agency to handle all public and private child care dollars for the county. State child care funds now get channeled directly to this agency, which then handles information and referral services, determines eligibility, and purchases care from a range of providers. Four different levels of standards applied to child care in North Carolina until 1985; and the prevailing standards for staff–child ratios, for infant care, for example, were among the lowest in the country. Since the agency is not permitted to provide evaluations to parents asking for referrals, the agency copes with the differential quality by explaining to parents the differences between the various levels of licensing standards and indicates what level applies to a particular child care service.

Clearly, the private sector programs are being operated at lower cost than the public programs were; the quality is lower, too, however. In general, privatizing the delivery of child care centers, in particular, increasing the proportion of proprietary centers, may have led to lower costs per child but at a "price" in quality that many would question: lower staff–child ratios, larger groups, larger centers, less equipment, lower caregiver salaries. Even the best of the for-profit chains will not locate in states with high minimum standards because of the costs imposed. They cannot meet the competition with regard to fees. Also, even the best of the proprietary chains define as a minimum size for a facility (100 to 150 children) one that many view as too large for an environment for the very young. A smaller facility is not viewed as economically feasible; yet 50 to 75 children is often cited by others as a desirable standard.

If we turn from per child costs to overall public expenditure, other issues emerge. The total federal expenditure for child care in 1980 was almost $3 billion and in 1986 about $5.5 billion (in current dollars); almost all the difference is the result of increased tax benefits. Moreover, the cohort in need of care has grown in size.

On balance? Per child costs for publicly subsidized care have been reduced as a consequence of increased private delivery and decreased public provision (also because some of the working poor, not eligible for aid, and those who spent Title IV-A "disregard" money, now can afford only low-cost unregulated family day care). But there has been a concomitant decline in quality (with unknown consequences for children) and a probable decline in caregivers' salaries—or a failure to adapt in any way to the inadequacy of the current minimum wage. Several executives among the leading for-profit chains acknowledge that their programs clearly "cream" and serve an affluent, relatively problem-free group of youngsters. That indeed is why a lower staff–child ratio can be satisfactory. With a more deprived group of children, needing more intensive care and attention, a higher staff–child ratio and therefore a more expensive service would be necessary. Finally, in terms of overall costs, privatizing the system has not led to a lower total expenditure. Instead, it has redistributed the expenditure, with less going to the poor and more to the better off.

The Case for—or Against—Privatizing Child Care Services

The child care service industry now, as earlier, is a "mixed economy." Service programs can be located on a continuum from the completely private to the completely public, with most somewhere in the middle. For example:

Private Funding & Private Delivery	Private Funding & Public Delivery	Public Funding & Private Delivery	Public Funding & Public Delivery

And there are various models for monitoring and regulating services under both public and private auspices.

Historically, the industry has always comprised a mixture, although previously the largest components were the private non-profit providers and the informal caregivers (domestic servants). Over the last two decades domestic servants have declined in numbers and importance, nonprofit providers have declined as a proportion of providers, and for-profit providers have increased significantly. At the same time, demand has increased many times over.

The Reagan administration announced at the onset a policy of privatization, to include a decrease in federal funding, an elimination of federal regulation, and encouragement and incentives for greater private sector financing and delivery. In the first half of the 1980s, federal direct funding for child care decreased in constant dollars, federal indirect funding (tax benefits) increased, state funding increased in some states, stayed the same in some others, and declined in a significant number. Private philanthropic funding and private employer financing increased modestly but still constitutes an insignificant amount overall.[25]

There has been some increase in the supply of services available, but it is unclear how much of this, if any, is attributable to the administration's policies of shifting from supply to demand subsidies and decreasing federal regulation. Some growth has occurred, clearly, in public school–based programs, but this development is independent of, and unacknowledged by, the administration. There has been a significant increase in diversity and therefore in the options available to some consumers. At the same time, the reduction in direct federal spending has curtailed the options of low-income families, in particular those preferring preschool programs.

More children, especially middle- and upper-class children, are receiving at least some public subsidy for child care, but the poor are receiving a significantly smaller proportion of total public child care expenditures than previously. There is some evidence of a decline in the quality of care available to low- and modest-income children; it is unclear what if anything has happened to the quality of care provided those for whom cost and fee is not an issue. There is some evidence that private programs operate more efficiently, but there is concomitant evidence that these lower costs carry with them poorer quality care for children and lower wages for caregivers.

Has privatization led to a larger constituency for publicly subsidized child care? It is difficult to sort out the effects of broadening the base through these policies versus the increase resulting from the continued and dramatic growth in labor force participation rates, especially among married women with children under age 6—more than 20 percent between 1980 and 1986. Indeed, one could argue that it is not the Reagan administration's stress on privatization that led to these developments but rather the growth in the middle-class constituency for child care that has had access only to a privatized delivery system and sought increased subsidies for themselves. This could also explain the increased attention on the state level to preschools, all-day kindergartens, and after-school programs—a development all but ignored in Washington.

On balance? *Privatizing the delivery of child care services* in the 1980s meant more public subsidy for family day care homes; more proprietary programs/service; and lower, less consistent, and less enforced minimum standards of care. For many it meant greater choice, whereas for others options were curtailed. The evidence suggests that the "costs" of a privatized delivery system in terms of quality can be minimized if adequate standards and monitoring are maintained; but they have not been thus far.

Privatizing the regulation of child care services has led to a decline in standards and enforcement and a greater stress on parent-consumer monitoring. Exaggerated claims for consumer education as an alternative to enforcement of licensing standards have been used to justify expenditure cuts. Quality appears to have declined as a consequence.

Privatizing the financing of child care has meant reduced subsidies for low-income children, higher subsidies for middle- and upper-income children, and a failure to maintain public support, given the growth in need/demand for care for children under age 6.

For the Reagan administration, privatizing child care has been first and foremost an ideological statement, an integral part of the administration's overall philosophy. Second, it has been an experiment in "load shedding," in reducing the social role and responsibility of the federal government.[26] Third, it has been part of a larger effort to reorient federal social policy, from concern for the poor to concern with the middle and upper class.

For many, such policy is suspect as ideology and counterproductive as load-shedding. The reduction of services to the poor is unacceptable. Society cannot in this era ignore its unavoidable contributions toward child rearing and child care. In the context of such responsibility, roles for the market, the nonprofit, and the government sectors may be explored and discussed. The following chapters deal with such specifics.

Endnotes

1. Jo Ann Gasper, Deputy Assistant Secretary for Social Services Policy, OHDS, HHS, Testimony, U.S. House of Representatives, Select Committee of Children, Youth and Families, *Child Care: Beginning A National Initiative* (Washington, D.C.: Government Printing Office, 1984), pp. 98–99.

2. U.S. Department of Labor, Office of the Secretary, Women's Bureau, *Federal Legislation on Day Care* (Washington, D.C.: USDOL, August 1982). Reprinted in U.S. House of Representatives, Select Committee on Children, Youth, and Families, *Child Care Services: What Can Be Done?* Hearings, (Washington, D.C.: Government Printing Office, 1984), pp. 905–911.

3. See Sheila B. Kamerman and Alfred J. Kahn, ed., *Privatization and the Welfare State*, forthcoming, 1987.

4. Carla Curtis, National Black Child Development Institute, Testimony, U.S. House of Representatives, Select Committee on Children, Youth and Families, *Families and Child Care: Improving the Options* (Washington, D.C.: Government Printing Office, 1984).

5. National Black Child Development Institute, "Child Care in the Public Schools: Incubator for Inequality?" (Washington, D.C.: 1986).

6. Jo Ann Gasper, *Child Care: Beginning a National Initiative*.

7. See, for example, Susan Rose-Ackerman, "Unintended Consequences: Regulating the Quality of Subsidized Day Care," *Journal of Policy Analysis and Management*, Vol. 3, No. 1 (Fall, 1983), 14–30; Dennis Young and Richard Nelson, eds., *Public Policy for Day Care of Young Children* (Lexington, Mass.: Lexington Books, 1973); Philip K. Robins and Samuel Wiener, *Child Care and Public Policy* (Lexington, Mass.: Lexington Books, 1978).

8. Helen Blank and Amy Wilkins, *State Child Care Fact Book 1986* (Washington, D.C.: Children's Defense Fund, 1986).

9. See Michelle Seligson , School-Aged Child Care Project, Wellesley College, for information on these services.

10. See, "The Child Care Industry," *Argus Research Report*, Vol. 5, No. 14, May

23, 1980, for the 1980 data; and Gail Schmitt, District Manager, KinderCare Learning Center, Testimony, in U.S. House of Representatives, Select Committee on Children, Youth and Families, Hearings, *Exploring Private and Public Sector Approaches* (Washington, D.C.: Government Printing Office, 1984), p. 72.

11. "How's Business? A Status Report on For-Profit Child Care," *Child Care Information Exchange,* No. 52 (November 1986), 26.

12. Katherine S. Perry, *Child Care Centers Sponsored by Employers and Labor Unions in the United States* (Washington, D.C.: U.S. Department of Labor, 1980). See also Women's Bureau, Department of Labor, *Employers and Child Care: Establishing Services at the Work Place* (Washington, D.C.: Department of Labor, 1981).

13. Sandra L. Burud, Pamela R. Aschbacher, and Jacquelyn McCroskey, *Employer Supported Child Care* (Dover, Mass.: Auburn House, 1984).

14. Dana Friedman, *Personal Communication*. See also *Corporate Financial Assistance for Child Care* (New York: The Conference Board, 1985).

15. Obviously, another important factor in this development has been the increased concern with the quality of education generally, and the growing conviction that early childhood education pays off in the primary and secondary school years. For discussion of the developments concerning school-based programs, see Chapter 5.

16. Other aspects of federal AFDC policy since 1981 have decreased from 15 to 16 percent to 2 to 3 percent the proportion of AFDC mothers holding jobs.

17. U.S., DHHS, *Report to Congress*. There is some debate about this, but it is not relevant to the present discussion.

18. Helen Blank, *Child Care: The State's Response* (Washington, D.C.: Children's Defense Fund, 1984), p. 27.

19. Karen Lehrman and Jana Pace, "Day Care Regulation: Serving Children of Bureaucrats?" (Washington, D.C.), Cato Institute Policy Analysis, No. 59, September 25, 1985, p. 1.

20 Ibid.

21. For a good history of this development see James A. Levine, "The Prospects and Dilemmas of Child Care Information," in Edward F. Zigler and Edmund W. Gordon, *Day Care* (Boston, Mass.: Auburn House, 1982).

22. See, for example, Angela C. Browne, "The Mixed Economy of Day Care: Consumer vs. Professional Assessments," *Journal of Social Policy*, Vol. 13, Part 3 (July 1984), 321–331.

23. James W. Newton and Sharon L. Kagan, "Survey on Profit and Quality Child Care: Progress Report, October 1985." Processed. We are uncertain about this preliminary report, which covers only a very small group of those in prekindergarten classes in private schools.

24. North Carolina newspapers were full of such statements early in 1985, when a proposal to establish a program for 4-year-olds in the school system was being debated.

25. Despite the administration's policies, little in the way of new "private" philanthropic funds have been contributed to support child care. United Way reported allocations for child care services are modest at best (2.4 percent of total allocations in 1981 and 2.8 percent in 1985). Although these have

increased by a little over 15 percent between 1981 and 1985, the base is so small to begin with that clearly the effort cannot be viewed as significant. (Data provided by Eleanor Brilliant from her forthcoming study of United Way.) Employers' financial contributions have been even more modest.

26. For discussion of "load-shedding" as a strategy, see Marc Bendrick, Jr., "Privatizing the Delivery of Social Welfare Service: An Idea to Be Taken Seriously," in Sheila B. Kamerman and Alfred J. Kahn, eds., *Privatization and the Welfare State*, forthcoming.

Chapter 5

THE SCHOOLS AND CHILD CARE

On one level, there would not appear to be need for any discussion—certainly not debate—about the role of schools in providing child care. Nursery schools, day care centers, and prekindergarten programs are all child care resources. In 1976 an expert panel who had spent several years examining many aspects of child and family policy under the auspices of the National Research Council, National Academy of Sciences recommended:[1]

> *For those families who, out of necessity or preference, elect some form of substitute care for their children, a range of alternatives should be available, including pre-kindergarten, kindergarten and nursery schools, in-home care, family day care, and center-based child care programs. The programs should be available free or at costs that do not require the sacrifice of other essential goods and services.*
>
> *Mechanisms should be established to ensure that alternative care arrangements meet minimum federal and state standards based on research findings . . . and on experience in administration of such programs. . . .*

Yet in 1984 when New York City decided to convert its kindergartens into all-day facilities, the Day Care Council and other day care advocates opposed the plan on the ground that children would have better experiences if the second half-day were turned over to the day care field. Moreover, there was concern that the public schools, which pay better salaries, would lure qualified day care teachers. Because they are free, they would attract children now in day care. (The program went ahead anyway. Day care centers lost 1000 5-year-olds [but retained 7000] and 200 teachers initially. The school-based program covers the school day but not most parents' work hours.)

117

Even more recently, a leading national organization, the National Black Child Development Institute, acted to slow down or halt the apparent growth of school-based programs in many states:[2]

> *The report raises serious questions, including: are existing public school-based programs serving the Black family adequately and fostering Black children's growth and development?; can public school-based early childhood programs still be molded to meet Black children's needs?; can public school-based child care models be developed that will not maintain the discriminatory tradition of our public schools?; and can the momentum toward public school-based child care be slowed long enough to allow a much needed and long overdue analysis of the record and the implications of continuing this experiment?*

While the report lists questions and calls for debate, it in effect is an antischool brief.

North Carolina is said to lead the country in the rate of labor force participation by mothers of young children. In the midst of a heated public debate in 1985, in response to a suggestion that public school become involved in day care for 3- and 4-year-olds, the lieutenant governor opposed, advocating upgrading of state day care regulations as an alternative: "It is my personal belief that the private sector can better handle day care. . . . The state . . . should encourage more industries to provide day care for the children of employees." In response, a leading newspaper referred in its editorial to the testimony of the state superintendent of public instruction to the effect that day care should be part of public education because "the preschool years are critical to a child's mental development." Most important, the editorial held, ". . . with more and more women working, there can be no doubt about the need for expanded day care services. It would be in society's best interest for day care to be as available as free public education and not restricted to children whose parents can afford it."[3]

The current debate has waxed and waned since 1974 when Albert Shanker, president of the United Federation of Teachers, surveyed the scene in a demographic context in which elementary school enrollment was falling rapidly and was expected to continue to fall; there were empty classrooms and underutilized teachers at the elementary level; and the situation would persist for at least five to seven years, as far as could be then predicted.

At the time comprehensive federal child care legislation was being discussed. Shanker argued that programs were desirable for two reasons:[4]

> *the early childhood years are the period in which the intellectual development of children can most effectively be aided; . . . services are urgently needed by mothers who cannot afford to pay for private services but deserve what well-to-do women now enjoy—the freedom to pursue a career.*

Shanker, in the widely circulated column, held that the time had come to decide where public responsibility for early childhood programs should be lodged. The basic principle should be equal access for all children. Therefore, the public education agency should carry prime responsibility for this field. Those who could afford them might turn to private alternatives, and private non-profit agencies might serve as subcontractors. "Profit-making entrepreneurs" would be eliminated. There would be no means test or sliding scales. Only if the schools in a given jurisdiction were not interested would other prime sponsors be considered.

Two major efforts to enact comprehensive legislation failed in the 1970s, so it was not necessary to resolve the issue. Then in the 1980s the following quite separate, if potentially interrelated, developments both revived and complicated the debate, which is still with us:

- Further explosion of participation of young mothers in the labor market increased substantially the need for child care services.
- Concern with the quality (and/or efficiency) of American education led some reformers to focus on the possibility of beginning school at age 4 or even 3.
- Responding to a variety of societal changes, many more parents, especially middle-class educated parents, began to send their children in the 2- to 4-year age groups to preschools, mostly private nursery schools. (By the 1980s almost all 5-year-olds were already in kindergarten or first grade, mostly in public schools.)
- A variety of research reports encouraged the media and the public policy community in the view that preschool resources should be expanded for deprived children because good programs would decrease problems in childhood and adolescence and result in more schooling, more employment, and less delinquency or expenditure for remedial education. One widely publicized report on the Perry Preschool Program calculated the value of such efforts in the language of cost/benefit analysis.[5]
- Concern with the large number of children of working parents alleged to be in self-care during the afternoon, between the

closing hours of elementary school and the return of parents from work, led to widespread discussion of "latchkey" children. To avoid abuse, exploitation, delinquency, physical danger, and so forth (or, at least, to ensure that children had time, place, and motivation to do homework and opportunity for wholesome and supervised recreation), it agreed that new provision was needed. Alternative proposals encompassed school buildings and staff, various types of community resources, and the day care community.

Thus by the mid-1980s the media heard regularly proposals for expanding education (and child care?) by creating and financing public prekindergartens for the 3- and/or 4-year-olds, ensuring all-day kindergarten for the 5-year-olds, and expanding before- and after-school facilities under one of several possible auspices and funding arrangements.

Everywhere, whether out of concern with employment of "welfare" mothers, providing an infrastructure for economic development, offering effective compensatory programs for deprived children, or upgrading U.S. education in an age of high technology, there now is exploration of how to move next. State legislatures receive proposals from diverse interests. Blue ribbon panels work at preparing reports for mayors, governors, or legislative bodies. Professional groups confer and publish resolutions. Government officials in their various associations take up the subject. Clearly, there will be more child care, and, clearly, there are a series of issues to be settled: What should or will be the role of the educational stream in the future architecture of American child care? What will be the relationship of school-based programs and those under social welfare auspices? Must the issue be settled in combat or is an agreed-upon coalition plan possible? Does a resolution involve hard and absolute choices among the options, or are there identifiable sound solutions to clarify possible and desirable combinations among them?

We begin with some brief historical perspectives.

Historical Perspectives

This is not the place for a full history. Indeed, the history is not yet completely documented, and some of the available writing is part of the contemporary policy debate.[6] What is immediately relevant is that a social welfare–day care stream and a nursery school–kindergarten stream are identifiable from the very beginning of

American child care and that many of their respective current characteristics, advantages, and problems have been long discussed.

There apparently were preschools, known as "infant schools," in the United States as far back as the 1830s; they were created by charitable sponsors to serve children of poor immigrant families. Not much is known about the operation of these infant schools, except that they coincided with the beginning separation of early education from religious control, that they stressed social development, in our terms, and (according to Greenblatt) first raised questions about selectivity or universalism, biological versus "social" parenting.[7] A short time later, beginning right before the Civil War and expanding later in the nineteenth century, "day nurseries" appeared; these were the original social welfare day care centers. The early cases cited by Greenblatt and others involve instances of "day orphans" who were to be protected while their mothers worked or of charitable groups that were responding to alleged or potential child neglect. Some programs were created to ensure mothers' needed posthospitalization recovery. Most of the early day nurseries were not available to children with fathers at home because their care was considered the mother's responsibility, whatever else she had to do. The early staffing for these services (as for much of late-nineteenth-century charity) was by leisured middle-class women volunteers.

Whereas the infant schools (which also had some day care characteristics) had limited development and most had faded early (after all, this was before free, universal elementary education), the German-initiated kindergarten movement of the mid-nineteenth century—reflecting the contributions of Froebel, Rousseau, and others and stressing the potential of "playschools" or "gardens for children" in drawing out children's capacities to feel, think, and create—became quite attractive in the United States. Private sponsors began the kindergartens, and the middle- and upper-class users seemed to predominate initially. In a late-nineteenth-century process, which was to be repeated in the 1960s, Progressive Era reformers soon saw the potential of kindergartens (plus home visits) in socializing and meeting deficits of poor and immigrant children. When private philanthropy could not expand kindergartens adequately, advocates turned to the public schools (first asking only for unused classrooms!). The movement was large, and more than half were public by 1900. It also had been sufficiently captured by the school bureaucracies and rigidified so that, by then, the new reforming progressive education movement also had begun.

Dewey and others had invented a view of a child-centered process in which "better" children created a "better" society. Some of the work was eventually to influence the formal educational system. From the 1920s private nursery schools, many of them based in university research programs and often known as laboratory schools, offered a new, special service outlet (often to middle-class parents) and became the locus of specialized child development knowledge and the training of a core of teachers for early childhood education. This movement elaborated parent education along with child development programming.

The day nursery movement remained limited in the latter part of the nineteenth century. There was some commercial development, a beginning of regulation, and some charity support for day care as a way of helping immigrant workers and avoiding institutionalization of poor children. However, given the model of the "typical" family with an at-home mother, the reformers assumed no need for day care for two-parent families and favored financial aid to widows so that the latter might provide care for their own children. The reformers initially backed private philanthropic aid and, later, mothers' pensions (the 1911–1935 precursors in state legislation of what was to become Aid to Families with Dependent Children). Where mothers nonetheless worked, day care became a form of charitable relief. After all, mothers' pensions were limited, coverage poor, stigma effects large, and public ambivalence considerable. Where, despite financial aid (or for lack of it), the child needed the protection of a child care center, day care also became a form of treatment (daytime foster care instead of a foster home or an institution). Later, too, building on what was learned in experimental nursery schools and in early child guidance clinics, some centers undertook more intensive work with troubled children. Trained nursery teachers were attracted to such work.

Nonetheless, public and private day care serving as care while mothers worked and as treatment was not a major development before the 1930s. Society had not yet accepted the idea that large numbers of mothers of young children were to be expected in the labor force. The proprietary center or private nursery school response also met a significant part of the need. There were important public exceptions, as in Los Angeles.[8] And, as paid staffs took over from the early volunteers, more teachers trained in early education appeared in day nurseries, so that in some instances only the distinction between an all-day and a half-day program could differentiate the nursery school and the day nursery (day care center). Elsewhere, day nurseries did not offer educational and "enrichment" experiences and were more custodial in their routines.

Preschool programs in the United States became large scale for the first time in the 1930s when the WPA (the depression work relief program) authorized such programs so as to provide employment for teachers and others. These year-round all-day programs, with elements of nursery schools, kindergartens, and day care centers, were located largely in the schools and had eligibility rules that covered a wide range of pupils. For the most part, the programs were conceived as educational. While they left no permanent structures, many eventually were folded into the federal programs that were established to provide child care during World War II under the Community Facilities Act of 1941 (Lanham Act).

Both the WPA and the Lanham Act had for the first time brought significant federal support to child care, and each had increased the level of involvement as never before. The Lanham Act programs were the first formal acceptance, too, of the fact that large numbers of mothers of young children could be needed in the labor force and that child care provision could therefore become an ongoing public responsibility. It is not that there was no opposition, ambivalence, or concern, however. The programs were overwhelmingly educational, but many had adopted the social service, nutrition, parent involvement, and developmental perspectives of the day care field, as well. Nonetheless, there was objection to a program that provided only centers and no family day care. Social workers and child welfare leaders feared that "the federal stimulus to day care would in the long run be destructive of day care and contrary to basic American values."[9]

There could be some acceptance of day care as meeting a wartime emergency labor force problem, but the "normal" circumstance in the family field was still conceived as one in which the mother was at home. Thus, the Lanham Act and other wartime child care programs were dismantled everywhere except in California and New York City, as the country was expected to return to normal (and despite continued, historically high female employment). For a while, at least, proprietary nursery schools were to grow and fill some of the gap in provision, but, of course, many lost public wartime day care space and many parents could not afford the middle-class nursery fees.

When the 1960s experienced even greater pressure for increased child care because of the rapid development of a new pattern of labor force participation, even by mothers of preschool and young school-aged children, the social welfare child care field as a whole remained fixed initially in a therapeutic-treatment-protective concept (with local exceptions). Applicants would be evaluated and assessed and social workers would see if there was a day care "need." The care had to have a social service component.

Where parents used care in the home of a nonrelative (rather than center care), it was often called "foster family day care" to signify its relationship to the substitute care for troubled or broken families. Even where casework staffing was weak or limited, as it often was, the "case" ideology pervaded the service.

Our mid-1960s reaction was to ask whether the time had not come to recognize the social reality that large numbers of normal women worked and that their children needed care. Should there not be an institutional response defined as serving typical—untroubled—families, a "social utility"? Should therapeutic day care not be differentiated and seen as specialized and for the few?[10] We recognized, as well, the reintroduction in the 1960s of a theme found in the early 1830s in the infant schools—and revived when kindergarten and even experimental nursery schools became available to the poor in the 1920s—what we now call compensatory education. For, by the late 1950s, a variety of preschool and related programs, many of them foundation-supported, with the Ford Foundation in the lead, were attempting to begin with younger children and thus to improve their learning "readiness" and eventual educational success. By the mid-1960s, in the context of what was to become the Poverty War, Head Start was elaborating the theme that educational and socialization experiences could help overcome deficits in child rearing inherent in social disadvantage. This theme also was taken up by the Elementary and Secondary Education Act of 1965.

Now all the elements of the tradition were on the table: self-expressive, developmental, and educational experiences for young children, beyond what the family offered; protective, therapeutic, and custodial care for children if the mother worked or the home was a place of neglect or abuse or danger; the early childhood educational experience as a compensatory one for deprived children. By the 1970s there had been a major cultural change, however. The bulk of parents could be interested in nursery school experience as normative. Children could grow, develop, and learn in public school or private group settings—and need not be deprived or handicapped to warrant such exposure.

Each of these themes was emphasized and protected in its own institutional niche; it had lay and provider constituencies, sanctions, and belief systems. As female labor force participation rates exploded in the 1970s, and child development knowledge and ideologies shifted, the question became whether the private nursery, public preschool, and social welfare day care center would remain separate and, perhaps, competing systems or whether new sorting out might occur.

Quite soon there were tensions. By the mid-1960s, for example, welfare policy had moved toward encouraging training for and work by AFDC mothers through reform efforts and the WIN program, work expense "disregards," and budgeting of child care costs. Now a welfare program did not compete with a day care strategy, as it seemed to when mothers' pensions began. Welfare departments began to sponsor and provide center care or family day care. At certain times they might encourage welfare mothers to become child care providers and thus self-supporting.

Similarly, the separation between the proprietary nursery school as education and the public day care center as custody eroded rapidly when in the late 1960s Title IV-A money and later Title XX funds increased the demand side of the child care equation. Proprietary program sponsors who wanted to attract publicly eligible clients spanned both systems, if state or local regulations were not too onerous, and all-day care was viewed by parents as a "school" option. (Others among the proprietary nursery schools remained completely unrelated to the public funding system.)

Day care centers, on the other hand, were increasingly related to early childhood education developments and training improvements. In high-quality jurisdictions they joined health, nutrition, social service, mental health, and parent-participation programming with sophisticated cognitive-development curricula, as developed at such centers of early childhood education leadership as Pacific Oaks College, Wheelock, or Bank Street.

Clearly, on one level, there was convergence and the joining of categories. Greenberg, in fact, after a careful review of the evidence, wonders whether the "ideal type" distinctions were ever pure and the differences ever as sharp in reality as in ideological discussion:[11]

> To recapitulate, evidence bearing on the program content of day-care centers and nursery schools reveals that the distinction between custodial care and education applied only partially and unevenly. The distinction bypassed historical exceptions, differences between programs under varied sponsors, and emergent trends . . . both our review of evidence and the history . . . show generally that neither program nomenclature nor auspices offer [sic] assurance of program content, let alone quality, in a loosely regulated service industry.

Almy, a leading expert in the field of early childhood education and a teacher of their teachers notes: [12]

> . . . the early childhood education engine has supplied the day care giant so generously that day care and early childhood education

programs are, for all practical purposes, identical. Unfortunately . . . day care has sometimes received less than the best of early childhood education, and the question of whether day care can afford to include early childhood education is still raised.

Day care might be defined by one group as child welfare for the poor, whereas nursery schools were described as contributing to the development of children, but parents often refused to make these distinctions; and proprietary programs offered both "care" and education as they appealed to diverse population groups and organized a very significant portion, perhaps a majority, of the service in the late 1960s. The 5-year-olds increasingly could go to public kindergarten, with space for only one-quarter of the cohort as World War II ended but accommodating two-thirds by the mid-1960s.

Grubb and Lazerson offer an instructive case study of California's Children's Centers.[13] Created during the period of Lanham Act financing and continued after World War II with state funding, this education-based system remained the largest in the country. Advocates could protect it because of the key role of women in the state's ever-growing labor force. Only a few local districts contributed to costs significantly, as the state legislature responded to the need; nonetheless, the program remained peripheral in the state education department as a peculiar combination of custody and education. Many waited for the end of a wartime "emergency," but by the time of the Korean War, they ceased to expect dismantling.

From a universal program during and after the war, the program took on more of a social welfare aspect as it introduced a means test and sliding fee scales. As early as 1951, 60 percent of the children it served were from single-parent families. Some advocates advanced arguments for support that were later to be associated with the "compensatory education" school. Others stressed that these programs allowed mothers to work and remain free of welfare aid.

In any case, despite debate the Child Care Centers (later to be called "Children's Centers") became a permanent, if not fully integrated, part of the state education system in 1957. They offered all-day care to preschoolers ages 2 to 5 and after-school care to elementary school children—sometimes in regular school buildings, often in special buildings on school grounds. Since the program has been controversial over the years, assessments are often in conflict. It would appear that they attracted both highly qualified and less well qualified personnel, that programs ranged in quality but that—here we follow Grubb and Lazerson—as of 1977, overall, "the average quality of the centers [was] rather high" from both the early education and the child caring sides. During the 1960s the centers had, in effect, become part of the Poverty War compensatory effort, and in the 1970s they were oriented increasingly to the social welfare preventive and work-supportive efforts to which social service and child welfare funds were targeted. California had not separated early education from day care, but it certainly had not created a universal preschool program. From the mid-1960s much of the financing was based on social service (IV-A and XX) and child welfare funds and, then, compensatory programs in the education system.

When, in the late 1970s, the state was ready for a new level of expenditure and a variety of new program models, it left this education-based system in place and used the social welfare route for its "resource and referral," "alternative payments," and other new efforts. Some observers believe it thus left California and the rest of the country with a sense of unresolved long-term issues and with bureaucracies and advocates in contention. Others feel that school districts, too, participate well in R&R and AP opportunities and that there is no sharp split.

The overview, thus far, has ignored the school-age child care question. It was not until late in the 1970s that the problem began to receive consistent, organized attention. Nonetheless, some elements of the background story should be noted.[14] One needs to be reminded, first, that it was the development of universal public education that constituted the most important, if largely unintended, public contribution to child care. All states had compulsory attendance laws by 1918 but enforcement was long to be uneven in some places. Nonetheless, even though the school day length does not coincide with the length of the parental work day—and schools are out for long summer vacations, for many holidays, and to allow teachers time for special purposes—the public school clearly has become the major child care resource.

Los Angeles apparently also created a large network of day nurseries as far back as 1917 and continuing until the 1930s, so that elementary school children would not need to skip school in order to mind younger siblings. Schools, then, have a preschool tradition independent of the nursery school and kindergarten programs already described.

What is now generally called school-age child care fills in the gaps before and after school, weekends, and holidays. From the latter part of the nineteenth century some of the day nurseries–day care centers have offered after-school care to children of elementary school age whose parents were still working when the school day ended. They also organized summer "vacation" schools. Then, as now, this coverage was limited.

The playschool movement, which developed out of the progressive education movement in the 1920s and 1930s, also offered after-school programming in settlement houses, community centers, and schools to limited numbers of pupils. Not designed as child care, and emphasizing enrichment and enhanced development, these programs were not reserved for children of working mothers but often did meet a child care need. As such programs spread, they became obvious recipients of Lanham Act funds during World War II and focused more deliberately on care for children of working mothers. Indeed it was said to be the recognition that day nurseries were now also serving school-aged children in afternoon programs that led to the adoption of the name "day care center."

The very large school-based, child care development of the Lanham Act came to an end with World War II, but some cities continued modest school-age programs for varying periods. The issue surfaced again as a subject of concern in the 1970s with efforts to enact comprehensive child care legislation, but died with President Nixon's 1971 veto. School-age child care returned to the national agenda in the 1980s with the growing proportions of mothers of school-aged children working full-time and with increased publicity about the so-called "latchkey" phenomenon, children alleged to be in self-care and endangered because they came home to empty houses and apartments while their parents worked.

Almost all of the threads in this historical story remain visible: the diverse perspectives, goals, stakes, and program forms. How do these interact with current realities? What may be expected next?

Developments

As we have noted in Chapter 1, child care could no longer be ignored in the 1980s, given the labor force participation rates of the married as well as single mothers of infants, toddlers, and preschool-aged children. Nor could the school-age child care question be put aside, in view of the widespread publicity given to the alleged self-care of many children of elementary school age between the end of the school day and the time a parent got home from work. Publicity about child abuse and neglect, delinquency, and failure to do homework kept the issue active in the public eye.

Effects of Federal Strategy

At the national level, the Reagan administration leadership could argue that they had no responsibility for supply, except to finance and enhance the program for poor children, Head Start, and this they did. They also encouraged corporate provision of child care services and could hardly be blamed if little came of that initiative. Their main response to the child care problem was to subsidize demand through the child care tax credit and by permitting employers to help meet employee costs or to provide service under favorable tax incentives. In short, they could be in favor of child care without commiting themselves to a particular delivery system, although it could be argued that the demand subsidy route tended to tilt toward the proprietary. This could mean family day care, private nursery schools, or private day care centers.

The main effect of the federal strategy was to transfer the major locus of action to states and local government. The Title XX social service funding had been converted into the Social Services Block Grant, which wiped out planning and public participation requirements, eliminated federal day care standards, and ended spending mandates. The Elementary and Secondary Education Act had become part of the block grant created by the Education Consolidation and Improvement Act of 1981, again leaving much of the decision about specific programs to the states.

Those states that chose to respond—and most felt they had to— would be dealing explicitly or implicitly with the preschool– kindergarten–day care choices. Would they utilize education or social welfare streams, both, or what? They were acting in an environment in which interest in education on an optional basis for the 4-year-olds was snowballing everywhere, as noted earlier.

Responses to Demographic and Social Change

Parental preferences, previous public policy, and existing provider responses had already created some facts. As noted in Chapter 1 and as shown in Table 5.1, by the early 1980s, 93 percent of all 5- year-olds were in nursery school, kindergarten, or first grade; 46 percent of the 4-year-olds were in preschool programs; and 29 percent of the 3-year-olds were in preschool programs. The number of 3- and 4-year-olds in preschool programs had doubled between 1970 and 1983, and the 5-year-old participation had jumped almost 15 percent, approaching universalism (and independent of income and the mother's work status). The especially rapid growth in nursery school attendance of 3- and 4-year-olds can be seen in Table 5.1.

Children age 3 and 4 of working mothers were more likely to be in care, and thus in preschool, than children of mothers not in the labor force, but the trend was obviously part of a cultural shift and not only a response to the need for care. Thus, in 1984, 49 percent

Table 5.1   Enrollment Data, Children Aged 3 to 5, 1970 and 1983

	Year		
Group	1970 (in thousands)	1983 (in thousands)	(1984) (in thousands)
Total 3–5-year-old population	10,950	10,252	10,612
% enrolled total	37.5%	52.5%	51.6%
% public	26.0%	31.5%	32.1%
% private	11.6%	21.0%	19.5%
Total 3–4-year-old population	7,136	6,986	7,188
% enrolled total	15.3%	33.6%	36.3%
% public nursery school	4.6%	11.6%	13.3%
% private nursery school	10.7%	22.0%	23.0%
Total 5-year-old population	3,814	3,266	3,423
% enrolled total	78.9%	93.0%	93.9%
% public kindergarten and grades 1–2	65.5%	74.0%	—
% private kindergarten and grades 1–2	13.4%	19.0%	—

SOURCE: Center for Statistics, U.S. Department of Education.

of the 4-year-olds with working mothers and 36 percent of the 3-year-olds with working mothers were in preprimary programs, whereas for those with mothers at home the respective rates were 42 and 22 percent. The more affluent and better educated made more use of these programs. In 1984, 53 percent of the 3- and 4-year-olds in families with median or higher income, but only 29 percent in lower-income families, attended preschools. Child attendance rates in preschool also rose with the level of the mother's education. For children of college graduates, preschool attendance rates were almost independent of the mother's employment status. About 70 percent of the 4-year-olds with college-educated mothers were enrolled in preprimary school programs whether or not their mothers worked. More than half (52 percent) of the 3-year-olds with college graduate mothers were enrolled; those whose mothers worked, in addition, were even more likely to participate in such programs (56 percent).

With about 52 percent of *all* 3- to 5-year-olds in a school-based program, and still more in educationally oriented group programs, it is appropriate to note that the educational stream is well represented in child care. The all-day nursery school enrollment is more than a third of the total and outnumbers the 3- to 5-year-olds in all-day day care centers. Together, over two-thirds of the group are in part-day or all-day *group* care; this total does not include some of the 450,000 children in Head Start and obviously omits a large group in full-time or part-time family day care arrangements. (It is estimated that only 15 percent of Head Start programs are school-based; about 20 percent operate all day. It is not certain whether and how these numbers enter into census or educational statistics totals since both mothers' answers and interviewer judgments are involved.)

Data problems and definitional inconsistencies preclude accurate generalization, but the point emerges: School as well as social welfare systems are heavily involved in child care. In the instance of group care, day care centers perhaps serve more "younger children" (under age 4) than do nursery schools, but kindergarten and first grade dominate for the 5-year-olds and nursery schools dominate for the 4-year-olds. Family day care meets a larger part of the need than does group care for those under age 3.

The data, however, are approximations and the changes rapid. What is most relevant and important is that despite these trends the country has not yet learned to think about the educational and social welfare child care streams as part of one development, certainly not to plan for them as one phenomenon.

On the level of data collection, Census Bureau experts and the Department of Education's Center for Statistics have gradually arrived at the view that child care "coverage" reports in the future must encompass nursery schools, prekindergarten and kindergarten programs, day care centers, Head Start, family day care and their several public, private-non-profit, and proprietary variations.[15] The Census Bureau now employs the term "group care center" to cover all program forms in the several systems other than family day care; but its reports are nonetheless incomplete and have methodological limitations (see Chapter 1). While the educational statistics series is currently confined to nursery school and kindergarten participation rates, a staff paper from the Center for Statistics noted in 1986 that the "distinction . . . between day care services (viewed mainly as custodial) and education . . . has been maintained long beyond its usefulness." The center was looking forward to more comprehensive data collection that would include the "variety of day care, nursery school and enrichment programs as well as kindergarten."[16] There was an agreement that such surveys should cover family day care as well.

Accurate user and provider information would contribute significantly to greater understanding of trends and assessment of needs. The issues about these interrelated and overlapping yet in some ways unintegrated streams would not thereby disappear. As indicated in our listing at the beginning of the chapter, these are systems in flux, and it is not easy to encompass them conceptually or deal with them in a policy sense. We devote the remainder of this section as well as the next to an effort to depict the action. Then we attempt to define the policy choices.

Initiatives

From one perspective, the increased part-time or full-time participation of 2- to 4-year-olds in organized group experiences may be described and explained as one unified, new social trend in a changing society. To the actors, these are separate phenomena, or one phenomenon with different interpretations.

First, there is the conviction that children socialize, learn, and mature at far younger ages than ever before. Whether because the development of children has been reassessed by researchers or because there is real social change that accelerates development, children are offered opportunities and do respond. Educated middle-class parents show the way, but, when they can, other parents follow. The visitor to a day care center or nursery school sees 2- and 3-year-olds in activity and interaction that would have been regarded as improbable in an earlier era—whether during the meal serving or eating periods or playing/learning on the computer. Parents in all social groups whom we have interviewed talk with pride of the accomplishments of their young children. Minority parents clearly hope that such opportunity will help their children escape the problems of many young people in their communities and open broad educational opportunities.

Many parents want their children to have such learning experiences. Others may be responding more to the smaller sizes of families. Children have fewer or no siblings. The preschool center offers a socialization opportunity once available at home.

Thus far, we have described the "demand" perspective, the parents' responses to demographic and social change and the encouragement they may receive from child development researchers and experts. There also is a degree of societal initiative, which may be described as a 1980s equivalent of the "Sputnick" phenomenon of the 1950s. In that latter period, traumatized by Russian space triumphs, the United States invested in educational upgrading, lest we lose out in the competition. Currently, the competitive successes of Japan in high technology, the shortages of U.S.-educated students to fill engineering and other advanced scientific training opportunities in our leading technical centers, and anxiety about the meaning of low national average scores in various mathematical, scientific, analytic, and verbal aptitude tests

have generated an important impulse to upgrade American education. Related to this is the belief in some states or cities that their
own economic successes during a period of considerable restructuring of local economies will depend on the quality of the local
"human capital." They want strong, local educational establish-
ments producing the personnel essential to local economies, particularly those economic activities that will position them at the
cutting edges to compete successfully in attracting new companies.

These impulses have come together in several official national
reports, several major reports from professional associations, and
the reports of a large number of national, regional, state, and city
blue-ribbon panels, task forces, economic development panels,
and legislative committees. Of immediate relevance is the fact that
a significant number of these reports have urged attention to
preschools. Many have argued specifically for offering educational
opportunities for the 4-year-olds.

Equal or even greater attention has been given to the case for
preschool for poor, deprived, and minority children. In an era of
social program cutting, 1981–1986, the President and Congress
have protected Head Start, one of the few program survivals from
the 1964 economic opportunity program. By fiscal 1985 Head Start
was enrolling approximately 450,000 children, almost all of them in
the 3- to 5-year-age group (26 percent were 3, 56 percent were 4,
and 15 percent were 5 in 1984). Expenditures were over $1 billion
a year. The program sites included 1200 regular centers (20
percent all-day; 15 percent based in schools), 25 migrant programs,
95 Indian programs, 30 parent/child program centers. These totals
allowed space for almost 20 percent of the 3–5 group in poverty in
the United States (since Head Start is limited to a maximum of 10
percent nonpoor children). In 1984 blacks constituted 42 percent
of the participant group, Hispanics 20 percent, and American
Indians 4 percent—a minority representation of two-thirds, which
reflects the U.S. poverty picture.

The excitement about Head Start accomplishments has been
stirred in recent years by research summations reporting long-
term success even though partly challenged still more recently by
a meta-analysis with what some interpret as mixed results.[17] There
has also been considerable positive national publicity and spillover
from the report of the longitudinal study by High/Scope of the
Perry Preschool Program, not a Head Start project and acknowledged to be programmatically superior to and more costly than the
typical Head Start effort. The positive impacts reported for the
Perry Preschool graduates hold a promise of better school achievement in reading, language, and arithmetic; higher academic moti-

vation; less need for special education classes; less unemployment after school; fewer arrests by age 19; fewer births by age 19. (The press and media enthusiasm, which reflect these positive results and report their impressive cost/benefits ratios, do not necessarily simultaneously remind readers that many of the graduates of these programs did not do well. They may be unemployed school dropouts and in trouble.)[18]

The Congressional Budget Office also has concluded that Head Start is clearly effective in providing useful services, even if the program impact on subsequent school experiences remains unclear. For present purposes we need not enter into the methodological problems of establishing adequate controls to measure and certify specific impacts of so complex and varied a national effort as Head Start. One wonders whether the first or second grade could be research-validated nationally in a similar sense![19] Drawing upon earlier and recent Head Start summations and their own studies, Schweinhart and Weikert do argue convincingly that "good preschool programs for children at risk of school failure *do* better prepare them for school both intellectually and socially, *probably* help them to achieve greater school success, and *can* lead them to greater life success in adolescence and adulthood."[20] However, Weikert contends in discussion that one need not prove impact to justify preschool for the 4-year-olds: Children need care and middle-class parents do send their children to nursery school. Now it is a matter of equal opportunity for the less affluent and the poor.

Although the idea of universal, publicly financed preschool for 4-year-olds has certainly not yet won broad public support, clearly, society, Congress, and the White House do see value in serving almost half a million deprived children in a program with cognitive, socialization, nutritional, mental health, social service, and parent participation components. With all the limitations, problems, and complaints, the positive reports and some research results are indeed impressive; communities and states now regard these as useful endeavors and seek to expand them.

On balance, one certainly can be encouraged. The positive impact is visible. Preschool is particularly effective in helping deprived children to learn. Enriched programs may accomplish even more. Society is properly impressed. In many states and cities not quite ready to respond to the considerable parental interest in public preschool for all 4-year-olds, there has been action on behalf of poor, deprived, or non-English-speaking children. These programs look like good investments to political leaders, businesspeople, and the media.

Thus far we have described educational and remedial initiatives with implications for the 3- and 4-year-olds. Although such provision also results in care for children during the day, perhaps while parents work, that is not the primary motivation. Indeed, as a largely part-day program, Head Start was developed with a strong requirement of parental involvement but gradually loosened in the face of the reality of parental work—still in many senses the original concept is viable since many of the Head Start children are in families in receipt of AFDC aid and with an at-home mother. Nonetheless, in the midst of the attention to educational opportunity for 3- and 4-year-olds or the advocacy of more enrichment programs along the Head Start lines, there also has been related attention to school-aged child care. Some studies and reports have documented the lack of care provision for school-aged children while parents work. Although a promised federally financed national survey was reduced to a two-state report with some debatable conclusions,[21] some cities and counties did their own data collection. A foundation-supported effort has been disseminating material about program models in different parts of the country and stimulating exchange of experience, public awareness, and further advocacy.[22]

If only gradually, states and cities are increasing their commitments to school-age child care programs or are converting kindergarten for the 5-year-olds from half-day to full school-day programs. And some all-day preschools for the 4-year-olds have expanded. Debates continue about public responsibility, locus, financing, and auspice, but some jurisdictions have moved ahead and the pace of action has accelerated.

Some of the specifics are of interest. Educators, school systems, or education departments have not undertaken an outright child care commitment or responsibility in competition with the social welfare or proprietary service systems; their interest, if any, is usually in preschool as compensatory education. Nonetheless, these several different impulses have resulted in significant child care action, and the programs could grow in importance. Early in 1986 a national magazine for directors of child care programs proclaimed that 1985[23]

> may be remembered as the year that the public schools rediscovered
> the early years. . . . By the end of 1985 at least 28 states had enacted
> early childhood initiatives. . . . The National Conference of State
> Legislatures cited early childhood education and child care as "the
> most significant new areas of legislative activity in education in
> 1985" . . . [and] the National Association of Elementary School
> Principals adopted the recommendation that states should create
> full day programs for all four years olds.

A similar assessment of accelerated action could have been justified for 1984. This is an arena of intense activity. Although no state provides universal public schooling for 4-year-olds and, indeed, few offer all-day kindergarten for 5-year-olds, enough is occurring or being proposed to justify attention and scrutiny and to encourage debate. We reported at the very beginning of the chapter the concerns and alarms of the National Black Child Development Institute and of opponents in North Carolina. One also could cite other reservations, as well as numerous speeches and resolutions expressing enthusiasm and expectation.

So rapid is the action that no summary would be valid for many months. We nonetheless report some recent developments to give a sense of what types of things are occurring.[24]

Kindergarten. A survey for the Illinois State Board of Education by Dr. Margaret Whaley completed early in 1985[25] found that whereas slightly over half the states were mandating provision of kindergarten services by local districts, most local districts, in fact, offered programs even in states where it was optional. Only Mississippi was not providing programs in most districts, and it planned to begin in September 1985. States require school attendance (first grade) either at age 6 or age 7 (Pennsylvania and Washington, at age 8) and admit to kindergarten one year earlier. Only five or six states compel kindergarten attendance (Delaware, Florida, Louisiana, Kentucky, and Maine; another source omits Louisiana but correctly adds South Carolina and Virginia!). As we have seen, practically all 5-year-olds are nonetheless in kindergarten or the first grade.

Most interesting, in recent years, has been a change from half-day to full-school-day kindergarten attendance, with the total now somewhere between one-third and one-half the cohort. In 1981 Dr. Sandra L. Robinson of the University of South Carolina surveyed full-school-day programs available to some or all children in 15 states, and the roster has been growing. The education literature of only four or five years ago is full of doubts, part-time/full-time comparisons, and curriculum models. Currently, the discussion for the most part is about such matters as program content, classroom space, supplies, teacher equipment, staffing levels, and resources.

The 4-year-olds. Despite the many initiatives for the 4-year-olds, by early 1986 there were only some 15 states with state-funded programs, and none offered coverage for all 4-year-olds in the state (New York, California, Pennsylvania, New Jersey, Maryland, Louisiana, Maine, Oklahoma, South Carolina, Texas, Ohio, Illinois, Florida, Michigan, Massachusetts, the District of Columbia). Four or five others belong on the list as we write. Including places where state government was not involved, there were some programs in two-thirds of the states at the time of the 1986 survey. A few other states were about to begin some funding or were funding programs through Head Start or community services programs, not through their education departments. Other states were making plans or considering initiatives. Attempts to move had been stalled elsewhere.[26]

The numbers of children thus far served are quite limited. Most of the laws for 4-year-olds are permissive, not mandatory upon the districts. A few fund in the state-aid formula pattern followed for kindergarten, but most set specific limits on the amount spent. A number permit preschools to cover the 3-year-olds. Despite New York City intentions, no jurisdictions offer universal coverage. All of the states target or give priority to the "at risk" children, and Texas requires any district with 15 such children to provide compensatory programs. The result thus far is that unlike the kindergartens, the preschool initiatives have been heavily compensatory to this point.

The programs range from those that use the kindergarten facilities, staffing ratios, and schedules for the 4-year-olds as well to others that attempt to approximate the Head Start model. Most offer half-day programs. In a few instances the state has been contracting with agencies outside the schools to provide kindergarten programs (Illinois, Michigan) or has provision to do so (South Carolina). Connecticut is shaping a public-private cooperative model. Several states place heavy emphasis on related parent education efforts. At least three contract with Head Start programs. Proponents can find examples of programs that compare favorably with the best of enriched day care; opponents can cite large, bureaucratic "kindergarten for the 4-year-olds."

School-Age Child Care.   The Wellesley group has published a list of 11 states that late in 1985 were reported as undertaking school-age child care initiatives. The range was considerable, as was the level of commitment.[27] No reliable funding stream exists as yet in most communities. Social welfare agencies rather than school systems have instigated most of these:

- The Arizona governor was mounting a campaign to encourage elementary school districts to offer care.
- California, in 1985, voted significant funds for one-time capital investment and also funding for ongoing operations.
- Indiana funded a pilot program in 1985 but did not renew it for 1987 when funding expired.

- Massachusetts had enacted a comprehensive plan that included a school-age component.
- New York had voted $300,000 for 1984 and again for 1985 for matching start-up funds. The grant for start-up was doubled for 1986. These are one-time $10,000 grants. Only districts with local matches can use the money, and ongoing operations are not covered. The grants are administered by the state social welfare and youth agency and are available to private nonprofit and government agencies.
- Wisconsin was funding three innovative programs at a total cost under $78,000.
- Rhode Island, Connecticut, and Florida were offering localities modest start-up help, and there were small beginnings elsewhere as well.

Some States Act

The system is a rapidly changing panorama, but it clearly is in motion. A role is being shaped for the schools, the nature of the action perhaps best understood with reference to a few specifics. First, a brief mention of the federal level.

There has been no school-related action except for what has already been said about Head Start and the Education Consolidation and Improvement Act, apart from a modest $20 million block grant authorized late in 1984 to expand both school-age child care and resource and referral (for dependent elderly and children). Funding was blocked until December 1985 when funds were included in an appropriation bill. In April 1986 the Office of Human Development Services finally announced that states could apply for formula grants for a dependent care block grant covering resource and referral systems (40 percent of $5 million) and school-age child care (60 percent of $5 million). The administration proposed elimination of the program for 1987, but it was reauthorized through 1990 and $5 million was voted for fiscal year 1987.

In Chapter 3 we noted how statewide comprehensive child care strategies in California and Massachusetts inevitably included education-based programs. We described two patterns. California has allowed both the school-based and community-based social welfare agencies to participate in its R&R and AP programs; these agencies and the proprietary programs all draw on state funds from the same pool. The initiatives are identified as school-based programs, community programs, latchkey, AP, R&R, and so forth, and the social welfare/school lines are blurred. The Office of Child Development in California's Department of Education, drawing only on state funds, administers a $310 million program serving 80,000 children in all the ways we have discussed. Of the "users," 70 percent are aged 3–5, 18 percent 6–17, and 12 percent under age 2. In encouraging increased prekindergarten offerings for the 3- and 4-year-olds, Massachusetts has protected the interests of community groups and ensured participation of all delivery systems from the social welfare as well as the education side in its expanding programs. It is not yet clear what the results will be as programs become operational, and whether the political "solution" will permit smooth operations.

Here we summarize developments in other states—the Carolinas, Minnesota, Texas, and New York—in an effort to view both possibilities and problems.

South Carolina

South Carolina has little service for the 4-year-olds as yet, but its approach clarifies some of the choices. Among its positive provisions, South Carolina legislation provides funding for developing half-day, voluntary early childhood programs for 4-year-old children who have significant readiness deficiencies. It also provides funding for home visits and parent education for 3- and 4-year-olds and makes kindergarten mandatory for 5-year-olds. The state will phase in services for "at-risk" 4-year-olds over a period of five years, at a cost of approximately $16 million for 1988–1989.

Further, the South Carolina bill specifically addresses some of the major concerns that early childhood professionals and working parents have had with part-day programs for 4-year-olds. The bill provides that programs must be at least one half-day in length. This policy leaves open the possibility of schools and communities eventually providing extended child care coverage while parents work.

The state has made it easier for parents to arrange for care during the second half of the day. Transportation policies have been modified so that school buses can leave children at child care programs, family day care homes, or with relatives.

The South Carolina bill also encourages cooperative approaches among all groups providing quality care for preschool children. School districts may contract with appropriate groups and agencies to provide part or all of the programs for younger children. This means that early childhood groups could run the programs.

In order to help ensure that programs are not developed by the education community in isolation from other interested groups, the bill also ensures that programs be developed in consultation with the Interagency Coordinating Council on Early Childhood

Education, which includes representatives from major state agencies concerned with children. This group must consult with the Advisory Committee for Early Childhood Education in developing proposals to submit to the State Board of Education. The Advisory Committee includes representatives from state agencies and child care organizations, Head Start, higher education institutions, and medical schools. In the event that a local advisory committee exists in a community to coordinate early childhood education and development, school districts must consult with the committee in planning and developing services.

The bill requires the governor to initiate the development of a state plan on early childhood development and education, which would assist the state in providing appropriate services for preschool children. In recognition of the special needs of younger children, the bill calls for the staff/child ratios of one teacher to ten 4-year-old children.[28]

None of this is simple. If public school programs become available to 4-year-olds and the traditional child care agencies merely "fill in" the uncovered hours, the latter will not be able to operate for their usual 7½ hours. Thus they argue for the opportunity to participate directly in the school-run programs. The South Carolina legislation does permit subcontracting, but many present providers of child care services cannot meet the state's formal teacher-certification requirements and will need to do some hiring. Will there be a supply of personnel? Would they be affordable?

Also, the South Carolina social service child care community has developed "comprehensive quality assurance standards" in health, nutrition, social services, and parent involvement through the state health and human services department. Such standards do not apply to school-based preschools. Should they? Can they? Will they?

Some fear that the schools will not reach out to those children not already known to existing programs. Some are concerned that if South Carolina eventually goes from a half-day to a full-school-day for 4-year-old children, the problem will remain of creating service to cover the period from 3:00 P.M. until parents return from work.[29] Obviously, the South Carolina situation moves on, but the problems and issues repeat in state after state.

North Carolina

We referred at the very beginning of the chapter to North Carolina, a state that has had long experience with all-day kindergarten for the 5-year-olds and is considering the 3- and 4-year olds. While the state's child educational officer was backing school delivery of preschool services and offering a rationale for a universal program to meet both educational and child care needs, other political figures were arguing the case for private sector (commercial as well as nonprofit social welfare) child care and urging more corporate child care initiatives.

The debate, in part, was about "turf." On the level of rationale, many believe that children need access to school at a younger age, that school can provide an integrating and universal experience, and that state financing would contribute to equity and access. In opposition were those who cited the bureaucratization and rigidity which had developed in the state's all-day kindergartens over its 15-year history and the fact that daily school hours and the year-long calendar and vacations do not coincide with the work schedules of parents. There were not enough properly trained teachers available; yet if teachers were eventually recruited for the 3- and 4-year-olds and paid at school salaries, not at current day care rates, cost would become prohibitive. Besides, schools have far less of a tradition of intense family involvement than do day care centers.

Added to this were the complaints from owners of proprietary centers that the schools constituted "unfair competition" by offering free or subsidized programs for 4-year-old children. "The schools," it was said, "already took the 5-year-olds from us. Let them leave us the 4-year-olds." Moreover, should the state begin to finance significant numbers of programs for the 3- and 4-year-olds, there would be a problem for the day care centers currently serving many 4-year-olds (and a good number are proprietary), and there still would be need for services covering the hours after 3 P.M., the weekends, summer vacations, and holidays. New transportation arrangements also would be required.

One has the impression that resolution of the several issues defined will require a somewhat mixed delivery system aided by state finance and that whether politically or practically the schools will not be able to take on the entire task. (See New York and Massachusetts.) It is nonetheless worthy of recall that the day care advocates opposing school-delivery of services to the 4-year-olds and complaining about school insensitivity and lack of a comprehensive concept of child care services are themselves operating in a state said to have among the lowest child care licensing standards and weekly fees in the country.

Minnesota

Much of the relevant state context is summarized in Chapter 2. As we suggested in describing developments in the Twin Cities, one cannot assess the emerging structural arrangements for initiating, planning, and facilitating child care services without considering the educational system. Two developments in Minnesota are relevant: the so-called "latchkey program" (Extended Day Programs) and a broader educational initiative known as "community education." Thus far, they are largely unrelated.

The latchkey program varies in size with district decisions: There were 19 before- and after-school programs identified in 1984, fewer in 1985. Apart from what districts do, there are some funds for Indo-Chinese refugees. Extended Day Programs are open before school hours and usually until 6:00 P.M. There are summer, weekend, and holiday programs. They usually have a well-qualified director, small staffs, and other part-time personnel, depending upon size and hours. The rule is that they must have access to some school space, on a limited basis, and to some central services. Several offer "drop in" service on a space-available basis.

Inevitably what occurs depends on the parents in an area and on the local board. There are several significant programs, but the requirement for self-support means that the poor districts of high-need tend not to be covered. Those parents eligible for sliding fee aid and reached on the waiting list may apply the voucher to before- and after-school service, but they do not constitute a sufficient critical mass anywhere actually to meet a program's financial minimum. In practice, then, the education-based latch-key programs and the social welfare-based child care centers and family day care home offerings (which may also be used before and after school) come into competition. Because schools do not need the licenses that are required by others, there has, in fact, been tension between the two systems.

The Community Education program is a separate one in the Minnesota school system and has been expanding in recent years. (Somewhat similar but interesting developments in Missouri will not be discussed, to conserve space.) On the basis of the efforts of State Senator Jerome M. Hughes, long the chairman of the State Senate Education Committee and, by the mid-1980s, president of the Minnesota State Senate, Minnesota enacted in 1981 an Improved Learning Law to complement and extend earlier (1974) legislation on early childhood family education. Further extensions have been passed in recent years. The legislation enacts a humanistic concept of lifelong learning and offers state support to districts to develop initiatives. Districts that take advantage of state "permission" to levy an appropriate extra small tax then obtain matching funds.

The opportunity is a broad one, extending both to the infants and the elderly. From a child care coverage perspective, its main limitation is that parents must participate with their preschool children in the offerings.

Thus, Rochester's Child Care Resource and Referral has been the subcontractor for a school-based series of local offerings, including:

- *Early Childhood Education* A once-weekly experience for children in a nursery school setting with highly qualified staff.
- *Parent Education* A parallel, simultaneous activity for parents.
- *Parent-Child Interaction* Parents and children are jointly involved in the program.
- *Informal Fridays* A less-structured sharing experience for parents, with child care provided.

These activities take place in a community service building and are open to all residents of the school district. They are once or twice a week programs that extend for 13 weeks, not child care for parents who work. Recently, the program has moved into child care centers for the period from 5:30 P.M. to 7:00 P.M., using school-paid staffs and providing food. The development is taking several forms in the state. One district has developed an infant-toddler program in a preschool in the context of the community education mandate.

Will these separate developments add up? Will there be further school expansion? Several child care leaders in the state who are not protecting boundaries see the potential for adding to coverage by converting kindergartens into all-day programs, gradually extending down to the 4- and 3-year-olds and building a more accessible program of before- and after-school coverage for all districts. Others resent the lack of school licensing requirements (but schools will need social welfare system licenses if they do not develop their own system within two years, according to recent legislation). Many in the day care center field believe that school systems are too rigid to be trusted with so large a part of the task, seeing them as completely cognitively oriented and bureaucratized. Others note the actual vagueness of the boundaries between day care centers and private nursery schools and the success of proprietary centers in bridging both domains.

We elaborate and discuss these claims elsewhere. Immediately relevant is the fact that the Rochester agency accommodates to the development and attempts to incorporate it, while the Twin Cities largely pursue a social welfare strategy. The state government has no vital center for coping with the subject. The governor's Committee on Children and Youth issued a new report on latchkey children early in 1986; there was some increased funding. The St. Paul Chamber of Commerce was also discussing the subject. Early in 1986 a state Department of Education task force, with cooperation from the social welfare community, was exploring both school-age child care (after school hours) and the issue of school-based programs for the 4-year-olds. A task force organized by the Pillsbury Corporation was completing a report and the Minneapolis mayor, Don Fraser, announced an initiative. Clearly the search for structure remains active.

Texas

If the issue is current or potential organization of child care resources, the Texas schools should not be ignored. (We have briefly mentioned some quite separate Houston school district initiatives in Chapter 3.) There are interesting beginnings at the state and local levels. A statewide task force has outlined a major effort to upgrade Texas education. There has been strong support from the governor. The details are not here relevant, involving as they do efforts to create greater rigor in high schools and colleges, to improve teacher competence, to enforce standards, while introducing computers and currently relevant educational content. The general concern is with upgraded education, not child care, but an initiative for the 4-year-olds may be relevant here.

In the context of the educational initiative (and concerned about the quality of the human capital on which its future industry must depend), Texas included a program for 4-year-olds in its 1984 legislation, voting $45 million for prekindergartens for fiscal year 1985–1986. Any school district with 15 or more 4-year-olds who are from low-income families (eligible for the school lunch program) or limited in English proficiency must offer such programs in the public schools. In effect this is a mandate to all but some rural school districts. A local match is required, but the funding formula offers most to the poorest districts. Once all educationally disadvantaged children are served, a district may open the program to all other 4-year-olds.

By 1986 about 35,000 4-year-olds were in a relatively low-standard program, judged by class size (a permitted ratio of one teacher to 22 children) and staff requirements. A state budgetary crisis has put many things on hold. It is noted as well that there is no requirement for an all-day program. Working parents will need to package the prekindergarten with day care or some other coverage in most or all districts. Child care advocates argue that the quality of the program as it is emerging makes it suspect both as education and as child care. There is little capacity for oversight and protection of children. Proponents respond that the effort has just begun.

All of these questions and caveats do not quite cancel out another observation, however. The state has been prepared for state leadership in education, although much is left to the locality. A minimalist government tradition, when confronted with current needs and social change, may find ways to move forward. This is in sharp contrast to the "social welfare" child care picture, where the state has largely withdrawn its funding commitments.

New York

The New York State and New York City story of efforts to expand school-age care and prekindergartens, and the ways in which social welfare and educational advocates have interacted with regard to proposals, may be instructive as to possible futures nationally. The accounting will require some detail.

In the midst of discussion of the newly documented successes of compensatory education and of the importance, for economic development, of generally increased educational investments, several elements came together in New York. The state already had since 1966 what was, after California, the country's largest "experimental" preschool program, but it was relatively small in relation to the total age cohort, with space for some 7000 children and with a compensatory emphasis. Early in 1983 the New York State commissioner of education, Gordon M. Ambach, proposed that children enter school sooner (kindergarten at 4, first grade at 5) because they were ready to learn sooner and ready for college earlier. The 12-year course of study could be condensed into 11 years. There would be an added bonus of efficiency, easing an expected elementary school bulge and teacher shortage and making better use of college teachers in surplus because of a declining population of 18-year-olds. The state reported that a 1980 five-year longitudinal evaluation and 1986 follow-up showed mixed, yet positive, learning (cognitive) effects, especially for the most deprived preschool children, and also showed that these effects persisted in the primary grades.[30]

The Ambach proposal set off an as yet unresolved debate among experts. It also yielded a modest expansion of state support for prekindergarten for 4-year-olds. At about the same time there was a city decision to convert its half-day kindergarten classes for 5-year-olds into an optional all-day program in September 1983. (Was this more urgent than admitting the 4-year-olds?)

The champions of traditional social welfare-based day care opposed this opening for the 5-year-olds based on the potential loss of children and the alleged kindergarten overemphasis on the cognitive as opposed to the socio-emotional. Some added that New York schools were generally unsuccessful with minority children: Why give them more to do? Others saw loss of opportunity for adequate parent participation. Why not, they asked, invite child care sponsors from among local community groups and social agencies to provide the programs for the second half-day or for the after-school hours?

All-day kindergarten was not completely new in New York. Some even went back 20 years. Some continued to be funded for special groups. When the school year had ended in June 1982 44,000 children were in half-day kindergarten and 8000 in the all-day program (7000 were 4-year-olds). School staff mounted an all-out curriculum development and training effort over the summer, directed by its then chancellor, Anthony J. Alvarado. Some 200 qualified early childhood experts were hired out of the day care system. Kindergarten teachers who had been on two shifts were now to remain with one group all day. Other licensed elementary teachers were assigned. (The department had dropped a special early childhood license some years before.) Within no time the enrollment grew, drawing some children out of tuition-charging nursery schools and day care centers, and soon there were 55,000 5-year-olds in all-day kindergarten.

The dominant curriculum development and training concepts were derived from the work of the Bank Street College of Education, widely respected by child development experts in both the day care and nursery school fields. There were inevitable equipment and supply shortages initially, and some of the space available was clearly inadequate. The target was a class size of 25, in contrast to the small day care center groups, and even this was not initially possible in districts that had 27 or 32 children in a room (with no funds, initially at least, for the aides or assistants common in the centers). In short, proponents could find much to applaud and critics much to question. The staff geared up to move ahead and the parents enthusiastically made use of this expanded and cost-free program for 5-year-old children.

Within a year it was clear that all-day kindergarten for the 5-year-olds would not wipe out center care for some of them. A school day from 8:40 A.M. to 3:00 P.M. does not provide adequate coverage for most working parents. Some also simply said their children liked the centers too much to move. In any case, when the enrollment of 5-year-olds in all-day kindergarten reached 55,000 in 1985 (there were also 8000 4-year-olds), the subsidized city day care system reported that it was still enrolling 7000 5-year-olds, down from 8000.

Parallel to this development was an explosion of interest in the after-school coverage question. If one juxtaposed data about working parents, on the one hand, and the sum total of known after-school resources on the other, it was obvious that many elementary school, kindergarten, and even nursery school children could be without adequate organized care from 3:00 P.M. until 5:00 or 6:00, or later, Many solutions exist on a small scale in some places. The use of the school buildings for programming either by community groups or by school personnel is one popular response. The debate as to who should do what and who should pay arrived in New York at about the time of the all-day kindergarten dispute.

There was a flurry of excitement during the summer of 1984 when the New York City Youth Board, with a mandate to operate or sponsor recreational programs in deprived areas, proposed to provide coverage for the all-day kindergarten children who needed it from the end of the school day until 6:00 P.M. They would start experimentally in 60 schools. In short, the all-day kindergarten project was to be connected to solutions for the child care problem more formally. Initial responses were enthusiastic, but the program was soon dropped in the course of the city government budget process for very inadequate "planning." (Among other questions to be raised is, Why all day for kindergarten and not for children in the early elementary school grades?)

There were some programs developing, however. The state legislature voted a modest School-Age Child Care Program in 1984, and in March 1985 the State Social Services Commissioner announced grants totaling $300,000 to 34 programs sponsored by school districts, day care centers, and other community-based organizations. The 34 grants were mostly in the $8000 to $10,000 range; the winning projects were chosen from among 134 proposals. Seven of the awards were in New York City.

In October 1985 another round of grants was announced based on a repeat of the $300,000 appropriation. Some 33 programs, designed to serve another 2377 school-aged children, had been selected. The effort was doubled for 1986. The state has not clarified whether it will go beyond these start-up grants; until this is clarified the significance of these projects cannot be gauged. In low-income areas there is no money to cover fees for poor parents. The projects, which require parent-participation components, are operated by school districts, day care centers, and community-based organizations. The legislation and the state report that provides their rationale suggest that approved programs may range

from the recreational to the athletic and remedial and are intended
to reflect parental preferences. They may be school-building-based
but may also be located in community centers, Y's, churches,
synagogues, or mental health agencies, as well as day care centers.
Family day care providers also are eligible.[31]

These and similar projects did not have ready access to New
York school buildings for after-hour space, however. A long-time
labor arrangement, in which unionized school custodians were in
some senses independent entrepreneurs using and controlling
public buildings but in other respects were employees, had resulted (through a process and logic too entangled for unraveling
here) in a situation in which community groups that wanted to
conduct after-school programs in school buildings were charged
very high "opening fees." One church-related social agency serving
adolescents in a Brooklyn neighborhood reported spending
$19,000, almost 20 percent of its annual budget, for fees to
custodians so that they might offer afternoon programs in two
public school buildings! This was a common situation.

Careful analysis and systematic planning for after-school offerings were complicated by the fact that the issue became entangled
in pre-election maneuvering involving the mayor, president of the
city council, and the comptroller. By early 1985 the latter had won
city approval for a program for 2550 children ages 5 to 13 in a
Queens school district. Some 60 percent of the $500,000 cost was
to be met by parent fees of $16 per child per week from those
parents who could afford it. The service would be free or partially
subsidized for families whose children were eligible for subsidized
school lunch. Another task force, under the aegis of the council
president, was working along similar lines. A state committee was
exploring other possibilities.

By the beginning of the September 1985 school year, the board
of education, in consultation with the mayor's staff of labor negotia-
tors, had made a "tremendous breakthrough," according to the
mayor. In completing a new labor contract with the custodians, the
issue of use of school buildings for activity after 3:00 P.M. had been
made a major priority. By increasing payment to custodian pensions, the city had, at a cost of $5.6 million, arranged for public
school buildings to be available to community groups every week-
day afternoon and during the summer without charge. A major
explosion of new after-school provision was expected but had not
materialized by early 1986. Agencies had to raise money for
administrative fees. The new "simplified" procedures were said to
require four months. But programs were gradually opening late in
1986, and school districts themselves expanded their offerings with

financial help from the central board if they committed themselves to coverage in 70 percent of their schools.

In the meantime, interest in prekindergarten for the 4-year-olds has been sustained. The governor has increased funding modestly, and the state education department is developing a plan. There are about 24,000 4-year-olds in publicly subsidized child care in the city, including about 5300 in public school prekindergarten, with perhaps another 1500 prekindergarten slots projected on the basis of optimistic funding forecasts. The mayor, however, escalated the issue: Why not a "bold experiment" in public education for the 4-year-olds beginning in September 1986? Supporters cited the positive research evidence that preschool programs avoid problems for many deprived minority children and thus pay off for society. Opponents preferred child care programs to what they considered to be insensitive teachers, overemphasis on cognition, and large groups. The mayor charged a commission headed by a former local college president to review the debate and recommend action.

Reporting early in 1986, the city's Early Childhood Education Commission urged a "bold city initiative." Eventually, state and federal backing should be forthcoming but the city should not "wait upon the results of extended negotiations amongst the three branches of government." The recommendations were dramatic:[32]

- Extension of early childhood education programs to assure universal availability to 4-year-olds; the programs should not be mandatory.
- A four-year phase-in plan that would begin with those neighborhoods with the highest concentration of children at "educational risk" (poor, near-poor, or from homes where English is not spoken).
- Building upon "the two existing administrative structures— the Agency for Child Development and the Board of Education—and their delivery systems."
- Coordination by a special office appointed by the mayor.
- Adherence to quality guidelines for curriculum, group size, staff qualifications, space, support services, parent participation, nutrition, and health.
- Careful planning with regard to space, staffing, monitoring, local coordination, and long-term fiscal sharing by the three levels of government.

The city has a 100,000 population of 4-year-olds of whom at least 25,000 are in privately funded programs (many unlicensed). In planning for 75,000 the commission ignored likely substitutability (a transfer from paid to free service). It did note that public programs for the 4-year-olds currently include day care (10,000 children), Head Start (7300), public schools (5300), and parks and recreation (1200). While the teachers in day care, Head Start, and the Board of Education "are engaged in fundamentally the same activity—educating young children—" they have different qualifications, salaries, benefits, and work schedules. The inequities "cause continuous staff problems."

The New York City school chancellor urged a national commitment to "universal prekindergarten programs." The mayor greeted the report positively but announced only a small beginning for 3000 children because of federal and state budgetary constraints. Observers noted several things: Defined in terms of the importance of early education, especially for deprived children, the proposed program is given an educational rationale. Parents will be asked to choose among school settings, day care programs, and Head Start. The funding, derived from an educational, not child care, rationale, will be for half-day programs.

The day care-preschool debate is resolved, temporarily perhaps, with a compromise or "hedge": both ACD and the Board of Education will be utilized for this initiative, and the money will be evenly divided, whatever the public response. Nonetheless, in the longer run much will probably be settled in the doing. For the moment, since only half-day programs are funded, it is not clear whether either of the options will be able to serve those children of full-time working parents needing all-day care, unless there are supplementary arrangements, too. High-quality programs that contain what both early childhood educators and the most experienced of social welfare day care experts profess are promised. The institutional consequences of all this are to be discovered. The program is evolving as we go to press, and a director, to be based in the mayor's office, has been appointed.

Parallel state developments suggest either difficult choices or the possibilities for public policy compromise up ahead. A governor's New York State Commission on Child Care has been meeting, holding hearings, collecting data, and issuing interim reports since 1984.[33] On the controversial issue of the 4-year-olds, the commission took a position reflecting the strength of the social welfare child care and community groups in its membership:[34]

> . . . *four-year-olds, especially economically disadvantaged four-year-olds should have access to quality early childhood education. As new funds are appropriated . . . they should be allocated to*

public school pre-kindergarten programs, day care programs, and Head Start in accordance with the needs of children and the desires of their families. . . . Particular attention should be paid to . . . families needs such as full-day programs for children of working parents . . . and to coordination between child care and early childhood programs in the community.

In an effort to bring together the educational and social welfare interest groups concerned with the 4-year-olds, new strategies have developed. One such proposal was offered in the midst of the debate about preschool for the 4-year-olds, all-day kindergartens, and sponsorship of school-age care. It is already part of the New York City under-4 plan, at least in spirit: Why not permit funds from the various educational appropriations to be expended within the social welfare-based child care (center day care) system? Why not use social services funds in school-age programs to strengthen components other than the educational? One has the impression that each of the sides envisions an implementation pattern protecting its interests. The interests on the social welfare side show the greater enthusiasm. They often argue that they do not oppose preschools in principle but are concerned that in the very areas where preschoolers need care the public schools are crowded and inadequate. They want to be sure that if there are resources for preschool, they will also be shared with the day care system. That is the New York City plan. However, social service funds to extend the school day for the 4-year-olds have not yet been suggested locally or seen as feasible.

For immediate purposes the New York case has yielded its conclusion: Groups are talking about and seeking to develop universal preschools for the 4-year-olds, not limiting themselves to the more common compensatory offerings. But only a subgroup is concerned with all-day programs, thus attempting simultaneously to meet child care needs. There are creative new ideas, positive responses, even increased resources, but all the issues remain, the competition persists, the future design is unknown. No local community agency or program alone, no matter how creative, inventive, or entrepreneurial can act without state context. It is not clear whether the child care picture ever will or should be outlined in a general policy and plan initiated by someone in city or state government, or in the private sector. However, it is difficult to believe that the economic and political marketplace will alone yield access, coverage, quality, and needed financing. Some basic issues may need to be faced, somewhere.

The Pro and Con

Many of these matters were, in fact, discussed early in 1940 at the White House Conference on Children in a Democracy. The lessons of the WPA were being absorbed, and the wartime Lanham Act day care expansion was yet before the country. Both compensatory education and the possibility of an ealier beginning for elementary school already had their proponents. An extended quotation may be of more than historical interest:[35]

> . . . *educators have been seeking the extension of school facilities beyond those of the traditional elementary and secondary schools as we know them. The task that confronts the educational world is, on the one hand, to reduce inequalities by improving the facilities where they are least adequate and, on the other hand, to press ever harder for still higher standards, even though they may accentuate the disproportion between the groups least favored and those most favored. The chief purpose of expansion of the school system is educational: It is to benefit children at an earlier age than the traditional first grade, and it is to help those who can benefit from organized educational instruction beyond high school, including those who are planning to enter college. . . .*
>
> *Opportunity for children of preschool ages*
>
> *Experiences of the child before entering school are of fundamental significance in the shaping of his adult life. During these early years physical and mental development occurs most rapidly, muscular coordination proceeds to increasingly complex levels, and social reactions that form the basis of character and personality tend to be established. During these years the broad patterns of conduct in later life are formed.*
>
> *Children at this stage would profit from a richness and variety of experience that few homes are able to provide unaided. School and home working together have a far better chance to provide it. Although teachers have much to contribute to parents regarding the learning processes of young children, they can also learn much from parents about the influence exerted on a child by his family life and relations. Moreover, nursery schools and kindergartens provide a suitable transition from home life to the more formal atmosphere of the elementary school.*
>
> *In the best nursery schools and kindergartens the child's health and nutritional needs also are carefully watched; good language habits may be established; self-management is encouraged; problems of adjustment are recognized and may be dealt with through corrective procedures. The child's range of experience is broadened and he becomes accustomed to playing and working with others of his age. His growing individuality is recognized and sympathetically*

guided through orientation of his activities rather than by repression; this tends to give him a sense of security and self-reliance. The beginnings of individualized education may be instituted here as they accord with the developmental needs of each child. . . .

. . . Kindergartens or equivalent experience ought to be made part of the public-school opportunities available to every child as rapidly as may be possible. Experimentation has proceeded far enough to indicate that children might well be permitted to enter the public schools at 4 or 5 years of age, provided educational content appropriate to the preschool level can be offered. Wider provision of this opportunity is contingent upon better school support, particularly in rural areas. Meanwhile it would seem good economy to incorporate the nursery schools established by the W.P.A. for children in needy families into the public-school system as rapidly as financial and other circumstances permit.

In the spring of 1985 a study group that had focused on the 4-year-old reported to Connecticut's State Board of Education. They had looked at what was developing in their own state, surveyed developments in the other states, carefully reviewed the relevant child development and child care research literature, and considered organizational stakes and resources. Their approach is of some interest.[36]

They saw three facts as creating powerful pressure to act: (1) the large increase in labor force participation of mothers, (2) the large increase in single-mother families and the need of these mothers to work, and (3) the large representation of deprived minority children. At the same time, they noted the convincing evidence that good-quality care can be of use and help to 4-year-old children. Clearly, there was a case for action. However, in view of the special capacities of other potential providers, and in the light of the diversity of needs, the committee did not envision an educational monopoly. The State Department of Education (SDE) was asked to share the responsibility:[37]

Our recommendations indicate that there is an important role for SDE with regard to four-year-old children, but that role must be sensitive to the critical functions of other state agencies and to private sector providers of services. Under no circumstances do we believe it appropriate for all four year olds to be involved in a "kindergarten-type" program within the public schools. We advocate, instead, a flexible open approach to serving four year olds, one that will encourage experiential learning and the active participation of many providers, and one that will encourage multiple forms of programs and services to co-exist and thrive in the public and private sectors. We find that SDE can take a leadership role in informing the public about these services and in helping to enhance

*their quality. . . . The creation of early childhood demonstration
districts will foster such developmental continuity, and will provide
specific information so that school districts, in concert with other
local agencies, can develop comprehensive and creative services for
young children and their families. . . . Not all families want or need
the same services for their young children. Recognizing this diversity, the committee strongly advocates the preservation of options so
that parents may choose the service or services that best meet their
needs at a given point in time. While preserving parental choice,
services must be afforded to all who desire them. Universal access,
based on parental option, must be the cornerstone of all policies for
young children.*

The Connecticut committee envisions a growing role for the
educational system but in the context of comprehensive local
strategies that include the traditional private "social welfare" system as well. Start-up funds were voted in 1986. A number of
initiatives in the states we have discussed are in this direction.
Others, as we have seen, concentrate on the educational system.

Three insights make it unlikely that future efforts to expand
child care will ignore the educational system:

1. Schools in the United States now provide most child care for
   children from age 5. It is not called or thought of as "child
   care," but the fact remains that the school day provides a
   diverse experience and relieves families of making other
   arrangements. Moreover, there is obvious advantage, if parental working hours require, to making coverage arrangements for the time before classes begin and after they end
   either at or in close cooperation with the schools.

2. The European continental pattern, except for Finland, Sweden, and the United Kingdom, is to provide a public or
   publicly funded nursery school for the 3-to-5 group, based in
   the educational system. These are usually free, universal,
   and used by 75 to 98 percent of the relevant age cohorts.
   These nursery schools cover the usual school day for elementary school, which can be a half-day (Germany) or a full-day
   (France). Coverage before and after the formal school hours
   is a serious problem in some places, whereas supplementary
   provision is good elsewhere (with fees in some places). In
   countries with such preschool systems the social welfare–day
   care (family day care and creche) system concentrates on
   infants and toddlers.

3. After years of confusion, misinformation, and controversy, it
   is now understood to be highly inaccurate to characterize the
   traditional social welfare day care centers as offering "only

custodial care," or to describe public or private preschools as "interested only in the cognitive." At the extremes, these characterizations are correct and may even be illustrated, but they are not warranted by much of the current situation and certainly do not express the announced aspirations and policies of the respective systems. The readiness of Department of Education and Census Bureau experts to combine preschool data from the several systems reflects this reality. The name of a program does not define a child's experiences.

The group services to children age 3 and 4 within public educational systems, proprietary nursery school and day care programs, and private nonprofit (social service-derived) day care centers are now dominated by the knowledge, insights, and aspirations of the field of early childhood education. They seek to recruit teachers and aides qualified through the same B.S. and aide ("child development associate") certification systems. They recruit directors with educational qualifications and relevant experience and share respect for the leadership qualities of M.S. graduates from Wheelock College, Bank Street, Pacific Oaks, and similar institutions. They all know that successful programs require a blend of cognitive, developmental, socialization, and parent-involvement programming. They respect the quality standards promulgated by the National Association for the Education of Young Children (NAEYC).

The truth remains, or course, that programs developed within educational settings often tend to think about curriculum, assessment, reading readiness, and the like—and may try to bring the first grade into the prekindergarten. Another fact is that many day care centers have few qualified personnel, pay very low salaries, and offer a "babysitting" milieu, although the best of day care from the social welfare tradition may look exactly like exemplary preschool programs and also have rich resources for social service, mental health, and parent involvement. Well-conducted Head Start programs, whether or not based in schools, have these resources and more, including health and nutrition programs. Clearly, the within-type variance is as great as that among types. Many or most parents view the entire domain as "school" or "nursery school" but use the program name prevalent in their communities. They want socialization, development, and cognitive content in programs serving their children (again with cultural and educational variations).

Where, then, are the issues? A large thrust for preschools in the educational system has obvious advantages. A professional practice, a research discipline, a knowledge base, and much administrative experience have grown around that part of the educational establishment known as "early childhood education." In many places, public officials and parents want to start "education" earlier. School systems have an established funding base that, whatever its problems, is far more reliable than the packaging of child subsidies from several means-tested federal social service programs as well as through possible tax credits. Many parents view the school as a "trustworthy" institution, one easy to locate and identify in every community. Most important, the creation of a general early childhood program for 3- and 4-year-olds in the schools could provide a universal, integrating experience, in contrast to our present system that tends toward a two-tier system— means-tested day care for the poor and working poor and proprietary or private nurseries for the middle class and the affluent.

Secondary arguments also prevail: the availability of school building space in some places, the potential for drawing on the existing school transportation system, and the location of elementary schools near children's homes. The schools, in fact, are already taking on more responsibility, a process that may be accelerating. Head Start lost most of its 5-year-olds when kindergartens became universal and is now 70 percent 4-year-olds. If schools take on more 4-year-olds in preschool classes, Head Start could pick up some of the many unserved and eligible 3-year-olds.

As we have seen, however, educators have not been interested in assuming a total child care function and developing a full-day program. Why, then, expect them to meet the need, some have asked. In its more vehement and bitter form, the argument of day care activists is this: Many inner-city schools are doing so badly with the education of minority children that turning the 3- and 4-year-olds over to them would be irresponsible. When asked why the schools fail, day care activists focus, variously, on the insensitivity of traditional teachers, the lack of adequate resources, the resistance of schools to parental involvement, the insufficient numbers of certified minority teachers, and the importance of program elements not traditionally the concern of education.

Not that this viewpoint is consistently held. Arguing for public support these same advocates cite Head Start successes (some school-based and some not), or the accomplishments of the Perry Preschool Project and programs under what was originally the Elementary and Secondary Education Act. Many acknowledge as well the schools' more secure funding base.

To all of these objections, those favoring a school system role respond: What about all the accomplishments of decentralization, parent control, and minority recruitment in inner-city school systems? What of the many school districts with minority school superintendents who are considered successful and who regard the charges quoted earlier as long outdated? Is much of the Head Start not a *school* initiative? If there are failings and evidences of unsatisfactory progress, they ask, are these inherent in education or simply to be seen as problems along the way? Why be so critical of the schools and completely uncritical of the many social welfare day care centers of very poor quality?

Evelyn Moore, head of the Black Child Development Institute, told a May 1986 conference at Yale's Bush Center that blacks must support the public schools: "That is where the children are." She conveys her concerns while calling upon schools and suggesting measures to "improve their track record with minority children." She stresses as well that in any case the schools cannot and should not take over completely and argues for a diverse system, whatever the schools' economic advantages.

Those sympathetic to a larger school system role acknowledge and cite other specific obstacles, among them the following:

- In most of the country nonschool child care centers are licensed; school systems operating preschools may in some place be exempt from standards relating to health, nutrition, group size, teacher qualification, physical space, and so forth.
- There is a genuine shortage of qualified teachers for preschool programs. Rapid expansion will lower standards and could introduce the teacher rigidity seen in some school systems. Higher school system salaries will raid personnel now in day care centers. (Obviously, those are contradictory concerns, applying to some places and not others.)
- Exposing 3- and 4-year-olds to long daily bus trips to school is not acceptable, yet busing could be necessary in some places. Would it be a good idea to expect these youngsters to share daily busing with junior high school students?
- Child care costs will go up significantly if systems convert from the typical exceedingly low day care center salary scale to the somewhat better (and occasionally very much better) school system salaries.
- The kindergarten system began with a strong child development orientation and by now has become traditional and rigidly academic. Why assume that school-based preschools will more successfully escape the administrative and bureaucratic forces for control now present in the school system?
- During the 1970s, seeing a need for care for children age 3 and

4, small private providers and large proprietary chains invested heavily and created a significant resource. If the public
system had acted in the 1970s, this resource would not have
grown. Should government now use its legal power and ability
to tax, and wipe out these small businesses by creating a free
service in the schools? Moreover, both nonprofit and proprietary centers are known to "need" preschoolers in order to
serve infants and toddlers at reasonable weekly rates; to
remove the preschoolers is to create a funding crisis for infant
and toddler care. Finally, given regulations everywhere, the
tight limits on numbers of infants simply make it financially
impossible to operate a center without a supply of preschoolers
to complete the census.

• If schools offer school-day programs for 3- and/or 4-year-olds,
even if they run all-day programs and not the half-day programs now operating or contemplated in many places, what
will be done about the rest of the work day, summers, vacations, holidays, special teacher meeting days? The present
social welfare day care system has a tradition of accepting
coverage responsibility. Educational systems have traditionally had short work days and short work years. The supplementary and school-age programs face a larger task if the
public schools take on preschool programs than they do under
the current patterns.

The arguments on both sides obviously are real, and many have
validity despite a tendency to exaggeration. Clearly, some of the
fight also is about turf, control, and jobs.

Directions

What do we conclude? We are convinced that if the United States
is to have adequate child care, the schools will necessarily have to
play a large part. The schools are the only institution with a societal
mission and potential capacity to serve a large portion of the 3- and
4-year-olds. Schools in the United States also have potential access
to needed resources. They serve the entire society and can play a
unifying and universal role where now we tend to a two-tier, two-
class system. The European continental precedent is instructive.

Yet there are caveats. School leaders have shown interest in
early childhood *education,* not in a school-based effort that also is
responsive to the need for full-day child care as well. With few
exceptions, states are ready now only for modest expenditure.

Most want to concentrate on deprived children. Those states that want to go further do have the problem of acquiring enough qualified teachers, setting standards, and ensuring that preschool will not be rigidified in the model of the elementary grades. They also will need to consider the questions raised about the quality of school-based programs, their responsiveness to the needs of black children, and their ability to overcome a "discriminatory tradition."[38]

The available sources suggest three elements in the discussion:

1. Basic organizational and program questions about the ability of schools to solve the problems listed and serve young children appropriately.
2. Questions about the readiness of schools to serve black and other minority children well, given the long history of discrimination and poor service.
3. Questions (to quote Velmanette Montgomery, a New York state senator interested in day care) about "who is going to control those programs . . . a tremendous political question." ("When New York City decided to go into all-day kindergarten, it reaped a windfall of $75 million.[39])

We assume that, rather than write off the school system, the black community, given its increasing success in the political process on all levels and its growing representation in the civil service and in education, will insist that the concerns about adequate attention to the problem of minority children be addressed. Black advocates will join the preschool initiative and help make it work. Legislative successes with preschool and school-age programs in several states suggest that this viewpoint has been adopted in some places. The coming era of implementation will show whether success is possible. We assume that a public system can and will choose a strategy of access, equity, and racial integration.

What will remain, even as careful efforts are made to respond fully to the needs and concerns of all parents, will be the generic limitations of the school systems and the issues inherent in an effort to establish large numbers of preschools within educational systems and in a significant child caring role. Will it be possible to overcome the real problems in school-based service to preschoolers? Is it realistic to expect the best of child care practice to locate in universal school programs in many places?

In our view, the record is indeed mixed and for American society to make a full and final choice would be premature. Although we believe strongly that the schools hold the key to the development of the universal child care system needed in the United States, we acknowledge that to commit public policy fully to a school monopoly in the field would be irresponsible at this point. The responsible course calls for an empirical approach: To what extent and at what pace can the school problems and obstacles outlined be overcome? What kinds of school-run or school-related models work successfully, satisfy parents, show good results for children? Can schools develop special administrative units to serve 3- to 5-year-old children in a developmental program that is not merely a downward extension of elementary education?

One can endorse the call for analysis, exploration, and debate. One can see advantages in South Carolina's decision in favor of cooperative approaches in which school districts may contract for some or all of the service for 4-year-olds, choose half-day or all-day programs, and decide to assign community agencies to run programs. One also can see value in the Massachusetts decision to allow school contracting with Head Start or child care programs while reserving three-quarters of the funds for low-income areas. Clearly, there is wisdom, too, in the almost unanimous conviction that before- and after-school programs should have access but not be limited to school buildings and be operated by school systems as well as by day care centers, boys and girls clubs, community agencies, parent cooperatives, recreation departments and many others! We see some advantages in New York City's initial plan to allow the local district to choose between a half-day preschool and a half-day community-based day care center, but note that at best this is only an interim step. Many of the children need all-day care and the eventual design should provide for it rather than assume that each parent must "package" a solution for each child separately. All of these approaches, then, are best regarded as "probes," "explorations," and political compromises en-route to model building.

In short, communities now have neither sanction nor resources to launch a universal school initiative. The states will commit at differing resource levels and will choose their own priorities. The diversity value is shared by the population at large and by minority constituencies who have been disappointed by insensitive school systems. A number of state initiatives are in the pilot, planning, or implementation phases. They become ideal circumstances for a large, national, natural experiment. Local school district options and community involvement are a way to protect diversity and ensure experimentation with alternative models—if the alleged compromises are not stacked and truly permit the several strategies to be considered. There are rich opportunities for trying things out and shaping a pattern to meet public preference. Among the options that should be considered are the following:

- Publicly operated and public school–controlled preschools.
- Publicly contracted preschools in the community using the nonprofit day care system.
- Community child care agencies operating within school buildings.
- Proprietary agencies providing publicly subsidized or purchased services and operating within the schools or in the community.
- Efforts to design special child care standards for the school-based programs or to adopt general child care standards.
- Efforts to train a sufficient corps of qualified teachers and aides to work with children at the needed levels of competence in all settings.
- Experiments with patterns of planning, administration, leadership. or monitoring, based in state and local departments of education yet appropriate for the achievement of the types of responsive programs sought.
- Experiments with transportation, food programs, and so on to answer questions about how these accommodate to different models.
- Experiments with parent involvement and parent education responsive to diverse parental needs, preferences, and circumstances and supportive of sensitive and child development-oriented preschools.

We envision, in short, a large school-oriented effort as well as community variations involving integration of day care programs as well. We see many kinds of social service–school cooperation, collaboration, coordination, planning. We also see before us a decade of exploration before the larger pattern is fully shaped. We expect that our complex and varied country, relying heavily on state funding and initiative in this area, will choose options that protect diversity and a mixed system in any case. Federal tax credits and funding through various social service streams for low-income families will continue to be needed. We hope that federal start-up funds, research support, and backing for technical assistance and training and for interchange and monitoring will contribute to good results. But we are sure that, eventually, the schools must be the major component in a universal child care system. The day care field here, as in other countries, would concentrate on infants, toddlers, special needs and, perhaps, before- and after-school programs.[40]

In September 1985 the press reported that the Prince and Princess of Wales had enrolled 3-year-old Prince William in a private nursery school in the neighborhood of the palace and requested that his privacy be respected. The school he attends stresses a "happy start" but not reading for children under 5. His parents considered it important, we assume, that he leave the palace and share a socialization, developmental, and learning experience for some portion of the day with a group of other young children. At the same time a significant number of American parents were arranging for similar opportunities for their children. Some were preoccupied largely with the child's need for care while they worked. Others, particularly the better-educated and more affluent, made the choice for a preschool whether or not the mother worked out of the home; they variously chose programs emphasizing the cognitive and the socioemotional. Because those who paid directly tended to exercise one group of options and those low-income parents at work or training had access to another group, access was unequal and a two-tier system was developing. The school initiatives discussed in this chapter seem inevitable and desirable to those concerned with access, affordability, adequacy, equal opportunity, and quality. To be sure, problems remain to be solved, questions still to be answered, doubts to be resolved, and diverse models to be perfected. Given the importance of the need, the goal seems worthy of attention and resources and to be perfectly achievable over the next decade.

Endnotes

1. Advisory Committee on Child Development, National Research Council, *Toward A National Policy for Children and Families* (Washington, D.C.: National Academy of Sciences, 1976), p. 6.
2. *Child Care in the Public Schools: Incubator for Inequality?* (Washington, D.C.: National Black Child Development Institute, Inc., 1986), p. 3.
3. *The News and Observer,* Raleigh, N.C., February 1985, p. 40; and Editorial, February 1985.
4. For more detail and quotation from Albert Shanker's November 8, 1974, column, see Sheila B. Kamerman and Alfred J. Kahn, *Social Services in the United States* (Philadelphia: Temple University Press, 1976), pp. 70–72.
5. John R. Berrueta-Clement et al., *Changed Lives: The Effects of the Perry Preschool Program on Youths Through Age 19* (Ypsilanti, Mich.: High/Scope Press, 1984).
6. The following sources offer the major documentation for this section and, in turn, provide more detailed notes:

    Bernard Greenblatt, *Responsibility for Child Care* (San Francisco: Jossey-Bass, 1977).

W. Norton Grubb and Marvin Lazerson, "Child Care, Government Financing, and the Public Schools: Lessons from the California Children's Centers," *School Review*, Vol. 86, No. 1 (November 1977), 5–37.

Sheila B. Kamerman and Alfred J. Kahn, *Social Services in the United States* (Philadelphia: Temple University Press, 1976), Chapter 2, "Child Care."

James A. Levine, *Day Care and the Public Schools* (Newton, Mass.: Education Development Center, Inc., 1978).

Anna B. Mayer and Alfred J. Kahn, *Day Care As a Social Instrument: A Policy Paper* (New York: Columbia University School of Social Work, 1965).

Margaret O'Brien Steinfels, *Who's Minding the Children?* (New York: Simon and Schuster Touchstone Books, 1973).

Edward F. Zigler and Edmund W. Gordon, *Day Care: Scientific and Social Policy Issues* (Dover, Mass.: Auburn House, 1982), Chapter 23 by School Age Child Care Project and Chapter 24 by Millie Almy.

7. Greenblatt, *Responsibility for Child Care*. We are heavily in Greenblatt's debt for our interpretations in this and the next several paragraphs. See also, Carl F. Kaestle and Maris A. Vinovskis, "From Apron Strings to ABCs: Parents, Children and Schooling in Nineteenth Century Massachusetts," in John Demos and Saranne Boocock, eds., *Turning Points* (Chicago: University of Chicago Press, 1978).

8. Ibid., pp. 40–41.

9. Mayer and Kahn, *Day Care As a Social Instrument*, p. 27.

10. Ibid. Also Alfred J. Kahn, "New Policies and Service Models: The Next Phase," *American Journal of Orthopsychiatry*, Vol. 25, No. 4 (July 1965), pp. 652–662.

11. Greenblatt, *Responsibility for Child Care*, p. 102.

12. Almy, "Day Care and Early Childhood Education," in Zigler and Gordon, *Day Care;* and ibid; p. 478.

13. Grubb and Lazerson, "Child Care, Government Financing, and the Public Schools."

14. Here we rely most heavily on the report from the School-Age Child Care Project at Wellesley, which constitutes Chapter 23 in Zigler and Gordon, *Day Care*.

15. In 1980, for the first time, the Bureau of the Census published a special study covering 1977 data comprehensively. The practice was continued in a 1983 publication. See U.S. Bureau of the Census, Current Population Reports, Series P-23, No. 129, *Child Care Arrangements of Working Mothers: June 1982* (Washington, D.C.: U.S. Government Printing Office, 1983). Unfortunately, thus far this series counts only secondary or primary care arrangements for the youngest child in each family under age 5, and only while the mother works. Moreover, June interviewing tends to lead to underestimations.

16. Mary R. Papageorgiou, "The National Preschool Data Base: Position Paper," Center for Statistics, January 1986, unpublished.

17. Consortium for Longitudinal Studies, *As the Twig Is Bent: Lasting Effects of*

Preschools Programs (Hillside, N.J.: Lawrence Erlbaum Associates, 1983); Irving Lazar et al., "Lasting Effects of Early Education," *Monographs of the Society for Research in Child Development*, Vol. 47, Nos. 1–2 (1982); R. H. McKay et al., *The Impact of Head Start on Children, Families, and Communities* (Final Report of the Head Start Evaluation, Synthesis and Utilization Project) (Washington, D.C.: CSR Inc., 1985). Also see the review and critique of the latter report by Lawrence J. Schweinhart and David P. Weikart, "What Do We Know So Far? A Review of the Head Start Synthesis Project," *Young Children*, Vol. 41, No. 2 (1986), pp. 49–55 and the authors' rejoinder in Vol. 41, No. 3 (1986), p. 20. There is consensus that "Head Start makes a difference in the lives of children and families and, with some program improvements, even longer lasting differences can be attained."

18. Berrueta-Clement et al., *Changed Lives: The Effects of the Perry Preschool Program*. Also See review by Kristin Moore in *Family Planning Perspectives*, Vol. 17, No. 4 (July–August 1985). For a *High/Scope* summary, placing the Perry Preschool in its perspective, see Lawrence J. Schweinhart, "The Preschool Challenge," *High/Scope Early Childhood Policy Papers*, No. 4 (1985).

19. Congressional Budget Office, *Reducing Poverty Among Children* (Washington, D.C.: U.S. Government Printing Office, 1985), p. 103.

20. Schweinhart and Weikart, "What Do We Know So Far?" p. 54. Also Schweinhart, *The Preschool Challenge;* New York State Department of Education, *Evaluation of the New York State Experimental Prekindergarten Program: Final Report* (Albany, 1982); and "Prekindergarten Improves Pupils' Performance Throughout the Elementary Grades" (Albany, March 1986). Also see summary by Fred M. Hechinger, "Preschool Programs," *New York Times*, April 22, 1986, citing David Weikart review in *Early Childhood Research Quarterly*, April 1986.

21. *School-Age Day Care Study: Final Report*, prepared for Administration for Children, Youth and Families, DHSS, by Applied Management Sciences, Inc., Silver Springs, Maryland, March 15, 1983. By including 12- to 14-year-old children who care for themselves in the uncovered group, the report tends to create alarm not justified by the self-care percentages for the 5–8 and the 9–11 group. See p. 11.

22. The files of the *SACC Newsletter* (School-Age Child Care Project, Wellesley College, Mass.) are a useful source on local studies, legislative developments, project initiatives, and so forth. See also Ruth Kramer Baden et al., *School Age Child Care: An Action Manual* (Dover, Mass.: Auburn House, 1982); and Levine, *Day Care and the Public Schools*. Also Michelle Seligson et al., *School Age Child Care: A Policy Report* (Wellesley, Mass.: School Age Child Care Project, 1983). For a state illustration, see Governor's Council on Children, Youth and Families, *You Can Make It Happen: A Manual for School-Age Child Care in Arizona* (Phoenix: Office of the Governor, 1985).

23. *Child Care Information Exchange*, No. 47 (January 1986), p. 7.

24. The School Age Child Care Project and the Bank Street College of Education launched a collaborative effort in 1985 under the co-directorship of Ann Mitchell and Michelle Seligson that should provide a more complete picture of state initiatives for the 4-year-olds.

25. Margaret Whaley, "The State of Kindergarten: A Survey of the States" (Springfield, Ill.: Illinois State Board of Education, January 1985, processed, unpublished).

26. Carolyn Morado, "Prekindergarten Programs for Four-Year Olds: State Involvement in Preschool Education," *Young Children,* Vol. 41, No. 6 (September 1980), 69–71. For additional data and a somewhat different list see Lawrence J. Schweinhart, "Policy Options for Preschool Programs" (Ypsilanti, Mich.: High/Scope Educational Research Foundation, 1985).

27. Ellen Gannett, "State Initiatives on School-Age Child Care" (Wellesley, Mass.: School Age Child Care Project, processed, unpublished, October, 1985). Also, Helen Blank and Amy Wilkins, "School-Age Child Care Initiatives May Often Fail to Help Low-Income Working Families" (Washington, D.C.: Memorandum, Childrens Defense Fund, September 1986).

28. "Preschool Programs Pose New Challenges," *CDF Reports* (June 1985), p. 5. Quoted with permission.

29. Ibid, pp. 5–6.

30. The State Department of Education, "Evaluation of the New York State Experimental Prekindergarten Program: Final Report" (Albany, February 22, 1984, processed). Also "Prekindergarten Improves Pupils' Performance Throughout the Elementary Grades" (Albany, March 26, 1986, 2-page statement).

31. New York State Council on Children and Families, *School-Age Child Care in New York State* (Albany, 1984).

32. *Take a Giant Step: Final Report of the Early Childhood Education Commission* (New York City: Office of the Mayor, 1986). Also, Mayor's response in letter of March 28, 1986 to Dr. Saul B. Cohen, chairman.

33. New York State Commission on Child Care, "First Year Report" (Albany: December 1985, processed).

34. Ibid., p. 7.

35. *White House Conference on Children in a Democracy, January 18–20, 1940, Final Report* (Washington, D.C.: U.S. Government Printing Office, 1940), pp. 158–159.

36. Committee on Four Year Olds, Their Families and the Public Schools, Sharon L. Kagan, Ed. D. chairperson, "Four Year Olds: Who Is Responsible?" (New Haven, Conn: The Bush Center in Child Development and Social Policy, 1985, processed.) Dr. Kagan has become the first director of New York City's new program for 4-year-olds.

37. Ibid., 2, 3.

38. Evelyn Moore discussion at conference on "Schooling for Four Year Olds," Bush Center, Yale University, May 22, 1986. See endnote no. 2. Also Evelyn Moore, "Day Care: A Black Perspective," in Zigler and Gordon, *Day Care,* pp. 413–444.

39. Quoted in *Child Care in the Public Schools,* p. 15.

40. A balanced overview of the options and considerable useful factual detail is offered in the following to-be-published review, which became available as we went to press: W. Norton Grubb, "Young Children Face the States: Issues and Options for Early Childhood Programs," 1986.

Chapter 6

EMPLOYERS AND CHILD CARE

A 1980 report on child care, issued by the Women's Bureau of the U.S. Department of Labor, begins as follows:[1]

> *As more and more mothers of preschool children in this country enter the labor market, the need for child care is increasing. Employers and labor representatives are recognizing the child care need as a major concern of employees and are exploring ways to alleviate it.*

With minor variations, hundreds of articles have appeared in this context in the last five years, stressing the theme of the inadequate supply of child care services in the face of growing female labor force participation and leading up to a statement concerning the need for employers to respond to this urgent and growing demand. Thus, for example, in *Personnel*, a professional journal for those in the personnel and human resources field, an article entitled "Employer-Sponsored Child Care Comes of Age" begins similarly but continues: "Finding reliable and convenient child care has always been a problem for working mothers, but only recently have employers recognized this problem and its impact on the organization and looked for ways to alleviate it."[2] In 1984 the national women's magazines agreed to make child care a priority issue. In addition to numerous articles on the state of child care in the United States, the major issues debated, how to choose good child care, and so forth, there were also innumerable articles on employer-sponsored or -supported child care services.[3]

Background and History

Employer-supported or -sponsored or -provided child care is certainly not a new development. Although such care was never extensive, mention is made of company day nurseries, nursery schools, and infant schools in several histories of nineteenth-century American welfare capitalism. Stuart D. Brandes reports, "Company education began almost at the cradle. In southern cotton mill towns children only 6 to 8 weeks old were admitted to company nursery schools—a convenience to mothers as it freed them to work in the mills."[4] Carnegie Steel established a day nursery to care for the young children whose mothers were the widows of employees who died while working for the company; the day nursery was set up to make it possible for these women to go out and work.

During World War II, companies such as W. J. Kaiser set up nurseries to provide care for the children of their women employees. As soon as the war ended the centers were closed. The concept was, that with the return of the men from the war, women workers would no longer be needed and therefore there would be no need for day care services.

The work place child care developments during World War II and the few efforts in the 1960s and 1970s stemmed largely from employer initiatives. Employers needed workers at wartime, when only women were available, or they needed low-skilled, low-paid female workers; they believed that an on- or near-site day care center would help to recruit workers and help to stabilize their work force. A few employers claimed positive conse-quences—usually, reduced turnover, often at relatively low costs, since quality of care was not an issue. A few others experimented with such programs and found them not worthwhile. Parents did not use the service to the extent anticipated; absenteeism did not decline; productivity was not increased. Several centers that were opened on an experimental basis in the late 1960s and early 1970s closed after a brief period of operation.

One well-known demonstration work-site program was es-tablished by KLH at the end of the 1960s with funds provided by the U.S. Children's Bureau, but it closed after two years. Fewer children were enrolled than were planned for, and costs were therefore much higher than expected. Parents did not participate, according to the finding of an evaluation study, because they preferred near-home care. Even those who did participate did not, as had been expected, join their children at lunch. The general employee response was limited—and even negative.

According to one assessment of "industry-sponsored day care" in the early 1970s, "Approximately 150–200 employer-supported centers have been opened, with over half in hospitals, health care facilities, and other non-profit institutions."[5] The author concluded her analysis by stating that[6] *[one] explanation for the continuing call for employer-sponsored day care is a strategic effort on the part of the advocates of universal day-care services. Clearly universal child care or child development services will not be available in the very near future. Present legislation proposes only a tiny proportion of the twenty to twenty-five billion dollars needed to pay for such an effort. Every additional source of day care service is viewed by the advocates of universal day care as a step in the right direction. Industry may contribute only a minuscule proportion, but it is one more institution that is involved, spending day care dollars and raising public awareness.*

Our Focus

Given this early experience, what happened to reawaken interest in employer-sponsored child care in the 1980s? What is happening now, and is anything different as compared with the earlier development? How significant is employer-sponsored child care as a component of the child care delivery systems today and in the near future? We will now try to answer these questions.

Clearly, the dramatic and continued growth in labor force participation rates of women with preschool-aged children is one important factor (see Chapter 1). If anything, the pattern of women's labor force participation has gone beyond what was anticipated.[7]

Paralleling this trend, as we have noted, is the significant decline in federal funds for subsidized child care, beginning in the 1970s with the failure to increase Title XX appropriations to reflect inflation and accelerating in the 1980s with the cutbacks in these funds under the Reagan administration, and the elimination of any requirement for a state "match" by turning Title XX into a social services block grant (see Chapter 4). The combination of enormously increased demand for out-of-home child care, coupled with a decline in federal subsidies for child care providers, led child care professionals and advocates to seek alternative sources of financial support and/or alternative strategies for expanding the supply of child care services.

Faced with a decline in federal subsidies for child care, severe constraints on state and local funding, yet growing demand for more services at prices parents could afford, child care advocates turned frantically to the private sector as an alternative source of support. Private philanthropy provides only modest support for child care, however; although contributions increased, this source remains a small factor in the overall picture of financial resources.

United Way allocations for child care, for example, increased by about 15 percent between 1981 and 1985 but, in fact, amounted to only 2.4 percent of its expenditures in the earlier year and 2.8 percent in the latter.[8]

Increasingly, child care professionals and advocates identified employers as the major alternative to government in seeking financial support. The rationale, of course, is that many employers, in particular those in banking, finance, insurance and service industries, benefit from the work of large numbers of women in the prime childbearing years. Furthermore, federal policy created or expanded all sorts of tax incentives to encourage employers to do more in the way of financial support for their employees' child care needs. Research in the late 1970s and early 1980s had pointed out the limited efforts made by employers to help their employees manage their job and family responsibilities with less stress.[9] The media, too, latched on to child care as an important issue for employers to address.

New community initiatives, designed to pool available public and private funding for child care, to administer the public child care food subsidy programs, and to facilitate consumer access to services, have also launched special employer-related activities. As described in Chapters 2 and 3, almost all the organizations include as part of their activities special provision of child care information and referral services for the employees of firms under contract with the community agency. Many have developed, or are trying to develop, employer-subsidized vendor/voucher programs for the parent-employees of firms under contract with them. And most are seeking to establish corporate development funds or to obtain corporate contributions.

Three Texas agencies illustrate these three approaches to increasing employer sponsorship of child care. Only the first has had any significant success. Austin Families, Inc. (see Chapter 3) became the local R&R agency for Work/Family Directions, the national information and referral agency that began in 1984 with a contract with IBM. (It has added several other contracts with major corporations such as MacDonalds and Kraft Foods.) In addition, Austin Families has since obtained contracts with several other employers and is continuing to market its services to other employers. Several firms have contracted with the agency for child care vouchers for their low- and moderate-income employees, providing a modest subsidy for each employee who qualifies. A few employers are purchasing "slots" or child care places in centers for their employees, also through Austin Families. Despite increased employer involvement within the last two years, however, the agency remains a minor player in the child care "industry" in Austin, and most of its financial support is still public.

This model of local child care R&R or I&R agencies contracting with employers to provide a "special" (more attention, more detail) service to their employees has become an increasingly popular pattern in much of the country. All the California statewide child care R&R services are enthusiastically marketing their services to employers with varying degrees of success, as are such other agencies as Child Care Inc. in New York City, the Child Care Resource Center in Cambridge, Massachusetts, the Minneapolis and St. Paul agencies, and so forth.

The second approach is that taken by Child Care Dallas. The agency received a grant from the U.S. Department of Health and Human Services (DHHS) in 1982 "to develop and demonstrate an employer-assisted family day home system as a new approach to solving the severe shortage of quality care for infants and toddlers."[10] The assumption was that this program could be done more rapidly and with less capital investment than could a center program and would be more responsive to employee preferences.

The DHHS grant financed the development of the program, the administrative costs, and a modest start-up subsidy for a two-year project. The expectation was that employers would subsidize their employees, at least to some extent, once the program was operating. Sixty-six companies with high proportions of young women in their work force were approached to participate in the program. Despite extensive recruitment efforts, only six were participating by 1985.

Much money was spent on promotion, publicity, costly brochures, and video tape. Each of the six participating companies wanted 15 or 20 spaces, for a total of 125, but by mid-1984, with the grant of $285,000 in its final phase, there were only 48 placements. Another 30 children were on the waiting list for whom the agency could not develop infant homes.

The initial design assumed that employers would pay part of the child care costs, but instead parents paid the full $49 weekly fee. The real costs were $87.50 per child per week, with the government grant providing the subsidy. From the total cost of $87.50 weekly, $38.50 was for administration, publicity, and other services. The parent user paid the $49 fee directly to the family day care mother.

Recruitment had been difficult, slow, and costly. The user population was heavily middle class: two-parent families, not single mothers, with incomes in the $30,000–$40,000 range.

Moreover, as in its regular family day care program, the agency had to recruit and screen enormous numbers of potential providers before it had a list of possible homes. The potential consumers in the corporate program covered a widespread area that had no family day care homes at all. Of 100 names assembled after long and extensive efforts, only ten seemed possible after further screening. Only one of these finally became part of the network. Inevitably, one must wonder about either the model or the viability of the program form.

As this nationally publicized "success" reached its end, only one of the companies continued its program and made a modest investment. Without a problem in recruiting mothers of young children, employers saw little reason to take on on-site operations or any heavy investment in provision of services. As Child Care Dallas concluded in testimony before the Select Committee on Children of the U.S. House of Representatives, "it would be very unrealistic to assume that employers are going to play an immediate or major role in resolving the child care crisis."[11] Currently, this agency is very successfully marketing an information and referral service to a significant number of companies, based on a successful start as the local outlet for the IBM network.

Similar efforts at getting employers to subsidize child care vendor/voucher programs for their employees, especially their low- and moderate-income employees who would not qualify for a public subsidy, have been carried out by the Orlando, Florida, 4-C program through its Child Care Assurance Plan, and in New York by Child Care Inc.'s program with Shearson Hamill-American Express. None has had any quantitatively significant success as yet.

A third model, whereby modest corporate contributions are used to leverage large amounts of public funding, has been the least successful of the three approaches, yet has received a great deal of attention nonetheless. The Corporate Child Development Fund for Texas, based in Austin and headed, when we examined it, by Bruce Esterline,* is a single-purpose agency designed as a new child care model to facilitate corporate support of child care. The "case" is instructive and informative.

The Fund was invented to meet a problem Texas has shared with some other states since 1971 requirements that federal social service funding (first under Title IV-A and then under Title XX of the Social Security Act) generate a local "match." One state dollar would yield three federal dollars; but, as already noted, some states, Texas among them, decided not to spend state money.

---

*In 1986 the director was Christine Nichols.

Federal money would become available, however, if private money (usually philanthropic money raised by agencies or by the United Way) became available. We have seen, in our reports on Florida and several Texas cities, how this requirement created opportunities that shaped several programs. California, Minnesota, New York, and Massachusetts are not in this group. Even though the conversion of Title XX to the Social Service Block Grant (SSBG) by the Reagan administration in 1981 meant the end of the local match requirement, Texas has retained it, as have some other states.

The result of such state policies has been perverse, recalling a similar pattern in Minnesota in which, in the mid-1980s, local school districts that can afford the required "match" under the education legislation offer after-school programs while the needy districts do not. Dozens of poor rural communities have been unable to afford local day care for lack of the local match. Texas actually requires a 30 percent match, keeping 5 percent for state costs.

The Levi Strauss Foundation, eager to encourage support for child care, turned to the Urban Affairs Corporation in Houston, a group with some success in using corporate money to leverage Title XX money. They did not want to undertake the child care project and made the referral to Esterline. The detail is of interest since it highlights the sense in which this model is truly an initiative of a corporation heavily involved in the state and of individuals who created a new organization—with the cooperation of the state Department of Human Resources.

The pattern of operation is suggested in a rather elaborate 1984 report:[12]

> *Typical of the programs that the Fund helps support is the Rapid Advancement Program (RAP), which contracted with the Texas Department of Human Resources (DHR) to provide day care to 45 Shelby County children, including some with single parents, a number in foster care, and several more in need of protective services. In November 1980, RAP had to postpone opening this program in the town of Center because it could not raise enough matching money to qualify for Title XX. The Fund came to the rescue in May 1981, offering the agency a $3,000 "challenge" grant on the condition that it raise another $750 in local contributions— much less than the normal state match requirement, but enough to demonstrate "a degree of self-sufficiency." Soon, an Atlantic Richfield representative—one of the Fund's private sponsors—was on hand to present the check, and a headline on the front page of the next day's newspaper (under a picture of a "future Babe Ruth"*

wearing a day care center tee shirt) read "RAP Growth Up Thanks to Industry."

To date, 28 companies and foundations have contributed to the Fund, and 17 programs have received private grants between $2,000 and $5,000 each. Corporate donors include—in addition to Atlantic Richfield—Shell Oil, Exxon, Getty, Sun Gas, Allstate Insurance, Crown-Zellerbach, Motorola, Zale, Haggar, Southwestern Bell, American General, Target Stores, Langham Petroleum, Great American Reserve, First International Bank, NL Industries, La Quinta Motor Inns, Valero Energy, West Texas Marketing, Texas Energy Reserve, Houston Oil and Minerals, and Del Monte. Many are "repeaters" who have contributed two or three years in a row, sometimes with renewal grants larger than their initial ones.

The Corporate Child Development Fund was launched in mid-1979, with a gift from the Levi Strauss Foundation, as a nonprofit, tax-exempt organization governed by a board of eight business executives, public representatives, and child development specialists. A second Levi Strauss grant, matched by the state DHR, helped the Fund with a contract to produce a periodical for state child care personnel. Levi Strauss eventually contributed $110,000 of operational funds over three years. There were two other small foundation grants as well. For four years the Fund functioned on the operational grants and channeled all money raised to the communities. By 1983 it was necessary to face the inevitable: With an operating budget of $68,000, the Fund would need to retain an increased portion of all money raised (from mid-1983 to mid-1984 the Fund raised $170,000 and spent one-third to operate).

Nonetheless, the leveraging continued to work. As the state began to vote some child care funds, the local match declined. The Fund reported in 1983 that its first $100,000 raised for grants to child care agencies produced $900,000 in state and federal money. This occurred in communities that previously had turned back potential Title XX funds, which were then reallocated to the more affluent communities. According to a June 1983 report, sponsor contributions to the Corporate Fund yielded the following:

Child Care Facility	Corporate Fund	Matching Public Funds
Nacogdoches, Community Action Agency	$5000	$40,000
RAP Shelby County, Center	8000	93,000
Rockdale, St. John's Day Care Center	1000	12,000
Lamera, West Texas Opportunities	3500	45,000

The Fund does all of the exploration of applicants, assessment, and program packaging. Contributors are spared that preparation and can rely on competent groundwork, an added advantage. The average grant continues at about $3000 to $4000. Over 40 corporations had participated by mid-1984, and the repeat rate was 80 percent.

With the inauguration of the White House child care corporate initiative effort during the Reagan administration, the efforts of the Corporate Child Development Fund were widely publicized in the media and presented as an illustration of an important private sector effort. A $3000 or $5000 gift by a big corporation with a local factory or plant to leverage ten times the sum in public funds becomes a large publicity opportunity. There are visits by officials, ribbon-cutting ceremonies, photos in the local paper. Close reading of a thick file of press clippings yields very little about the role of public funds in supporting the major portion of the operation launched this way. As much may be said of the explorations, application process, and the training activities launched with the funds and of the occasional modest capital investments.

From the perspective of public social policy, the questions are obvious: Should one spend nine public dollars to attract a $1 corporate contribution? Should the general public not have the full story? Is the fact that much of each $3000–$5000 local grant is also saved at the tax end not relevant? Should the decision of a locally operating company with regard to a fund-raising proposal by a private group determine whether local children have access to needed care while their parents work? Should the experience of this kind of program be defined as supportive of the White House claim that a significant part of the child care burden could be carried by private industry? (Not within our purview is the complaint from some big-city United Way groups that money which should go to them is raised from locally based corporations and "exported" to rural towns where the corporations also have operations.)

By 1986, with the decline in the price of oil, the core group of energy-related corporate givers had largely withdrawn from the program. Those remaining were increasingly interested in serving only their own employees (not the low-income community) and in addressing such needs as latchkey child care, not care for younger children. And the Corporate Child Care Fund was concentrating heavily on obtaining public funds.

The stories are similar around the country. The child care community agencies are striving hard to market their services to employers. Some employers are receptive, but when they purchase a service it is usually I&R—an inexpensive if worthwhile service with high visibility, but one adding little to the supply of services or to the ability of parents to pay for the services they want. Many agencies have sought corporate contributions, with modest success. Many have sought employer sponsorship for child care services either through establishing on-site programs or more often via financial subsidies and/or vouchers for their employees. Very few employers have funded such programs. They are more likely to help employees pay for care by establishing a salary reduction, Dependent Care Assistance Plan (DCAP). These programs, however, offer no support to the child care planning and coordinating agencies; they do not add to the supply of care; nor do they assure financial support to existing child care providers. We turn now to a more detailed picture of what is available.

Employer-Sponsored Child Care: The Numbers, The Different Options, The Activities

A comprehensive 1979 survey of employer-sponsored child-care services, updated in 1981, documented its rarity at the beginning of the 1980s.[13] The survey found only 19 day-care centers sponsored by industry, 7 sponsored by labor unions with funds from employers of the members, 14 sponsored by government agencies, and 75 sponsored by hospitals. In addition, 200 centers were sponsored by the military. The extremely limited involvement of private industry was particularly notable; in fact, the number of industry-sponsored centers actually declined between 1970 and 1980.

A 1982 survey identified 415 civilian employers that were supporting some child-care related activity. About half were hospitals. Among those programs supported by private industry, only 42 were on-site child care services, 10 were voucher programs, 20 were information and referral services, and 78 involved some form of support to community services, usually in the form of a modest financial contribution.[14]

By 1986 somewhere between 2000 and 3000 employers nationally were estimated to be "sponsoring" child care services in some form or providing some form of "child care assistance."[15] The figures are not precise and reflect much of the public relations atmosphere surrounding developments in this field. The "sponsorship" or "assistance" involved actually ranges from a very limited number of employers operating or contracting for the operation of work site child care services to those holding occasional seminars to inform parents about how to choose a child care service or helping employees to segregate some of their wage and salary income before taxes in order to pay for child care services.

The types of child care services currently supported by some employers thus include the following:[16]

- Employer-owned and operated child care services at or near the workplace. Employers usually pay all start-up costs and partially subsidize fees or operating costs, albeit modestly.
- Employer-contracted-for child care services provided by an independent operator located at or near the work site.
- Discounts on child care services owned and operated by an independent, private child care provider and located at one or more sites in the communities where employees reside. Through a contractual arrangement with the employer, these services are offered to employees at a modest discount (5 to 10 percent off the fee for each child) as long as the employer guarantees that a specified minimum number of children will be enrolled.
- An off-site child care center established by a consortium of employers located reasonably close to one another. The companies usually provide seed money for initial construction or remodeling of a facility and may underwrite some of the operating costs of the facility or provide a partial subsidy of tuition costs for children of employees.
- A vendor program in which the employer purchases a number of "slots," or child care places, in one or more centers or family day homes and makes these available to employees at a partially reduced rate.
- A voucher program in which employers provide a "coupon" to the employee worth a specified amount toward the purchase of child care from any licensed provider. The employer may either fully fund the cost of service or subsidize the child care cost based on the income and/or family size of the employee; the employee may choose among all available licensed providers.
- Employer-provided child care information and referral services. The employer hires an employee specifically to provide this service, among others, or the employer assigns an employee responsibility for this task.
- An independent information and referral service. A child care consultant or organization provides the service to employees through a contractual arrangement with the employer.
- Child care as a fringe benefit. This benefit is included in a

flexible benefit plan, so that employees may choose a small subsidy for child care as one of their fringe benefits. The employer either pays a small amount toward employees' costs of child care or reimburses employees for a part of the costs.

- A salary reduction plan that includes child care as one of the benefits. If this course is followed, employees may allocate a portion of pretax salary to pay for child care each year. (This is a benefit that usually costs the employer nothing and provides the employee a subsidy that varies in amount depending on the employee's tax bracket. It is paid for, in effect, by the taxpayer. In some cases employers also contribute modestly to employees' salary reduction plan.)
- A philanthropic contribution by the employer of money or services to a child care center located in the community where the employer is based, or where the employer has a facility.

According to the informal estimates of Dr. Dana Friedman, a nationally respected expert on employer-sponsored child care who is affiliated with the Conference Board, the national picture of 2500 employer-sponsored child care services looked something like this in 1986:[17]

- Approximately 400 hospitals had on- or near-site child care services.
- Approximately 150 corporations (and 30 public agencies) had on- or near-site child care services. Except for those operated directly by the corporation or a subsidiary, almost all were contracted out to private independent providers and operated by them.
- About 300 employers had contracts with one of the large proprietary child care chains that offer a modest discount to employees' children; and about 50 of these employers actually contributed as well. (Dr. Friedman estimated that about half of these were with one large child care service chain.)
- About 500 companies were either operating child care information and referral services themselves or had contracts with another organization to do so.
- About 150 firms had cafeteria-style or flexible benefit plans, and half of these included child care as an optional benefit.
- About 800 firms had flexible benefit or salary-reduction plans, but only about 10 percent of these included child care.
- About 25 firms had voucher plans.
- About 20 firms had sick-child-care initiatives.
- About 75 companies were involved in some way in after-school child care.

- In addition, about 200 employers made some form of contribution to local child care centers and about the same number had held "parenting" seminars and workshops to which outside speakers are invited to discuss various aspects of parenting problems ranging from child care for infants to the substance abuse problems of adolescents.

We will now discuss in further detail some of the most important of these different "models" of employer-sponsored child care.

On-Site or Near-Site Child Care Services

Initially, when employer-sponsorship of child care services was first discussed, the most frequent proposal was for a child care center located at the work place and operated either directly by the corporation or as a separate subsidiary corporation responsible to the parent corporation or operated by others but under contract to the corporation.

An obvious way to provide care for children whose parent or parents are employed, so the discussion would go, is to bring the children to work. While the parents work, the children can be cared for in some group arrangement. With this proximity, parents have the opportunity to see their children at certain times during the day, regularly check on their progress, and be readily available for any emergency. Nursing is possible. It is an arrangement that seemingly can reduce the typical disjunction between work and family life. Other possible advantages for families include the convenience of not having to commute to another location in order to drop off and pick up children.

Certain disadvantages of work-site child care, documented in earlier U.S. experience, were largely ignored in these discussions. Most notable, for example, was the experience of American Telephone and Telegraph, the company that was the country's largest employer of women until 1984 (when it carried out the court-ordered divestiture plan, spinning off seven regional operating companies and thereby becoming a far smaller company than previously). For three years, from 1971 to 1974, AT&T operated day care centers at two of its locations, Washington, D.C., and Columbus, Ohio. Given the company's large female labor force working at thousands of locations across the country, in particular in heavily urban areas, the argument was that "If Bell could demonstrate the viability of industry-run day care centers in large urban settings, a powerful impetus could be given to this type of child care.[18]

Despite great expectations and much publicity, the Washington center, with a capacity for 110 children, opened with only 16 children, and the Columbus center, with a capacity for 50, opened with 22. The occupancy rate averaged 65 to 70 percent at both locations and never exceeded 80 percent for any sustained period of time. By mid-1974 the company closed both centers.

In evaluating the experience, the company conducted a longitudinal study of an experimental group (working parents using one of the two centers) and a matched control group of nonusers. The following were its major findings:

1. Lateness was reduced in the experimental group as compared to the control group. However, reducing lateness had not been a major objective in establishing the centers.
2. Absenteeism, which was a major company concern, was *higher* among parents using the center because when their children became ill, parents had no readily available home-based or near-home support and therefore had to stay home to care for the child.
3. Turnover, another company concern, was no lower among those in the experimental group than among those in the control group.
4. The evidence was not adequate to indicate whether the centers provided a recruitment device because the company's own hiring policies changed during the period the centers were operating.
5. Far fewer employees were interested in the service than was expected.

Although the labor force situation is very different now, more than one decade later, and the same problems, successes, and same failure may not necessarily hold true today, the findings of this unusually rigorous effort at evaluating an on-site child care center do suggest that this approach is certainly not necessarily the definitive answer to employees' child care problems. These and other findings raise serious questions about on-site care and employee responses to this type of care. Of equal interest, however, they suggest how important it is that employers carefully monitor and study whatever approach they choose, if they have specific goals in mind when developing a child care policy.

Some companies that established on- or near-site child care centers in recent years have been very satisfied with them; but usually the success of the arrangement has to do with factors that may be unique to the particular company involved. Several of the companies that view their experience with on-site child care centers positively are located in communities that resemble "company towns," where they are the primary employer or a major employer and few alternative child care arrangements are available. A large group among the employers who have on-site child care services are hospitals or medical complexes of some sort. These organizations, employing a large number of professional women (nurses) and nonprofessional cleaning and support staff, largely female, and open 24 hours a day, 365 days a year, face special problems in recruiting and retaining staff and have unusual work schedules; on-site child care services may be highly attractive and appropriate for their personnel.

A precise figure on the number of on- or near-site child care centers is still not available, but current estimates, excluding hospitals, range from 42 to 80 to 150.[19,20,21] Even among these relatively few such programs, there are substantial differences. Thus, for example, those at Wang Laboratories and Hoffman La Roche are completely in-house operations where center staff are considered corporate employees. Intermedics operates its child care center as a wholly owned subsidiary. Corning Glass, through its corporate foundation, provided start-up funds as well as some ongoing support for the establishment of an autonomous, nonprofit child care center. Merck Pharmaceuticals, similarly, provided start-up funds for the establishment of private, nonprivate centers; employees' fees for the services are expected to cover the operating costs. Other companies with on-site centers include Connecticut General Life Insurance Company, Stride-Rite Shoe Corp., and Zale Corporation. Several governmental agencies have also established on-site child care centers, including one in Albany, one in Boston, and several in Washington, D.C.

Another approach to providing at- or near-site child care is to contract with one of the large child care chains to offer employees a discount on their child care fees. Sometimes the employer provides a small subsidy to the employee, but usually the discount is offered by the provider for the assurance of a guaranteed minimum enrollment of employees' children. At Disney World, the center is operated by Kinder-Care, a private, commercial (for-profit) child care company on contract with Disney. A similar pattern exists at Allendale Insurance Company in Rhode Island and Union Mutual Life Insurance Company in Portland, Maine, where Living and Learning, another large commercial child care chain, leases space from the insurance companies. The companies guarantee a certain minimum enrollment, and Living and Learning provides a 10 percent discount to employees.

Except for those centers operated on a contractual basis by an independent child care organization, often a commercial child care chain, employers typically bear start-up costs. In almost all these centers, the fees for employee-parents are partially subsidized, usually very modestly. In several the center also serves children from the community whose parents are not company employees, although employees' children do have priority if space is tight. Often community children are needed to make adequate use of the available space and staff.

Many in senior management in other companies that considered but rejected development of an on-site center have commented about the earlier negative experiences. The following are among the reasons that management in many companies have decided against on-site child care:

- The costs of establishing and operating a center.
- The complexities of a business that is new and unfamiliar and the regulatory maze involved in starting and operating a center.
- The difficulties in monitoring the quality of service provided and the potential problems of liability if accidents occur.
- Siting and transportation problems.
- The unreliability of employees' actual use of such centers despite expressions of positive interest (sometimes the issue is convenience, sometimes cost, often preferences about programs).

Labor unions have also been involved with the development of child care centers near their members' place of work.[22] The Amalgamated Clothing and Textile Workers Union (ACTWU) has been the most active union where child care is concerned. In 1981 there were six ACTWU child care centers, five located in the east and one in Chicago. Most were operated out of the ACTWU health and welfare fund, to which management contributed as part of a collective bargaining agreement. In Baltimore, however, there is a special child care fund under joint control of the union and management. In all these centers fees were heavily subsidized; indeed, in the Chicago program, until 1978 child care was free for union members.

Of some interest, given the negative attitudes of many in management about operating a work-site-based child care service, is the increasingly similar attitude expressed by union officials. Several of the ACTWU centers have closed in the last few years, including the Chicago center. The Baltimore center in 1983 had only three members' children! As one senior union official said: "We would not establish day care centers again. Day care centers are expensive facilities and need permanent financing. The labor force changes in a plant. Members get older. The communities where plants are located change, and the members with young children move to different neighborhoods. Plants move. Parents want child care near where they live, not near where they work."

Among the most positive current reports of on-site child care is one from the staff of the Governor's Day Care Partnership Project in Massachusetts. As noted in Chapter 3, below-market rate loans have stimulated the establishment of on-site facilities and 63 employers now make provision. The reports state that there is heavy use for infants and toddlers and that the availability of care is very popular. All of this has occurred in a tight labor market and during an economic boom in the state.

An illustration of an unusual combination of a union-sponsored, government- and management-financed work-site- and community-based child care center is one in New York City's Chinatown, under the auspices of the city's child care agency and the ILGWU. Here, in a unique situation, federal child care funds and city and state child care funds together with funds from management are supporting a community-based child care center for the children of the very low earner Chinese employees-union members who qualify for publicly subsidized child care. Management's contribution enabled the center to serve almost twice as many children (70 instead of 40) as it would have if only public financing was available. In effect, this is a publicly funded center in which supplementary funds are provided by local employers in order to increase the numbers of employees' children—who would qualify for public child care if it were available—that can be served. It is very small and meets special circumstances. Moreover, by 1986 management funding had ended (the commitment was for the start-up and phasing-in period only), and the program became a publicly funded program, seeking private foundation assistance as well.

Additional objections by parents to work-site child care, in part documented in earlier and more extensive experiences in European countries (which are increasingly eliminating such services), have been supported by the findings of parent surveys in the United States. These objections include the potential for disrupting a child care arrangement if they wish to change jobs; the problems of transporting children long distances during peak commuter hours, often on mass transportation; the lack of neighborhood friends when a child's relationships are limited to the children of other employees; and preferences for neighborhood-based care.[23]

More important, there are a variety of other potentially very attractive options whereby employers can support, facilitate, and subsidize child-care services for employees; these options, often far less expensive than on-site child care, are receiving increasing attention. Among them are several types described earlier:

- Organizing a consortium supporting community-based services.
- Providing a voucher covering a full or partial reimbursement to employees for the costs of child care.
- Subsidizing a number of slots in various community-based facilities near employees' places of residence.
- Contributing to the support of one or more existing child care centers located near where employees work.
- Including child care within a flexible benefit plan.

Child Care Consortia

In theory, at least, among the most feasible models for small- or medium-sized employers is a consortium. As one report suggests,[24]

> . . . one of the least used, but perhaps the most feasible for the majority of companies, is a consortium. In a consortium, employers can join efforts by sharing resources, liabilities, and costs and by pooling their populations of parents and children.

For the most part, what is needed to start a consortium is a group of employers located relatively close to one another geographically or at least drawing their work force from a common residential community or communities. Centers can be started in industrial parks or complexes or even in shopping malls. Some have been started by employers in the same or related industry.

One child care consortium was begun as a collaborative effort by employees and employers, a university, and the National Academy of Television Arts and Sciences, Inc. This center, the Broadcaster's Child Development Center, was started by four television and two radio stations and serves the children of local television and radio station personnel at all levels.[25]

Another consortium was established in the early 1970s by a group of Minneapolis companies under the leadership of Control Data. This consortium, supporting the Northside Child Development Center, included such companies as Dayton-Hudson, Pillsbury, Northwestern Bell Telephone Company, Northern States Power, Minnesota Federal Reserve Bank, and Farmers & Mechanics Savings and Loan. Over the years, participation by employees declined as participation by community residents who were not employed by the sponsoring companies increased. The center became increasingly dependent on government funds for survival. By the late 1970s the center had essentially become a community child care facility. Of the 120 children in the center, recently only 12 were reported to be the children or grandchildren of employees.[26] In commenting about the changes over time, the center director said, "The workforce at the plant (Control Data) has remained relatively stable over the last decade. As a result, few of the employees have children young enough to enroll in the center."[27] Her statement sounds remarkably similar in context to a statement made to us by the president of the Amalgamated Clothing and Textile Workers' Union. Although Control Data continues to provide financial assistance and in-kind services to the child care center, the company no longer offers child care benefits within its fringe benefit package to its employees. In effect this is a consortium that was; it is no longer operating as such.

Still another consortium was established by six high-tech companies in the Silicon Valley. The city of Sunnyvale approached four subsidiaries of TRW and several other companies, including Hewlett-Packard, about the possibility of joining together to support the establishment of a local child care service. The local companies were very enthusiastic about the possibility and agreed to provide some funding to get the center launched. Some were so enthusiastic that they tried, unsuccessfully, to get some additional funds from their parent company. Management in the local high-tech companies were convinced of the need for additional child care services and saw this as a way to encourage the development of more services and provide some aid to their female employees without getting to the costly and complicated effort of actually operating a program. The companies make a financial contribution to the center, and, in return, employees are entitled to a 5 percent discount off the regular fee and are given priority for places when space is tight.

The human resource manager of one of the participating companies described the consortium as "fairly successful." He said that the center provides very high quality child care, but that it is expensive and beyond the reach of many of the single mothers who are employed as support staff and were originally viewed as the primary consumer group for the center. The subsidy provided by employers is only modest; it is not adequate for most of their women workers, who tend to earn low or at least modest salaries. Over the years since the center was first established there has been a decline in the numbers of employees using the center. Thus, for example, in 1984 only about ten female employees out of a total labor force of 3000 in two firms in the consortium were using the center. Moreover, not only are the costs of the service a problem, but over the intervening years residential patterns have shifted somewhat. As a result, although the center is located where many young families lived initially, by now most of these firms' employees who might use the center live in a different area; they prefer using a child care program that is nearer their home. Here, too, the situation is somewhat reminiscent of the on-site child care programs. The labor force is dynamic, and over time needs change.

Contracting with a Private Provider

In this "model," employers identify one or more private providers, usually large corporate child care chains with several facilities in the area, and contract with the provider(s) to offer a small discount to employees on the basis of the employer guaranteeing a certain minimum enrollment of employees' children. An alternative approach involves an employer's encouraging a provider that has facilities in other communities not too far away, but none in the immediate area of the employer's work site, to establish a new facility nearby. In neither case does the employer have any financial obligation to the child care provider; nor does the employer provide any subsidy to employees to purchase child care. Employers using this approach merely act as "facilitators," and if enough children are enrolled, the employee benefits from a modest discount.

Minneapolis Honeywell established such an arrangement with Learning Tree (the name under which Children's World operates in Minnesota) at one site that had recently experienced employee relocation. A relatively large number of professionals had been relocated, and the company wanted to be responsive to their problems. Child care was viewed as a potentially important problem for employees, in particular because no child care facility was located near the work site or in the surrounding community. Management initially explored the possibility of an on-site child care center but rejected it for a number of the usual reasons. They then explored the possibility of a local public school operating such a program but dropped that when they discovered that a leading commercial child care chain was in the process of establishing a center near the plant. An employee survey had revealed that about half preferred having child care available at a facility located near the work site while the other half preferred a facility located near home. A contract was negotiated with Children's World, whereby

Honeywell employees would get a 5 percent discount (later raised to 10 percent when the employee participation rate was higher than anticipated). A similar contract was negotiated with two other commercial providers with facilities located in the nearby communities where employees lived. In 1984, out of approximately 2500 employees at this location, about 100 parents, with slightly over 100 children, were participating in this child care discount program, located at 30 centers. The fees for care are $60 to $65 a week for preschoolers and $90 to $100 a week for infants; the second child gets a 15 percent discount. The company provides no subsidy for employees; in effect, it is a discount based on numbers—the company assures these three providers of a certain minimum number of child participants.

Subsidizing "Slots," or Places, for Employees' Children

In this model of employer-sponsored child care, employers guarantee payment for a number of places in established child care centers, which are reserved for employees. Commercial child care chains such as Kinder-Care, Children's World, and La Petite Academe offer an employer a 20 percent discount for its employees' children, for which the company pays 10 percent and the center absorbs a 10 percent reduction in fees. Equitable Life Assurance had a pilot project with Kinder-Care in Atlanta, Georgia; Albuquerque, New Mexico; and Columbus, Ohio. The project was ended because employee participation was much lower than anticipated, in part because of the inconvenience of the sites. Equitable is now moving in a different direction regarding its child care policy (I&R services).

An alternative way to subsidize individual places in different child care centers for employees' children is for employers to contribute funds to a nonprofit agency that can then provide vouchers to pay for child care to those who qualify for the service. For the most part, these efforts have received very limited support, and the practice exists on a very modest scale. Among those places in which such a model is found are Austin, Texas; Minneapolis and St. Paul, Minnesota; and San Mateo County, California. A few organizations have obtained small contributions from employers, which they have used to leverage public child care funds. The main advantage has been to help communities obtain public funds that they might not have been able to otherwise and to expand the number of places that would have been available.

Although anything that expands the availability of reasonably good child care services deserves attention, these programs, which have received a great deal of publicity, thus far provide very little in the way of new child care money, for very few, if any, additional children.

Voucher Systems

The term "voucher" is used to describe a subsidy provided by employers to employees to purchase child care at any licensed facility or, sometimes, from any licensed family day care provider. Two companies, the Ford Foundation and the Polaroid Corporation, are among the very few employers using this approach to help employees defray a portion of their child care costs.[28] Each had initially considered establishing an on-site child care center and chose instead a system of financial assistance. Polaroid Corporation, in Cambridge, Massachusetts, pays anywhere from 5 percent to more than half of the child care costs of employees whose income is below a certain level. Similarly, the Ford Foundation reimburses employees who qualify for the subsidy for up to 50 percent of their child care costs, to a defined maximum. Both organizations limit the subsidy to employees with incomes under a specified ceiling. Polaroid chose the voucher model because it operates out of many different locations and could neither establish a center at each site nor establish a center at one site and ignore all the others. The Ford Foundation rejected the concept of an on-site center because it was convinced employees would not want to bring their young children to a mid-town program but would prefer to use a service near their homes. Moreover, both organizations were convinced that the problem was not availability of child care services but affordability of a good quality program for their employees. They concluded, therefore, that what was needed was a child care subsidy, not a specific place. Polaroid has since found that for its evening shift workers, a subsidy is not enough; there are just not enough services around. Polaroid provides another child care service for employees who do not qualify for financial aid (see below).

Here, too, developments have been very modest; at best, a handful of companies have established this model.

Information and Referral (I&R) Services

Child care information and referral services are expanding everywhere, in part in response to the growing diversity of programs and the concomitant problems of parents trying to locate them and be assured of the quality of care provided (see Chapter 2). One new development is employer sponsorship of these services, either by employing someone on an in-house basis to provide the service or by contracting with an existing child care information and referral service or a child care agency to provide such services for their employees.[29] This is an inexpensive yet highly visible way for employers to "do something" about child care that is simple to establish yet is helpful to employees.

Three companies that were among the first to establish in-house I&R counselors are Mountain Bell in Denver, Colorado; Polaroid; and Steelcase, Inc., in Grand Rapids, Michigan. Steelcase, the largest manufacturer of office furniture, is a nonunion, family-owned business with about 6000 employees at the Grand Rapids plant. According to one report, its Human Resources Department offers a counseling and referral service on a range of issues to company employees seeking help. Employees discuss child care needs with a counselor, who suggests possible alternatives. Parents are told about the characteristics of a good child care program and are helped to develop criteria for choosing a service that will best meet their needs. Counselors are knowledgeable about community resources and make referrals to both center care and family day care providers.

An alternative model, whereby services are provided on a contractual basis, is the approach taken by IBM. Beginning in mid-1984, IBM contracted with Work/Family Directions, a Boston-based private organization, to provide child care information and referral services as well as parent/consumer education to its employees located throughout the country. The service is delivered through a nationwide network of about 250 local agencies and individuals with whom Work/Family Directions contracts. Most of these community resources are thus also available to serve other employers as well as the general public. Work/Family Directions contracted with I&R services where they existed and helped create such services where they were lacking. By 1986, 90 percent of IBM employees were covered by this service through contracts with I&R services in 45 cities, while about 200 contracts in a variety of organizations around the country carried the remaining 10 percent.

According to Work/Family Directions, all IBM employees who call the referral service receive child care consultation, referrals to available services, and a parent handbook that describes how to choose a good service. IBM also sponsors training workshops for child care providers as a way of improving the general quality of services available and provides financial support for recruitment and development of new providers. The costs of the information, referral, and parent education services are prepaid by IBM (which has also provided personal computers to many services), but the employees pay for the child care service itself.

The IBM development seems to have constituted something of a breakthrough. Several large employers now seem interested in making I&R services available to their employees, and Work/ Family Directions has contracts with MacDonalds, Kraft, Merrill Lynch, and several other large companies. The agency serves only large, multisite corporations; single-site employers are referred directly to a local I&R service in their area. As more employers decide to make this service available to their employees, the IBM "model" of purchasing the service through a community agency or a national network is likely to become the prevalent information and referral mode.

A variation of this model was developed earlier by Child Care Inc (CCI) in New York City, currently one of the local agencies under contract with Work/Family Directions to provide services to IBM employees in the New York City area. An experienced and well-established child care information and referral service, CCI developed a relationship with several large corporations interested in providing child care information and referral services to their own employees. On a contract basis, CCI provides this service to employees of a corporation, including information about what is available, the criteria for making choices, and referrals and recommendations to a range of services that seem to meet employee-parent needs and preferences. The employee pays no fee for the service. CCI also initially organized parenting seminars for corporations but later simply facilitated access to specialists. It is presently exploring options in providing "sick child care" services. Among the 25 companies contracting with CCI in 1986 were International Paper, Phillip Morris, Time, American Express, Equitable Life, Morgan Guaranty, and Conde Nast.

Parent Education

Closely related to the information and referral services, and often provided along with these services, are a variety of parent education programs.[30] We include a brief discussion of these programs as one variety of child care assistance because one type of seminar is designed to educate parents about the characteristics of "good" child care services, about how to differentiate between "good" and "bad" services, and about the criteria to use in choosing among existing services, be they centers, preschools, or family day homes.

Among the most popular of these parenting seminars are the

"noontime" or "brown bag" seminars sponsored by employers and provided at the work place, usually during the lunch hour. They address a variety of parenting, child care, and work and family issues. Thus, for example, in addition to the child care information needs of working parents, other child and family issues may be discussed—for example, coping with work and family responsibilities, surviving divorce, managing as a single parent, dealing with the school system, communicating with adolescent children or with stepchildren, and recognizing substance abuse problems in an adolescent.

A visible indication of employers' interest and concern, these programs are easy to carry out and the most inexpensive of all types of child care assistance to implement. Illustrations of organizations providing these seminars include the Texas Institute for Families, the Bank Street College "Work and Family Seminars," and the Parents in the Workplace program conducted jointly by the Greater Minneapolis Day Care Association and St. Paul's Resources for Child Caring, Inc.

Sick Child Care

When enumerating the problems of managing work and family life, working parents frequently list the difficulties of coping with the need for emergency child care right after talking about their child care problems generally. Many parents, even when they manage to find an affordable, reliable, and satisfactory child care arrangement, still speak with something akin to horror when they describe their fears about a child getting sick on a work day. While most employers permit time off when an employee is ill, very few companies specifically allow the use of those same sick days to care for an ill child. Furthermore, many employees who would return to work after the acute phase of a child's illness is past cannot do so because they are unable to make arrangements for their child to be cared for while convalescing. Sometimes, even if able to take some days off, an employee has to be present at his/her job "for a little while" or "for an important meeting or task" and cannot make a care arrangement.

For many parents, an ill child means that whichever parent has the "less important" job, or the more flexible job, or the more sympathetic boss or supervisor will stay home. Needless to say, for single parents, there is no choice. For the parent who has to stay home, this may mean taking off a day or two and losing pay, or if the parent has paid sick leave at work, it may mean the parent-employee lies to her boss (and it's usually *her* boss), and takes time off by saying that she is ill herself. She then runs the risk of eventual job loss for excessive illness and unreliability.

Employers are becoming increasingly convinced that caring for an ill child is one major cause of absenteeism, and employee-parents agree. Among the responsive options, some employers have instituted the following policies:

- Employees may use their own paid sick leave to take care of an ill child, or in some cases, an ill dependent such as an elderly parent.
- Employees may use their paid personal days for personal emergencies, including the illness of a child.
- Employees are allowed a specific number of paid days off, in addition to their own sick leave, to take care of an ill child. (More and more, European countries are including such entitlement in their social security systems.)

One alternative or supplementary approach is an in-home sick child care service, a special service that provides a trained caregiver to come to the child's own home in the case of illness. Two such services exist in the Minneapolis–St. Paul area: Child Care Services, Inc. and Control Data Temps. Similar services exist in a few other large cities. These services involve either a kind of babysitter who is trained to care for a mildly ill child or a home-health aide who is trained to work with children. In each case the caregiver goes to the child's home on a temporary basis. One major problem with this service is the cost, usually between $35 and $50 a day for the babysitting service and far more than that for a home-health aide. Few employees can afford such a service, and not many employers are likely to offer the service or provide a significant subsidy for it.

In Tucson, Arizona, the Sick Child Home Health Care Program is now in its fifth year of operation, staffed by trained and certified health care aides and available to help working parents meet sick child emergencies. A call at 6 A.M. can lead to the dispatch of an aide by 7:00. The aides care for children with common childhood ailments. They may also provide nonspecialized care for children with special needs and terminally ill children. They are available, too, in special instances when a child is not ill, as when the usual caretaker is ill or there are other gaps in child care arrangements.

The minimum service unit in this program is four hours. In 1984 the fees were set on a sliding scale basis between $1.50 and $4.25 per hour. To the extent that parents' fees did not meet the full costs, there was funding from a woman's service organization, a foundation, the City of Tucson, and the United Way. Two electronics firms have contracted to share the costs of the aide with their employees.[31]

Another approach is that of the family day home or center that permits mildly ill children to be brought to child care. There, the ill child may rest or play quietly, with some supervision, in a separate room. Medicine can be given as needed.

Still another pattern is found at the Berkeley, California, Children's Service, in its satellite sick child care program, Wheezles and Sneezles. This program was established in 1978 in a three-bedroom apartment adjacent to the child care center. The program is licensed as a family day care home, and the caregivers are familiar to the children because they sometimes staff the regular child care program. All the children have opportunities to visit and familiarize themselves with the sick child care facility, should they become ill. Probably as important, the ill children all come out of the same contagion pool, so children are unlikely to be exposed to new illnesses while convalescing from the old. A variation on this plan involves a community medical facility, staffed by a registered nurse with a doctor available on an as-needed basis, that has a few rooms set aside in a special wing for ill children.

Thus far there are few such services of a formal kind. One of the newest is "Chicken Soup" in Minneapolis, Minnesota, with room for 20 children. It plans summer closings. The San Juan Batista program in San Jose, California, is a year-round, more medical operation.

Other approaches include employers who operate summer camp facilities for the use of employees' children (Fel-Pro Industries, Skokie, Illinois) and employers who have established special loan programs for the construction and renovation of child care facilities (Bankers Trust Co., Chase Manhattan Bank, and Citibank, all in New York City).

Child Care and Flexible Benefits or Flexible Spending Plans

Two other approaches to providing child care financial assistance for employees are flexible benefit plans and flexible spending (salary reduction) plans. Both models involve providing child care assistance as an employee benefit, either with a subsidy from the employer or through the use of employees' pretax income or both. Providing child care aid this way permits employers to avoid the issue of a discriminatory benefit and often even to avoid spending any of their own funds—yet to contribute to a reduction in the out-of-pocket costs to the employee. Several companies have gone this route, including Northern States Power in Minneapolis, which has included child care in its flexible benefit plan, and about 100 other companies that thus far are known to have included child care in a flexible spending plan (consultants in the field report considerable additional activity even as we write). The flexible spending plan, created through establishment of a salary reduction plan as permitted by the Internal Revenue Service, allows employees to reduce their salaries by a specific sum, depositing that amount into a fund from which an employer pays one's child care bills using pretax dollars. Another variation on this permits employees to pay for child care directly and then at the end of the year apply to their employer for reimbursement from such a fund.

The Montgomery County Council (Maryland) was the first governmental body in the country to establish such a plan,[32] which of course can also become available to public employees and staffs of nonprofit organizations. Several universities have such programs.

It is not likely that the tax changes enacted in late 1986 and their constraints, as well as their lower tax rates, will decrease the attractiveness and potential of these plans.

An Office Furniture Manufacturer Assembles Several Components

Steelcase, the leading office furniture manufacturer, employs 10,000 workers countrywide, 7300 of them in Grand Rapids, Michigan. Its child care initiatives are embedded in a total program and philosophy expressed as follows in a statement by its vice president for human resources:

> *The Steelcase family commitment is comprehensive: from an innovative child-care referral program that has gained national publicity . . . to a gerontologist-conducted, eight-week pre-retirement program for employees and spouses . . . to a Steelcase-sponsored Retirees Club where former employees can maintain their "family ties" participating together in picnics, cruises, and other social events . . .*
>
> *That commitment to employees and their families is inherent in the Steelcase corporate philosophy: while change is Steelcase's constant partner, people are Steelcase's constant future. Steelcase's employees, dealers, customers, stockholders and suppliers are partners in profit. Steelcase believes the key to corporate success is three-fold: (1) the identification of the needs of each of these people groups; (2) balancing individual group needs for the mutual satisfaction of all groups; (3) supporting the individual group needs for*

*the collective benefit of all the groups. And so what's good for the
employee is good for the company.*

The company's strong and committed paternalism involves services as well as a comparatively generous benefits program and
profit-sharing. It has never had a work-stoppage leading to a labor
dispute since 1912. Especially noteworthy, apart from the child
care efforts, are family-oriented recreation programs at a large
1178-acre camp ground (as well as city-based programs), flexitime,
many aids to students, an unusual food service, a van transportation service, and a company-operated rehabilitation program.

The child care offerings are quite unusual in national context:

> *Steelcase also offers employees assistance in obtaining and paying
> for quality child care. Steelcase screens prospective child-care
> providers and makes recommendations to employees seeking indi-
> vidual child care in their own neighborhoods. Steelcase also offers
> dependent care reimbursement (in tax-free dollars) as part of its
> flexible benefits program. The referral program is advantageous for
> both the company and the employee. The company doesn't have to
> build and staff a central child care facility. The employee has the
> privilege of individually tailored child care.*

Two full-time on-site staff members individualize the referral
service, visit potential family day care homes to be sure of a good
"match," and help upgrade provider services (even lending providers furniture and equipment!). The program has been in operation since 1980. Its quality assurance components parallel what a
number of other companies are now doing under special contractual arrangements with local information and referral services.

Employers, the Government, and Child Care

Unlike the nineteenth-century employer initiatives or those that
occurred during World War II, what is occurring in the 1980s, with
a few exceptions, is not occurring because employers are trying to
recruit and retain their female workers but because employers are
undergoing pressure from government, from the media, and from
child care advocates to do something more to respond to the child
care needs of their employees.

The governmental pressures include:

• The White House Private Sector Initiatives effort that organized a series of luncheon and breakfast meetings around the
  country, with the CEOs of major corporations and a few child

care advocates, to discuss what corporations could do to sup-
port child care services for their employee-parents.
- Discretionary research and demonstration grants provided by
  DHHS to encourage the development of employer-sponsored
  child care services and related activities (for example, Child
  Care Dallas, the Employer-Sponsored Child Care Project in
  Pasadena, California, the Work and Family meetings carried
  out by the Conference Board).
- Limited grants by state and local governments to encourage
  employer involvement (for example, Massachusetts, Texas,
  New York City).
- Some activities designed to make state government a "model
  employer" (for example, North Carolina).
- Initiatives stressing the economic development function of
  child care services (for example, North Carolina and Massachusetts).

The primary factor acting as a spur and catalyst in the development of new forms of employer-sponsorship of child care services
is the support and encouragement provided by recent developments in the Internal Revenue Code.[33] One major development is
the ability to establish a "Dependent Care Assistance Plan"
(DCAP), legislated as part of the Economic Recovery Tax Act in
1981.

Employers have generally ascribed their reluctance to provide
child care services for the employees to problems of high costs;
possible liability in operating on-site facilities; a concern that such
a policy would be viewed as a "discriminatory" benefit by the
majority of their employees who do not have very young children
or do not need such a service; and a reluctance to appear too
"paternalistic." One other obstacle, however, has been tax legislation which required that, unlike many other employee benefits,
employer payments for child care assistance be considered as
taxable income to the employee. Except in situations where an on-
site facility was established, identifying the specific amount of
employer subsidy to be counted was easy. Thus, any increment
employers might provide for child care offered no more benefit
than a straight wage or salary increase.

Of particular importance, the 1981 legislation establishing these
DCAPs (known also as "Section 129 Plans" because of the locus of
this tax advantage in Section 129 of the Internal Revenue Code)
permits an exclusion from gross income for the value of employer-
provided child-care services. In addition, the legislation provides
for an increase in the credit available to taxpayers for dependent-

care expenses necessary to their employment and a new depreciation system for employers who improve facilities by creating on-site or nearby child care centers for employees' children. The tax-free status of the benefit and the increase in the dependent care tax credit (and thus the child care tax credit) have been most important in generating these new developments. The employee takes advantage of the child care tax credit at the time of filing the annual tax return. A special employer initiative is needed to establish one of several possible programs subsidizing employee child care in a tax-free fashion.

A second incentive or device created as a result of changes in the Internal Revenue Code (IRC) is the development of various flexible compensation plans, including flexible benefit plans and flexible spending plans. Section 401 (k) of the IRC permits employers to establish deferred compensation arrangements with their employees. Through such arrangements employers, with the agreement of their employees, can reduce an employee's salary and place these pretax dollars into an account that can be used to pay for various services such as group legal services, extra health insurance, dental or vision care—or child care services. Some employers may even contribute to their employees' "flexible spending account," but by and large it is the employee who contributes through a salary reduction plan established by his or her employer.[34]

Thus, federal tax policy has created a strong impetus for employers to provide a child care subsidy as a tax-free fringe benefit to their employees and at no or low cost to themselves. And parents, employed in firms offering a generous fringe benefit package, have a strong reason to encourage their employers to establish such a benefit. The employee benefits, the employer incurs very little costs, and the benefit is paid for out of the public purse. It is worth noting that this is one of the two forms of employer-supported child care that have grown most.

The new ceilings on employee contributions and the lower tax rates enacted in 1986 could very well decrease the potential impacts of these measures.

Employers and Child Care: Toward the 1990s

The 1980s developments in employer-supported child care can be characterized by growing pressure by the Reagan administration, federal and state governments, and the media as well as child care advocates for employers to *do more* and by a continued search by employers for acceptable and inexpensive responses. Both the Reagan administration, with its goal of reducing federal social expenditures, and the child care advocates, with their goal of expanding the supply of affordable services, have played a major role in developing and selling alternative child care strategies to employers.

At the beginning of the decade, work-site child care services were viewed as the primary form employer support should take. By the second half of the decade, this model was viewed increasingly as acceptable only in special situations or under special circumstances but otherwise as only a minor form of employer support. Despite some growth in the numbers of such programs, the statistics show quite clearly that these programs constitute only a small part of the totality of employer activity in the child care arena, and a declining proportion over time. Indeed, a major change in the debate about employer-supported care is the growing disenchantment with on-site care. Most employees do not like it, and most employers will not support such programs because they are too expensive to establish, too risky to operate, too complicated to administer, and too likely to be underused.

The two most significant employer-sponsored child care developments are low-cost items and characterize large, generous firms primarily: providing child care information and referral services and establishing salary reduction plans that include a DCAP (a child care tax and spending benefit). I&R services became a more important and extensive development nationally in the 1980s largely in response to an expanding but increasingly diversified child care service delivery system. Child care agencies sought out employer financial support for these services, marketing them as both useful and inexpensive, and employers seized on this service because it is a cheap form of "image-building" and of announcing a policy of "family responsiveness." The services are certainly worthwhile, but one must not lose sight of the fact that they are of value only if there is an adequate supply of good quality, affordable care. Under those circumstances they can help parents find care and choose among different options. Except for recent modest family day care recruitment efforts, they do not, however, add to the supply of care available or help parents pay for care they cannot now afford.

Salary reduction plans may offer quite significant subsidies to employee-parents. A plan that permits employees to set aside up to $5000 a year in pretax dollars to pay for child care (decreased from $9000 by 1986 tax reform) can provide an important subsidy for an employee. But most employees are not covered by such plans, and most of those who are cannot put aside that much money for child care. Moreover, the employee whose income is subject under the new law to only 15 percent tax rate would be better off using the federal child care tax credit—and would not benefit from anything else nearly as much.

At best, the employers who are doing something to support child care services for their employees are a minuscule group among the six million employers in the United States. A recent survey by the administrative management society found that among 312 responding member companies, only 4 percent offer or sponsor child care programs for employees' children.[35] Only a limited number of employees can qualify for the salary reduction plans or other forms of employer sponsorship. The BLS survey of employee benefits in medium and large firms in 1985 found that only 1 percent of the workers in the firms surveyed were entitled to some form of child care subsidy as a fringe benefit.[36] And employees who leave their jobs—are let go, discharged, or just change jobs—would suffer the additional loss of child care aid also. Finally, at a time when employers are monitoring their benefit costs more carefully than ever before, it seems highly unrealistic to expect them to add a significant new benefit—and a new benefit cost—on to their already expensive benefit packages.

Given the current stress on employers, however, one question that remains is, What role can employers play that could address some of the pressing child care issues? One response is that employers could play an informed, "good citizen" role, taking positions on federal and state legislation, encouraging greater public support for child care, and taking the financial burden off the individual employee. Another approach is to follow the model of the new initiative launched in 1985 by the Bank of America Foundation, whereby employers, private foundations and public agencies joined together in funding a series of pilot projects established and operated by the California Statewide Network of Resource and Referral Services to expand the supply of family day care homes, especially for infants and toddlers (see Chapter 3). Here is an appropriate and socially responsible role for employers concerned about child care, going beyond a focus on the individual firm and that firm's employees.

A 1985 survey prepared for New York City's Human Resources Administration, Agency for Child Development, found that employers overwhelmingly report themselves as unlikely to offer benefits designed to meet their employees' child care needs, and that even among the very small group (10 percent) of employers who said they might consider doing something, by a 3 to 1 margin they responded that if they did anything it would be to provide information about child care rather than financial assistance (while employees, by a 2 to 1 margin, wanted financial assistance).[37]

Repeatedly, in interviews with employers and in the testimony of those trying to encourage greater employer involvement, the findings are similar. The theme is the same. Employers do not want to get into the business of child care. They do not want to increase their benefit costs. And they certainly will not establish a "special" expensive benefit for employee parents. They recognize the changes that have occurred in the society and in their work force. They know that more women are working and they sympathize with their problems. The costs of paying for child care may be high, but the burden is not the employer's—at least until the parents of young children become a much larger part of the work force than the 20 percent they now are or unless government mandates employers to do more.[38] Employers will do "something" if the costs are modest. Otherwise, they may begin to recognize that they will be better off if the costs of providing child care are shared and responsibility for funding and for operating programs becomes a community or societal responsibility, not just a parental responsibility and not just a responsibility for some employers.[39]

Endnotes

1. Kathryn Senn Perry, "Child Care Centers Sponsored by Employers and Labor Unions in the United States" (Washington, D.C.: Women's Bureau, Department of Labor, 1980).
2. *Personnel*, November–December 1980, p. 45; see also, *Community Focus*, the United Way Magazine, February 1981, p. 3.
3. See, for example, Dana Friedman, "How Are We Really Doing?" *Working Woman*, November 1984; U.S. Department of Labor, Women's Bureau, *Employers and Child Care: Establishing Services through the Workplace* (Washington, D.C.: U.S. Department of Labor, 1981).
4. Stuart D. Brandes, *American Welfare Capitalism*, 1880–1940 (Chicago, Ill.: University of Chicago Press, 1976), p. 53.
5. Susan Stein, "The Company Cares for Children," in Pamela Roby, ed., *Child Care Who Cares?* (New York: Basic Books, 1973), pp. 245–261.
6. Ibid., p. 260.
7. Howard Hayghe, "Rise in Mothers' Labor Force Activity Includes Those with Infants," *Monthly Labor Review*, Vol. 109, No. 2 (February 1986), 43–45.
8. Data provided by Eleanor Brilliant from her current study of United Way.
9. Sheila B. Kamerman, *Parenting in an Unresponsive Society: Managing Work and Family Life* (New York: Free Press, 1980); Sheila B. Kamerman and Paul W. Kingston, "Employers' Responses to the Family Responsibilities of

Employees," in Sheila B. Kamerman and Cheryl Hayes, eds., *Families That Work: Children in a Changing World* (Washington, D.C.: National Academy Press, 1983).

10. Roberta L. Bergman, Executive Director, Child Care Dallas, Testimony, in U.S. House of Representatives, Select Committee on Children, Youth and Families, *Child Care: Exploring Private and Public Sector Approaches* (Washington, D.C.: Government Printing Office, 1984), p. 4.

11. Ibid.

12. "Corporate Child Development Fund for Texas, Austin, Texas," in *The Child Care Handbook* (Washington, D.C.: The Children's Defense Fund, 1982).

13. Perry, "Child Care Centers."

14. Sandra L. Burud, Raymond C. Collins, and Patricia Divine-Hawkins, "Employer-Supported Child Care: Everybody Benefits," *Children Today,* Vol. 12, No. 3 (May–June 1983); National Employer-Supported Child Care Project, *Child Care Programs in the U.S. 1981–1982,* (Pasadena, Calif.: National Employer-Supported Child Care Project, 1982). A 1983 survey of a selected group of 80 major employers in New York City found that three hospitals had on-site or nearby child care centers, five employers had some form of flexible spending or benefit plans that included child care, five provided information and referral services, and six had offered some kind of parent education seminar. This is not a discrete count of employers; in some cases the same employer provided a child care benefit, information and referral service, and parenting seminars. See Kristin Anderson, *Corporate Initiatives for Working Parents in New York City: A 10 Industry Review* (New York: Center for Public Advocacy Research, 1983).

15. Bureau of National Affairs, *Employers and Child Care: Development of a New National Benefit,* A BNA Special Report (Washington, D.C.: Bureau of National Affairs, 1984). Dr. Dana Friedman is quoted by the *New York Times* (May 16, 1985) as stating that 1800 employers were "sponsoring" child care services. In early 1986 Conference Board press releases, she cited expansion to 2500 employers and, then, 3000.

16. For some descriptions of these, see Clifford Baden and Dana Friedman, eds., *New Management Initiatives for Working Parents* (Boston: Wheelock College, 1981); Dana E. Friedman, *Encouraging Employer Supports to Working Parents: Community Strategies for Change* (New York: Center for Public Advocacy Research, 1983); "Employers May Find It Easier to Help Working Parents with Child Care," *World of Work Report,* Vol. 7, Number 9 (September 1983); and Sheila B. Kamerman, "Employers Sponsor Child Care Services," Vol. 8, Number 11, (November 1983); Bureau of National Affairs, *Employers and Child Care: Development of a New Employee Benefit.*

17. Dana Friedman, "Is Business Good for Child Care? The Implications of Employer Support," *Child Care Information Exchange,* No. 47, January, 1986, pp. 9–13 (Table, p. 11). To underscore the softness of current data on these employer-supported/sponsored child care services, we note that nowhere is there a list of the employers referred to. Furthermore, there may be a significant amount of overlap across categories, since some employers are counted as having a near-site program as well as having a contract with an independent provider and most who provide information and referral ser-

vices also have held parenting seminars. See also, Friedman, "Child Care for Employees' Kids," *Harvard Business Review*, Vol. 86, No. 2 (March–April 1986), 28–34.

18. "AT&T: Two Experimental Day Care Centers That Closed," *World of Work Report*, Vol. 2, Number 2 (February 1977), 16.

19. Burud et al., "Employer-Sponsored Child Care: Everybody Benefits."

20. Friedman, *Encouraging Employer Support to Working Parents*.

21. Friedman, "Is Business Good for Child Care?" see endnote 17.

22. In 1969, the Taft-Hartley Law was amended to permit unions to include child care as a bargainable item when negotiating contracts.

23. Sheila B. Kamerman and Alfred J. Kahn, *Child Care, Family Benefits and Working Parents* (New York: Columbia University Press, 1981).

24. Baden and Friedman, *New Management Initiatives*.

25. "TV Stations Join Forces to Provide Day Care," *New York Times*, January 12, 1980.

26. BNA, *Employers and Child Care*.

27. Ibid., p. 28.

28. The Ford Foundation has a special brochure describing the company's plan; the Polaroid plan is described in Baden and Friedman, *New Management Initiatives*, and by Joann S. Lublin, "The New Interest in Corporate Day-Care," *The Wall Street Journal*, April 20, 1981.

29. Catalyst, *Child Care Information Service: An Option for Employer Support of Child Care* (New York: Catalyst, 1983); Baden and Friedman, *New Management Initiatives*; Friedman, *Encouraging Employer Supports to Working Parents*; Press release, Work/Family Direction, Boston, Mass, 1984.

30. See Baden and Friedman, *New Management Initiatives*; see also, Lublin, "The New Interest in Corporate Day Care."

31. Jacqueline S. Anderson, "Who's Minding the Sick Children?" *Children Today*, Vol. 13, No. 1 (January, February 1984), 2–5.

32. "Montgomery to Let Employees Set Aside Pay for Day Care," *Washington Post*, July 14, 1983.

33. For additional details, see Dana Friedman, *Corporate Financial Assistance for Child Care* (New York: The Conference Board, Research Bulletin); EBRI, *Fundamentals of Employee Benefit Programs* (Washington, D.C.: Employee Benefit Research Institute, 1985).

34. Ibid.

35. *World of Work Report* (Elmsford, N.Y.: Pergamon Press, 1986).

36. U.S. Department of Labor Bureau of Labor Statistics, *Employee Benefits in Medium and Large Firms, 1985* (Washington, D.C.: BLS, 1986), p. 81.

37. Stephen Leeds et al., *A Survey to Assess the Potential for Employer-Supported Child Care Services in New York City* (New York: Lieberman Research, 1985).

38. Moreover, although almost 25 percent of the work force has preschool-age children, estimates of the percentage of employees in large firms who might utilize employer-sponsored child care services remain low. Thus, one estimate suggests that in the average work force of a large company less than 10 percent of employees will use a child care program at any given time. Other data report fewer than 4 percent. See BNA, *Employers and Child Care*.

39. For a more extensive discussion of the appropriate roles of employers and government in responding to the personal and familial needs of employees, see Sheila B. Kamerman and Alfred J. Kahn, *The Responsive Workplace: Employers and A Changing Labor Force* (New York: Columbia University Press, forthcoming).

Chapter 7

FAMILY DAY CARE AND THE FUTURE CHILD CARE PROGRAM MIX

Nobody pretends to have an exact number, but all concerned are agreed that family day care homes are a significant part of the child care supply in the United States. Nobody could possibly claim an accurate picture of family day care providers—since most operate in the underground economy—yet there is consensus as to sufficient diversity to feed both enthusiasms and anxieties about the quality of this important resource. Public officials are counting on an even more important role for family day care as the child care demand accelerates, yet some analysts urge caution—for a diversity of contradictory reasons.

What is the picture? Why the interest, support, enthusiasm—and why the doubts? How should family day care be regarded in the future child care policy and program mix? Is it possible to make informed choices?

An Overview

At the most fundamental level, champions of family day care see it as the form of substitute care most akin to care by a parent: a "motherlike" person caring for the child in her own home, if not in the child's home. This view is counterposed to the impersonal institutional nursery with a line of cribs and unattended, crying babies. Who could question the attractiveness of such a service?

The informed realize at once that much family day care is not and could not be quite like the former view, but many nonetheless argue its indispensability and attractiveness as a public policy vehicle on several grounds. First, family day care is the largest current supply for infants and toddlers. Second, it is cheaper than licensed group programs. Third, it is quite elastic, capable of rapid start-up in response to demand, involving little capital investment, no construction of buildings, little administrative complexity. Finally, proponents refer, as suggested above, to alleged parental choice or preference. Family day care is what parents select when and if they have the opportunity to do so.

The Numbers

No one fully satisfactory source on the numbers of family day care is available, but several components suggest the range. Recall that in the United States about 10 million children under age 6 have mothers in the labor force (Chapter 1). In its 1977–1978 National Day Care Home Study,[1] the Department of Health and Human Services estimated that 1.8 million unregulated providers and 115,000 licensed/regulated providers gave care to 5 million children. Some 23 percent of these children were school age and cared for before or after school. Adams, reporting on an early 1982 telephone survey of all states and territories, found 137,865 licensed, registered, approved/certified family day care homes.[2] These or similar numbers recur in congressional testimony and the literature today: 1.5 to 2 million providers caring for 5 million children, mostly in unregulated care. The unregulated care is variously estimated over the past decade as constituting between 60 and 90 percent of the supply.

These numbers are consistent with the last large consumer survey of the subject (the UNCO study), which reported that in 1975 some 1.3 million family day care homes served 3.4 million children full time (30 or more hours a week) and 2.8 million from 10 to 29 hours a week. The children in family day care constituted 45 percent of all children in care.[3] (We omit the casual babysitting and brief care for many other children for less than 10 hours weekly, also reported by UNCO.) However, 25 percent of all children in care were in the care of relatives, and 20 percent were in family day care with strangers. Since the age range reported is 0 to 14, we estimate that there were at least 4.6 million preschoolers in the group (assuming that one-quarter are school age children in part-day care).

What current judgment may be made about the numbers? The decade since the UNCO study has seen an explosion of labor force entry and continuation for mothers of infants and toddlers— historically the family day care constituency. As already noted

(Chapter 1), available reports of numbers of children in different modes of care are somewhat flawed. Nonetheless, it is here relevant that whereas in the 1977 National Day Care Home Study there were reports of 115,000 licensed family day care homes, Hofferth and Phillips report state licensing officer listings of 167,680 licensed homes in 1985.[4] Assuming the reasonableness of calculations that the unlicensed and unregistered supply is 60 to 90 percent of the total, this yields a supply estimate of between 419,200 and 1,167,680 homes.

Obviously, this supports a wide range of estimates of the numbers of children in family day care. The 1977–1978 study, which may or may not still be relevant, reported a mean of 3.5 children per home and a median of 3.0 children. If one applies the 3.5 figure to the provider estimates, the national total would range from 1.5 to 4.0 million children, including school-aged children, in family day care. If the average is above 3.5, the total of 5.0 million, a widely used estimate, could be correct.

We have attempted our own estimates of children of working mothers in family day care using the National Survey of Family Growth (NSFG) findings on the percentage in family day care of all children in nonparent care, their best estimates of the full-time and part-time working mother percentages for each age group, and the very uncertain extrapolations of the percentages of children still in parental care while going to school. The results must inevitably be read as rough approximations and await an updated consumer survey for improvement. They do nonetheless fall within the parameters already found in the preceding supply estimates and provide "ballpark" figures for current discussion of children of working mothers in family day care:

Age Category of Children in Family Day Care	Total No. in U.S.
Under 3	1,270,000
3 and 4	1,054,080
5	277,000
6 to 13	2,500,000
Total	5,101,080

We have no basis for family day care estimates for children of nonworking mothers but do note that most current supply estimates are exhausted by the reported usage by children of working mothers. Age breakdown and survey differences are shown in Table 7.1, which is constructed from the Hofferth-Phillips data.

Table 7.1   The Role of Family Day Care as Seen in Two Surveys[a]

| | 1982 Current Population Survey[b] | | 1985 National Survey of Family Growth[c] |
	% of Children not in parent care or self-care	% of all children in care	% of children not in parent care or self-care
All Employed Mothers			
Child Age			
Under 1	33.6	23.0	40.4
1–2	34.9	25.2	37.6
3–4	23.1	17.3	
3–5			26.9
6–8			35.2
9–12			25.8
Total	30.7	22.0	31.9
Mother Employed Full-Time			
Child Age			
Under 1	37.2	28.0	44.4
1–2	34.9	27.2	45.3
3–4	21.9	17.7	
3–5			28.0
6–8			35.9
9–12			25.3
Total	35.6	24.1	34.8
Mother Employed Part-Time			
Child Age			
Under 1	25.3	14.1	26.4
1–2	35.0	22.0	24.4
3–4	26.6	16.5	
3–5			25.0
6–8			30.3
9–12			32.9
Total	32.2	18.4	26.7

SOURCE: Hofferth and Phillips, "Working Mothers and the Care of Their Children," forthcoming.

[a]Percentage of children who are not in care of parent or in self-care while mother is working, and are reported to be in family day care.

[b]The CPS survey has several limitations: It took place in June when school was out in many places and when arrangements are therefore not representative of the year. It asked only about care arrangements for the youngest child under age 5. It distributed its 8.6 "not ascertained" responses proportionately among the care categories. See Martin O'Connell and Carolyn C. Rogers, *Child Care Arrangements of Working Mothers: June 1982*, constituting U.S. Bureau of the Census, Current Population Reports, Series P-23, No. 129 (Washington, D.C.: U.S. Government Printing Office, 1983). Discussed in Hofferth and Phillips; see endnote 4.

[c]National Survey of Family Growth (NSFG), as analyzed by Hofferth and Phillips. Only 1 percent "not ascertained." Questions asked about *each* child in household. Whereas CPS (above) carefully distinguished primary and secondary care forms, NSFG did not code most multiple arrangements.

Several observations are of interest. First, within the group using nonparent, nonrelative care while a mother works, the heaviest use (referring to rates, not totals) of family day care is—as expected—for infants and toddlers. Here the CPS and NSFG are in agreement. According to CPS findings, of the children under age 1 in nonrelative care, 66 percent are in family day care (the NSFG figure is 67 percent); for the 1–2 age group, the CPS proportion is 59 percent (and for the NSFG 60 percent). For preschoolers, however, the *overall* proportion in group programs (see Chapter 1) is greater than that in family day care, except that children of mothers working part-time are slightly more likely to be in family day care. Further, family day care dominates for those school-aged children in before- and after-school care. These data are offered not as a count adequate for administrative purposes but to suggest the reason for current attention to family day care in almost all city and state discussions.

Some further explanation is in order, however. In the most intensive look available, the National Family Day Care Home Study found that of the care in use in three major cities, some 94 percent of providers operated informally and independently; another 3 percent were independent and licensed or registered, meeting state or federal standards; and another 3 percent were regulated and part of day care systems or networks, under the auspices of sponsoring agencies.[5] Although the distributions of family day care providers among these categories vary by location and over time, since there has been considerable effort in recent years to register providers (rather than to license them) and to organize them into systems, there is consensus still that the vast majority are unregulated. On the other hand, over 94 percent of this care is also monetized. These, in short, are formal—but largely invisible and unprotected—transactions in a major mode of care that affects many children. Small wonder that many people see this service as an important resource not to be invaded by the strong arms of government, whereas others sound an alarm to action.

Costs

Currently, federal, state, and local officials and advocates have displayed much interest in family day care as a most economical way to increase supply. This line of discussion is best buttressed with reference to the payment rates for unregulated care, as seen in the 1980 data in Table 7.2, taken from the National Day Care Home Study. That study found a very considerable tendency for

Table 7.2   Comparative Fees and Hourly Wages for Family Day Care Type

	Mean Hourly Fee Per Child[a]	Mean Weekly Fee Per Child[b]	Mean Net Hourly Wage[c]
Sponsored Care	$0.70	$26.36	$1.92
Regulated Care	0.63	22.65	1.39
Unregulated Care	0.54	17.80	0.85
Weighted Average	0.59	20.85	1.25

SOURCE: National Day Care Home Study (1980 data), pp. 96, 97, 98.
[a]Includes children cared for without charge.
[b]Does not include children cared for without charge.
[c]Net income after expenses deducted: some items incomplete.
NOTE: These are obsolete data, used only to compare prices by regulation status.

state and local officials to use group and center care rather than family day care. Since the 1970s, as noted earlier, the concentration has been on the 3- to 5-year-olds among subsidized children, and thus on centers. (More recently, we have noted, schools have received increasing attention.) Moreover, since family day care is largely not system organized, dealing with such providers has not been easy even when they were sought. Thus family day care as a field has been less subsidized out of public social services funds than has center care and reflects market fees somewhat more. In a sense, unsubsidized low-earner mothers could not afford to pay good salaries to the women caring for their children.

Table 7.2 should be examined not as a source of current cost data but to note the alleged cost "advantages" of unregulated care. As used in Table 7.2, regulated care is family day care that is licensed, registered, or certified in some way but operating independently. The sponsored care is in some way tied to a network of homes or a system related to a public or private administrative agency. Most or perhaps all children in sponsored family day care homes have their care partially or completely subsidized out of public funds and the child care food program.

The unregulated care has a considerable cost advantage over center day care, whereas regulated care has some significant advantage. When one compares sponsored and regulated care with center care, the differences become modest. Centers involve greater capital costs initially, of course. But if centers and family day care are sponsored by nonprofit or public agencies, "the differences are not great." The major differences are in caregiver earnings.

We have reproduced in the chapter appendix reimbursement rate data for 1985, assembled in a Children's Defense Fund telephone survey, which helps explain the continuing cost attraction of family day care in many states to the parent who must pay the fee partially or unaided and to the public official concerned with budgets. Recall that for some states these fee levels may omit in both categories the higher-cost providers who do not accept public referrals or payments, since they exceed them, as well as the underground family day care providers who, in some instances at least, charge considerably less than state reimbursement rates— and in other instances charge more.

In recent years in many discussions of the needed increase in the child care supply, one could hear a double-barreled theme: Family day care is most like mother care and therefore desirable; family day care is least expensive and therefore the best arena for expansion. The current validity of such analysis will be explored subsequently; the potency of the claims is seen in the efforts everywhere to incorporate more family day care providers in local I&R rosters, to make such programs available to parents eligible under vendor/voucher systems, to encourage family day care providers to "surface" from the "underground" by substituting registration for licensing on a state level and by simplifying all forms of regulation. Moreover, as will be seen, efforts have been made to increase the attraction of system or network membership.

As state after state has established task forces or blue ribbon panels to plan for child care, they also have made the point about the elasticity of family day care. If the governor or legislature increases subsidy or sliding-fee funds, the eligible parents may be accepted quickly and providers will be found. If funds are cut, nobody has a large capital investment, a contract, a commitment to a work force.

Preferences?

The assumptions about preferences clearly are part of the case for concentrating on family day care. As indicated, the case for family day care seems obvious at first consideration but erodes soon thereafter. It does not take a parent very long to know that the typical day care home is not really an extension of one's own home. As we carried out our field work, we heard again and again of a large turnover annually in the family day care provider supply and of a large percentage of parents who shifted their arrangements annually, on average, out of dissatisfaction or a perception that the child's needs were changing. A center can, in a sense, offer a group of teachers and a repertoire of experiences, changing as a child grows, where a family day care mother is only one inflexible

program, either meeting needs splendidly or not meeting a particular child's needs at all.

In connection with an earlier work we reviewed the systematic
preference research in the United States and found that it did not
generally support some of the claims of family day care champions.
Some authors argue that what people use should be interpreted as
displaying their "preferences," but they ignore issues of access or
affordability. This argument would make inexpensive, unlicensed,
underground care the most attractive as well. The reality is that
preference responses in a developing field such as this, where
information is often limited, seem to reflect what is known and
experienced (unless the survey itself completely structures the
perceptions). The most complete U.S. survey suggests that parents
prefer the care mode they are currently using: Parents respond
that they are satisfied with the care their children have. However,
significant numbers of parents would prefer a change for their
children, from family day care with nonrelatives to group care (or
care in one's own home). Rarely do parents of children in centers
want a shift to family day care.[6] This may, of course, be a function
of a child's development: By the time the parent begins to think
about change, a group may be considered. Certainly, most of the
parents in the current day care market seek out and use a family
day care home for infants and toddlers either because they prefer
this type of care, it is all they can find, or it is what they can afford.

All recent analyses call attention to the increased parental
interest in group experience for their children by age 2½, or even
2. One assumes that this trend may reflect the smaller families,
leading parents—seeing advantages in a center organized around
group activities conducted by personnel trained to lead such
activities ("teachers")—to seek socialization experience for their
children who have no brothers or sisters. Parents are affected as
well by the increased understanding in the society that children
begin to learn while very young and that centers more often are
organized for learning than are family day care homes. Caught by
the competitive environment and the desire to ensure opportunities for their children, many put these two considerations together,
the desire for a good socialization experience and an early start on
"learning," and they look toward transfer to a center as their
children approach 2½ or 3. It does not necessarily mean that they
regret the initial use of family day care or are dissatisfied. Some, at
least, are responding to a child's development. The at-home
mother with an at-home child also may be thinking of a nursery
school for a child of that age. We also have encountered many
working-class minority parents who have heard the lessons of Head

Start and want to ensure their children access to essential opportunity.

Nonetheless, all this said, many or most parents cannot conceive of placing infants in centers, and some feel the same way about toddlers. Indeed, such sentiments are part of recent discussion about the importance of maternity, parenting, or infant-care leaves, which allow a parent to be home and to defer the use of out-of-home care for some months. Until recently, the conventional wisdom in the social welfare and child development fields was that if it was truly impossible for a child to be home with a mother, the "foster" family day care was the desired alternative. This view remains strong in both personal preferences and some agency policy preference structures. Family day care retains strong support.

The Policy Environment

All of these elements have had their impact. Family day care is where the numbers are. It is believed to be the economical and elastic child care supply and to reflect parental preferences. It suits the priorities of those who would like developments to be as localized, community-based, and informal as possible. As we have seen, and understandably, family day care has been the center of intense interest and activity. New York voted a fund to seek ways to stimulate provider development in 1985. California found that its alternative payments (vendor-voucher) program moved public policy from a heavy reliance on centers to family day care, as it served infants and toddlers. Several corporate contracts with local R&R agencies in several states involve commitments to provide and guarantee a supply of high-quality family day care. In the leadership states, efforts are made increasingly to find incentives for family day care mothers to be better trained and to include them in training. Everywhere there is evidence that some providers are becoming more like small businesspeople or semi-professionals and less like mothers' helpers. Family day care has begun to organize. What, then, is the overview? What is family day care like, beyond the numbers?

Family Day Care as Care

A sophisticated family day care advocate and former provider captures both the burdens and contributions of the role, as well as some of the attractions to parents:[7]

There are many dimensions to the service of family day care. They include flexibility of times that family day care is available; the willingness of family day care providers to serve lunch twice every day when they agree to care for two kindergarten children, one who attends morning kindergarten and one who attends afternoon kindergarten; and providing care for the child who comes early in the morning, eats breakfast, goes to school and returns after the school day, has a snack and is supervised during the remainder of the afternoon until the parents arrive back from work. Additionally, that provider cares for that school-age child full-time on any school holidays and in Minnesota on any snow days, plus often cares for that child during the summer when full-time care is again required. Many providers do the basic toilet training for children when they are ready. Providers tell me they also train the parents. They provide the opportunity for learning various skills that are appropriate for the ages of the children, i.e. large and small motor, cognitive, conceptual, language. Many providers work with children who have learning disabilities. Many providers give basic parenting education to first-time parents who do not have another support group such as extended family members to help them in the very important job of parenting.

Because a larger proportion of day care centers and nursery schools than of family day care homes is licensed, regulated, or publicly subsidized, more is known about the experiences of children in group care than in family day care. Also, group situations involving a number of adults more readily absorb observers, researchers, and even one-way mirrors than do family day care homes. Further, the arrival of a consultant, inspector, specialist, or even of a parent at a family day care home with one adult and three to six children present inevitably changes things enough so that one is not quite sure what the picture may be when no visitors are present. Not surprisingly, the small- and large-scale research that reports center and nursery school practice and process is not matched in the family day care field. Available micro studies almost without exception do not lend themselves to program generalizations, however useful clinicians and practitioners may find them to be.

The National Day Care Home Study is an exception.[8] Intensive study of 793 homes (143 sponsored, 298 regulated, 352 unregulated; caregivers 46.2 percent white, 32.7 percent black, 25.9 percent Hispanic) with a mean enrollment of 3.5 children and a median of 3.0 per home in Los Angeles, Philadelphia, and San Antonio provided information about providers, group composition, the parents who make use of family day care, and most important, ultimately, what occurs during the care day. We already have reported on fee and earnings data from this study in Table 7.2.

In addition to collecting descriptive information, the researchers were able to observe a sample of caregivers and children in both spontaneous and standardized interactions. Although a variety of sampling and methodological difficulties were present, the consensus in the policy and professional community was that this was a creative and highly competent study whose results could be accepted in the codification of family day care standards by the federal government in 1981. (As we report elsewhere, the standards were never implemented because late-1981 legislation converted Title XX to the Social Services Block Grant, dropping all federal day care requirements.) While confident detailed generalization to the entire country and to 1986 is not justified, this is the best available quantitative analysis by child development experts of family day care as a living, operating system, useful for our purposes.

Caretakers

The caretakers in this and several less ambitious studies are classifiable into three groups:

1. Young mothers in their late 20s and 30s with their own children at home.
2. Women in their 40s and 50s with at least one child of a relative (often a grandchild) in the care group.
3. Women who range from the 30s to the 50s in age and who are not caring for the child of a relative (having remained in the work after belonging to one of the earlier categories or, we would add, having decided to enter into this activity as a "business" or "career").[9]

The caretakers are a diverse group, described as "young and old, married and single, rich and poor." They talk both about being motivated by love of children and interest in the money to be earned. As a group, three-quarters describe family day care as a permanent role for themselves, yet for half of the unregulated caregivers it is clearly a short-term activity. The young mothers at home with their own child are overwhelmingly white and the youngest subgroup, barely over 30 on average, compared to a median age of about 42 for the total group. These white mothers are serving as family day care providers because their own children are young and they want to be at home with them. They are a relatively higher income group than the others—although almost all are low income by general standards.

Black and Hispanic caregivers are relatively older, many caring for a child of a relative, often a grandchild, and then adding others. The fees earned are proportionately more significant for the income of these latter households. Nonetheless, overall, over half of the caregivers have at least one relative's child in care, often beginning this way; this is especially true among the unregulated

Despite considerable variability, the "mean" level of education is a bit over 11 years—not quite high school graduation. Black caretakers are at the mean, Hispanics two years below, and whites almost a year above. There are a good number of high school graduates (57 percent of the total) and some college course-takers, but few college graduates. Small percentages have had day care center or preschool-elementary school experience. Fully one-quarter of the interviewed group had less than a year's experience, but half formerly had been day care providers from one to seven years and a quarter for even longer. Follow-up a year after initial contact showed that one-quarter were no longer providing any child care. About 80 percent of sponsored and regulated providers of family day care in the study sample could be found, but only two-thirds of the unregulated.

Children

The children were found to belong to three groups. Some entered care between birth and six months. These children were most often with a relative and remained in care longest. Another group entered care between 6 and 12 months of age. Of those in the third group, entering family day care after age one, half were gone in less than two years.

We have mentioned that the median home had three children. Hispanic homes had fewer. Sponsored homes had more children (4.3) than regulated homes (4.0); unregulated homes had 2.8 children on average. But these trends did not hold in all cities. The average home had .6 resident children and .5 nonresident related children; but here, too, there were city variations, and the vast majority of nonresident related children were in unregulated homes.

If centers are dominated by preschoolers (age 3 to 5), family day care homes are dominated by toddlers (32 percent) but have as many infants (23 percent) as preschoolers (22 percent), with about one-quarter school-aged children coming before and after school. Some are one-age group homes (31 percent of all), some two-age group (39 percent), and the remainder have three or four age combinations (29.9 percent).

Parents

The parents of these children often live close to the caregivers. Black and Hispanic parents are of economic backgrounds similar to those of their counterparts elsewhere, but the whites are below average in that respect, living in lower-income areas than do median whites. Nonetheless, they constitute the highest income users of family day care. While the distribution is broad, the parents concentrate in lower-status occupations as well. Forty percent of the parent-users are single; as the lowest-income parents, the single parents more often have their children in sponsored-subsidized care.

Experiences

The National Day Care Home Study offers a picture of the daily experience of children through the eyes of experienced observers. Our objective here is to convey a picture of activity and of what is offered to children. We therefore reproduced as our Table 7.3 a rich NDCHS summary table.

Obviously, much of this conceptualization of activity comes from sophisticated child development experts. One is impressed with similarities but also with the more frequent occurrence of "teaching behaviors" in the sponsored homes, making them, in the words of the researchers, "more suggestive of a preschool environment." Also of interest is the fact that direct involvement with the children ranges from 42 to 50 percent of the care-day in claims on the caretaker's time, increasing from the unregulated, to the regulated, to the sponsored home. Housekeeping, conversation with the adults, and relaxation time add up to a considerable portion of the day, most of all in unregulated homes, and there also is time for task-related supervisory and preparatory activity. Nonetheless, family day care providers, in the researchers' view, "spend nearly two-thirds of their days in child-related activities" even if the unregulated caregiver and untrained personnel generally are more likely than the others to be focused on the household's—rather than the children's—needs.

Of much interest to those who were at the time trying to define basic criteria for quality, as part of a federal regulations system, the NDCHS found that both group size and age mix needed to be considered in achieving a reasonable burden for the provider,

Table 7.3   Distribution of the Caregiver's Time by Regulatory Status

	Sponsored	Regulated	Unregulated
Direct Involvement with Children			
Interaction with one- to five-year-olds:			
Teach	17.0	12.8	12.1
Play/participate	8.6	7.3	7.3
Help	9.3	9.5	8.2
Direct	3.9	3.8	3.8
Converse	3.4	3.3	3.0
Control	3.6	3.8	3.5
Subtotal	45.8	40.5	32.9
Interaction with baby	3.4	5.3	2.5
Interaction with school-aged Children	0.8	0.7	0.9
Negative emotional affect	0.2	0.2	0.4
Total Direct Involvement	50.2	46.7	41.7
Indirect Involvement with Children			
Supervise/prepare	18.4	17.2	14.2
Noninvolvement with Children			
Converse	5.5	5.8	6.8
Recreation alone	4.8	5.7	13.0
Housekeeping	17.9	17.8	22.0
Out of range	1.7	1.4	1.2
Subtotal	29.9	30.7	43.0
Total[a]	98.5	94.6	98.9
Activities Facilitated:			
Language/information	10.6	8.4	7.8
Structured fine motor	6.1	3.1	3.5
Work	1.4	1.3	1.3
Physical needs	8.2	8.9	8.1
Dramatic play	1.1	0.8	1.2
Music/dance	2.1	0.7	0.4
Television	1.8	2.6	2.0
Exploratory fine motor	1.2	1.0	0.9
Gross motor	2.2	1.8	1.5
Total facilitation	34.7	28.6	26.7
Positive Affect	6.0	5.6	4.6

SOURCE: National Day Care Home Study, Vol. I, *Family Day Care in The United States: Summary of Findings* (Washington, D.C.: U.S. Department of Health and Human Services, 1981), p. 81.
[a]Observation of helpers, averaging 2.2% overall, were deleted from the analysis. This accounts for total distribution of caregiver's time equaling less than 100%.

flexibility for the children, and a setting for the kinds of behaviors—responses deemed best for socialization, emotional development, and cognitive stimulation. A limit of approximately six children to a home, varying by age mix, was recommended as desirable. Review of the relationship between caretaker training, on the one hand, and caretaker behavior as well as child behaviors, on the other, led the researchers to encourage and support caretaker training and credentialing for child care. Since the issue was specialized yet modest training rather than formal education, the finding was considered one that might reasonably lead to serious policy responses in the form of courses, workshops, in-service training, perhaps even capped by credentialing.

Relevant to this present discussion is the summing up of observations by experts of the homes in all categories and of family day care providers of all types:[10]

> *In general, the observations showed family day care homes to be positive environments for children. It was observed that caregivers spend a considerable portion of their time in direct interaction with children, and the time spent with children seems to be appropriate to the needs of children of various ages. Caregivers rarely expressed any negative affect toward the children. The caregivers' homes were generally safe, home-like environments which were less structured and homogeneous with respect to children's ages than day care centers.*

Much earlier work by Emlen and a later 1970s study by Wattenberg are more circumscribed if consistent with the NDCHS.[11] Emlen has discussed the special family day care advantage as the creation of opportunities for provider-child provider-parent relationships. Wattenberg has highlighted the distinction between the "traditional" provider who is intuitive and sees no need for training and the "modernized" who seeks training and the opportunity for a professional role. There are "novices" with unstable commitments and "traditional" types, as well. More recently Abbot-Shim has begun to report on an Atlanta, Georgia, study, admittedly unrepresentative in a number of ways yet containing a descriptive overview of providers consistent with the NDCHS. Great variability in educational backgrounds of providers was reported, however, with some 32 percent in this group of self-selected respondents having completed two-year degrees and 11 percent holding college degrees.[12] It is not clear whether this variability reflects expansion of training for this field in the years since the NDCHS, a sampling difference, a regional difference, or some combination of these reasons.

Effects?

Of course, the more basic question frequently asked is: Beyond the description, the observations, the search for "process" considered desirable by child development experts, what of the specific effects of family day care—of all family day care and of particular modalities within the whole? Definitive answers are not at hand. Experimentally designed studies, random child assignment, and strong research controls have generally been beyond the scope of interested researchers and may continue to be. One cannot deliberately manipulate the environment for or withhold services from these young and very vulnerable subjects. In a seldom-matched effort in the 1970s Golden and his colleagues in New York found that infants placed either in family day care homes or in centers did as well as or better than home-reared children on intellectual, social, and emotional development measures. The differences between the two modes were minor and only suggestive, with group programs perhaps having some advantages with regard to enhancing intellectual performance and family programs perhaps doing more for social competence. But many of these findings could be specific to the particular New York programs.

Riley and Cochran question the value of more comparisons of family day care homes with centers, given the self-selectivity problems and the fact that such studies repeatedly show more similarities than differences in cognitive and social development of the children. In a recent comprehensive review of family day care research, Betsy Squibb of the Yale Bush Center argues that available family day care research is in "an embryonic stage" and "fraught with methodological weaknesses." Her summing up of work on social, emotional, and physical development suggests the need for studies in natural settings that specify programs being examined and children being studied.[13] One suspects that there cannot be one answer about day care or center care. Outcomes will vary with parents and their motivations, their relationships with their children, the age at which the child is placed, and the quality and particular characteristics of the care relationships.

Many parents affirm a very positive impact of family day care on children's development. Skeptics may respond with concern about occasional media stories of abuse, neglect, or horrible physical and safety conditions. Professionals in the field express concern about parents who never enter a provider's home from the time that they make a "care" arrangement by telephone. Any of this can be convincing, yet most family day care remains underground, not inspected or regulated. On balance, we conclude that family day care offers a considerable amount of needed care. It also would appear that when regulated, sponsored (or even visible), and related to its community family day care can be attractive, satisfactory to parents, and not harmful to children. For some there may be many more positive effects. The overall assessment will vary with the particular family and with parental and community objectives:

- Are we seeking to respond only to the historical goal of meeting a parent's need to obtain care for a child in a wholesome environment?
- Is the program also expected to demonstrate specific capacity to promote the child's cognitive and/or social development in specific, measurable ways, while avoiding endangerment?

Licensing, Regulation, and Philosophy

The state is responsible for family day care standard setting and standard enforcement, and the public has been ambivalent. The popular comments are on all sides of the debate: Why interfere if people want to leave their children with a neighbor? Why not ensure that children whose parents must leave them in care—and who cannot themselves report much about their experiences—are in healthy and safe environments? Must everything become professionalized and expensive and make work for government inspectors and bureaucrats? Will the public not act to protect infants and toddlers against ex-criminals, addicts, or perverts who may exploit or endanger them? Is it not difficult enough to get people to do this low-pay–low status work; do we need licensing or registration to drive people away; do we need to spend scarce public funds on inspectors when there is not enough money to help pay the fees of low-earner mothers who need care for their children?

The debate is an old one, but in the funding squeeze that began in 1982—with federal day care requirements eliminated—states with licensing laws considered and sometimes enacted less stringent or token registration alternatives. State licensing inspection staffs were dismantled or decreased in size so that a generally loose system became looser or nonexistent. Some jurisdictions gave up all requirements, and others, having geared up to comply with what were to have been new stringent federal standards, stopped in mid-stream. Moreover, as we have seen in the early chapters, many child care advocates in leading states such as California and New York have accepted a new ideology or rationale that says that the ideal pattern is financing by voucher and standard protection by parents as educated consumers. Many militant child care advocates who defended federal interagency day care requirements through the long legislative and regulatory battles of the 1970s made a similar switch. Thus the I&R agencies counsel parents and encourage families to read brochures and attend seminars on how to select child care. In the face of anxieties about child abuse, parents are urged to visit care facilities and homes frequently and not to enroll children in places that do not permit drop-ins. At the same time many of the I&R and advocacy agencies we have described—arguing that state monitoring has in any case been a mere token and that it is best to encourage new providers now and to make them visible—have lobbied for "experiments," with registration plus parent monitoring, or state monitoring based on visits only after there are complaints, or simplified registration. They also have encouraged or participated in the creation of new training opportunities for providers and urged better fee scales.

Georgia, with a virtually unenforceable licensing law, switched to registration as far as back as 1980, with monitoring based only on complaints. The switch to registration permitted Texas to increase its family day care home rosters by 200 a month, where previously only 15 or 20 were added to the licensed rolls monthly.[14]

Massachusetts is an exception. It switched to registration in 1974. Its recent major reform combined fee upgrading and training increases with enhanced capacity for the state agency responsible for licensing and monitoring. It chose to seek better-qualified, better-paid providers while strengthening state responsibility for actually ensuring compliance with requirements. No family day care licenses are currently issued without home inspection visits.

The national picture continues to change. Paralleling the state tendency to relax licensing laws is a new nationally supported initiative for mandatory criminal record checks for center staffs and family day care providers—a response to the abuse scares of the mid-1980s. Given the dismantling of the federal child care technical assistance, funding, planning, and reporting apparatus, an ongoing picture of licensing/registration that covers all variables is not possible. A comprehensive federally funded six-volume report covering 1981 is now in some ways out of date and does not report all dimensions of interest.[15] As of that review, six states did not regulate family day care at all and 29 had no experience requirements for family day care providers. Adams's 1982 report noted that many states were in transition. She found five states with no regulations except for publicly purchased care. Some 31 states, three territories, and the District of Columbia still required licensing, but some required it if even one child was in care, some for two, three, or four children, and five states only if as many as five or six children were in a family day care home. Many of these states were actually exploring registration. Eight states offered mandatory registration as an alternative, and three had voluntary registration. Three states had both options, varying with the funding mode.[16]

CDF's 1985 phone update does not identify the children to whom the prevalent forms of regulation of family day care apply. Some form of licensing is required or available in 27 states, varying by numbers of children in some places, and these states offer no alternatives. On the other hand, 13 states require or offer voluntary registration, again varying in some states by numbers of children or sources of funds. Four states combine the two modes in various ways for family day care, depending on either provider choice or funding source. In addition, six states have an approval or certification procedure if a provider will receive federal funds.[17] The informal consensus is that for the most part this does not constitute an accountability or monitoring network. However, there is no consensus, as indicated, that the absence of accountability or monitoring should be defined as a problem. Many call for an open market and educated consumers who have cash or vouchers.

Even if there were enforcement, the prevalent standards for health protection, safety, staff training, adult-child ratios, and group composition are so varied that family day care would continue to be many things. As noted in Table 2.1, of our five "leadership" states, only Massachusetts maintains a standard of a maximum of three children per caretaker for infant care. Florida's standard is 1.6. Currently, many states accept a 1.8 infant and/or toddler standard. Yet the proposed federal standard promulgated for 1981 and then dropped was (in homes with one caretaker) 1 to 3 for homes with all children under age 2, 1 to 5 for mixed ages but only two children under age 2, and 1 to 6 if all children were older. The National Association for the Education of Young Children is currently implementing (for centers) a research-based voluntary standard of 1 to 3 (in groups of six) and 1 to 4 (in groups of eight) for infants and toddlers.

In short, despite the NDCHS picture, which showed that regulation and sponsorship were associated with characteristics deemed desirable in family day care (Table 7.3), the concern with supply, costs, diversity, and parent initiative and use of markets rather than government administration, where possible, have converged to support deregulation. While the Reagan administration's ideological rationales have not been adopted in all states, there has been a joining of purpose by advocates from many different locations on the political spectrum—or a giving up on standards by those who see no way to finance them.

Family Day Care as Work

Much has already been said about providers, the types of people they are, differences among subgroups, the stability and turnover in their family day care roles, their backgrounds and neighborhoods, their very low hourly earnings in the late 1970s—especially in unregulated care—and the kinds of experiences they make available to children when things go well. The National Commission on Working Women adds yet another perspective, family day care as work.[18] How does family day care look as a job or as entrepreneurship in a cottage industry?

> *People sometimes call them babysitters, but most family day care providers resent what that word implies. Providers find that running a family day care home requires good health; a knowledge of children; an ability to communicate, organize activities, and keep records; a willingness to take on responsibility; and a great deal of patience and energy. Their days begin as early as 6:30 or 7:00 A.M. when parents drop off sleepy, and sometimes irritable, children at the provider's home.*
>
> *Throughout the day, the child care provider is called on to prepare special educational projects that require creative resourcefulness, read stories, comfort and cuddle youngsters in need of affection, settle arguments, prepare meals and snacks, change diapers, and supervise outdoor play and trips.*
>
> *The provider's work day usually ends 12 hours after it begins—at 6:30 or 7:00—when the last parent arrives to pick up her child.*

No national update of earnings levels has been available since the 1978 statistics cited earlier (net income of $50 to $62 weekly), but local surveys in 1984 found little relative improvement. Despite considerable variability, these caregivers would appear to be below-minimum-wage earners caring for the children of other low earners. Even the lack of taxation on these earnings (they are so advised by some sponsoring agencies) does not make the weekly net competitive with even low-pay salaries. As self-employed people they often undertake for themselves what employers could not do by way of exploitation!

Those for whom this income supplements a spouse's earnings and justifies deductions of home costs as a business expense may find this satisfactory. The many single mothers in the group (20 percent of the whites and Hispanics and half the blacks at the time of the NDCHS) are living at the margins. Most have no right to sick leave, paid vacation, retirement or pension income, or (if injured) to workers' compensation.

Clearly, the National Commission on Working Women notes, people do this work despite its physical requirements, isolation from adults during the day, and low monetary returns for a variety of reasons: to be able to provide care for their own children, to earn core or supplementary household income, because they find care of developing children and ties to their parents to be appealing. Some are attracted by the autonomy involved, others by a sense of community service. Still others, we would add, have identified themselves with an emerging semiprofession. On balance, however, the result is instability in this occupational group. There is a solid, continuing core but many family day care providers enter and leave the field each year, so that constant recruitment is necessary. For children, this means frequent shifts unless or until they "graduate" to a group program.

Why Remain Underground?

Recruitment, monitoring, and upgrading would all be easier if family day care were everywhere identifiable. Yet the bulk of it remains in the grey or black market. Family day care is "underground" in many types of locations, yet is often quite visible to neighbors. A few children are dropped off daily at the very small home in a poor working class district. Others are left with a caretaker in a fourth-floor walk-up apartment in an inner-city neighborhood. Some are with a provider on a quiet, attractive street (but not one with the more expensive homes) in a moderately prosperous suburb. And an 11th-floor apartment in a near-luxury highrise receives infants and toddlers throughout the morning or afternoon.

All of these providers are breaking the law or evading regulations. Why do these family day care homes not get licenses, or register, or affiliate with agency "systems" to get help and support? Some, in fact, meet or exceed all local licensing, registration, or certification requirements, but others do not.

Given the nature of the phenomenon there are no definitive answers. Kappner has reported on a New York group.[19] The NDCHS interviewed in unregulated homes in four cities. I&R agencies and family day care systems administrators have shared their insights with us in six states.

Some providers see themselves as temporarily caring for the children of neighbors while raising their own children. They may not know about formal requirements or may see the licensing process as frightening, complex, or costly, or not relevant to them as informal, short-term providers. Some regard licensing as a "complex government hassle and unnecessary intrusion." Why take it on if there is no recruitment difficulty, especially in high-income neighborhoods, where one can charge fees above the rates for public reimbursement? Indeed, higher-paying parents may not want their children in a home with government-subsidized children.

Others are motivated by the desire to avoid income taxes and social security taxes or to hide income from public welfare authorities. Tax burdens had become exceptionally heavy at low income levels before the 1986 tax reform, as tax brackets had not been adjusted to inflation. Married providers have the social security protection, and often the health coverage, which accrue from their husbands' employment. The single family day care mothers sometimes do not understand the value of social security coverage or are willing to forego it for the reasons given.

Why, then, emerge and participate openly in the family day care system? Kappner's interviewees affiliated with agencies or made themselves visible because they needed referrals. They wanted to be listed by I&R services. Others, we have found, want the advantages of the child care food subsidy. Still others want to be eligible to receive public agency referrals and to care for publicly subsidized children. Some providers wish to reassure parents and to have liability insurance. Finally, those who are developing the concept of a semiprofessional activity and a small business need to be visible to function properly, to interact with peers, and to satisfy their own sense of dignity and self-respect.

Throughout the country agencies and public officials are working at expansion of the visible family day care supply with these considerations in mind, and apparently with some success. Family day care systems have a role in this process.

Family Day Care Systems

The NDCHS estimated that in 1978 some 30,000 caregivers serving at least 120,000 children were operating as part of day care systems, which they identified as "networks of homes under the sponsorship of an administrative agency."[20] A provider in such a network was described as having access to training and referral services. The systems had developed largely as a result of state or local requirements as they subsidized children's care through Title XX funds. In the instance of group care, governments could contract for "slots" in a center meeting state and/or federal requirements. Payment, audits, inspection, and referral could be routinized. A state or locality had no comparably efficient way to deal with individual providers in the unstable day care market. However, if a child care agency would develop a "system" undertaking to provide a specific number of "slots" in homes, to pay providers agreed rates, to guarantee specified standards, and to be responsible for referral, vacancy control, bookkeeping, and payment, the operation would become possible. Since the major system organizers were child care agencies operating centers, or agencies created because of a perceived need for subsidized family day care, it was inevitable that they also would offer training and referral services. Many collected both parent fees and state/local funds and provided access to fringe benefits as well. Later, book and toy libraries, shared activities, opportunity to arrange for "respite" by dropping in at a center with one's charges, and other services appeared in some places.

Despite this mechanism, federal funding was and is directed disproportionately to group care because it remains easier to manage. Moreover, until recently, child care services concentrated on the 3- to 5-year-old group. The system has opened up family day care somewhat as an option, especially for infants and toddlers, and those who would develop family day care further currently see the need to expand systems.

Child Care Food Program

In 1975 the federal Child Care Food Program (CCFP) was expanded from day care centers to include participants in sponsored family day care and group day care homes. The responsible administrative agency is the Food and Nutrition Service of the U.S. Department of Agriculture (USDA). A CCFP sponsor is required to submit an application and reimbursement claims for a group of homes, consult on nutrition, and monitor actual compliance with the food program rules.[21] A sponsor may be a system in this sense, but also may be an association of family day care providers, a United Way agency, or a public welfare department.

Since the early 1980s the opportunity to add food program sponsorship to the other activities of family day care systems has provided a decisive impetus to the launching of new systems. Family day care providers are attracted by the added financial support (currently over $2.00 per child per day). They may bill daily for each child for breakfast, lunch or supper, and a snack at a specified rate. Payment is indexed to the consumer price index. As of July 1, 1985, it amounted to the following, per child, per day:

Breakfast	$ .57
Lunch/supper	$1.1175
Snacks	$ .33

At the same time the sponsoring organization was reimbursed as follows, per home per month, for handling records, payment, nutrition education and consultation, and inspection:

For the first 50 homes, $50 per home per month.
For the next 150 homes, $38 per home per month.
For the next 800 homes, $30 per home per month.
Additional homes, $26 per home per month.

Family day care systems range in size and function. Some do little more than what is required by the CCFP. However, the administrative support we found in California, Minnesota, and elsewhere can be very important to the basic operation of a new style local-initiative organization with broader functions. The pattern of nutrition education and consultation may be integrated with a technical assistance operation for the general upgrading of family day care. For the provider, these extras—including bulk food commodities and the considerable add-on to fees—can make the activity financially possible and a credible part of a professional service network. Quality Child Care, described in the next section, has demonstrated in eight states how an entire movement of consciousness-raising and the cultivation of provider self-respect and sense of direction could be built on this foundation.

Some 800 systems in the USDA CCFP served 78,000 homes and 336,000 children in 1985. These homes received reimbursement of about $171 million. In the late 1970s one-third of all family day care systems did not participate in the food program. While the nonparticipation rate is currently probably considerably lower, it would not be unreasonable to guess that there now are 1000 family day care systems in the United States. Clearly, a significant portion of regulated and subsidized homes are in systems. The effort to organize additional systems thus is at the cutting edge of the effort to bring family day care out of the underground, standardizing and regularizing it as an occupation. The process has been threatened in recent years by a move in the Reagan administration to introduce a means test and eliminate financially ineligible children from receiving subsidies from the family day care program. Opponents argue that the administrative complexity and cost thus imposed would destroy this very hopeful development. They cite the much lower rates of participation in the food program before family day care homes were permitted by 1978 legislation (implemented in mid-1980s regulations) to drop the means test.[22]

One of the developing questions, as yet unexplored, derives from the fact that much of the increase in family day care home participation in the food program, and thus in "systems," has come through the growth in very large umbrella sponsors (like Quality Child Care), in contrast to small family day care associations. It would be useful to understand the relative advantage of each in increasing access, quality, provider competence, and identification with an occupational group.

Quality Child Care: Organizing Family Day Care "Systems"

Whatever its problems with the food program of the Department of Agriculture in 1984 and 1985, Quality Child Care, located in Mounds, Minnesota, offered the most impressive argument yet that family day care could become visible, improved, and made a more important child care resource. Moreover, although a nonprofit agency, Quality Child Care was in many ways like a proprietary family day care chain, paralleling the proprietary child care center chains. It thus provided the model of a pattern of child care administration and operation based neither in state nor in local government (although in need of licensing and monitoring). It is a pattern particularly congruent with demand subsidies (child care tax credits or vouchers). It should thus be discussed even though it has unraveled since we studied it, and its sponsorship functions have been picked up by several large statewide groups and some smaller systems. Its difficulties, if we understand them, do not suggest that the model could not be repeated.

Quality Child Care could be developed because the U.S. Department of Agriculture cannot deal with individual family day care providers in offering access to the child care food program. Under law and regulation the providers must be organized in "systems" capable of certifying their eligibility for the food, guiding them in nutrition, inspecting their food service, and administering the subsidy.

Pat Maltz, who developed and led Quality Child Care, began as a family day care mother. Her experience convinced her that it had to be developed as an occupation with self-respect, rules, and protections; these would develop only if family day care mothers became more assertive and defined their roles. A variety of experiences eventually put her in a state leadership role, representing family day care providers. She created Quality Child Care to offer services and publish a newsletter.

The big opportunity came in 1978 when, having learned of the federal food program, she began as a system sponsor. By the summer of 1984 Quality Child Care operated in eight states (Minnesota, North Dakota, Wisconsin, Nebraska, Illinois, Massachusetts, Connecticut, and Texas). It was serving 8300 family day care providers who cared for 57,000 children each month and reimbursed a monthly average of $1.2 million of federal food funds.

The 8300 homes constituted 13 percent of the 63,700 homes in the program nationally. Minnesota remained the center of the operation, serving 26,800 children. No state had fewer than 2400 children. Only three major proprietary chains of child care centers had greater impact on numbers.

Since the program requires reimbursement to providers within five working days after billing, Quality Child Care had developed a large and efficient payment, clerical, and accounting operation. State coordinators, supervising a team of regional coordinators, recruited, trained, supervised visits to homes and inspections, and supported the billing and payment system. The national office staff of 25 in Mounds was responsible for the coordination, accounting, clerical support, management, and payroll operations. There was there, too, a separate Minnesota state office. The total national staff, heavily professional and semiprofessional, included specialists in training, home contacts, nutrition, editorial work, and several of the successful spinoffs, many of which supported the core operation and were the reason for the expansion and dominance of the field.

To summarize briefly:

- Quality Child Care administered the Bonus Community Food Distribution Program, bringing such surplus foods as butter and cheese directly to family day care providers. They helped providers learn to use these surplus foods. The operation required leased trucks and drop sites.
- A National Commodity Processing contract allowed discounted prices on products, added surplus commodities to other products, and offered them at reduced prices. Quality Child Care had heavy discounts because of scale.
- Nutrition and related training activities were carried out as required by the child care food program.
- More elaborate training weekends were offered for which family day care parents had to pay—and were pointed toward consciousness-raising, education, and increasing professionalization in the role. This was a new developing program.
- In several states and communities they accepted contracts which permitted them to license or register family day care homes, with final formal state approval to follow; in some places they undertook certification of eligibility for the food stamp program for people above the assistance level.
- A special spinoff nonprofit organization known as Day Care Fair was created to offer day care providers management

supports. It had not developed very far before Quality Child Care had to disband. Family day care providers were to be taught essential small-business skills in a program of training, information, and supply of essential materials and forms. There also were to be tax management consulting services and group insurance (liability, accident, and disability).

- The Quality Child Care publication program produced a variety of handbooks, information pieces, training materials, a monthly training newsletter, and a basic provider handbook, *Family Day to Day Care*.
- In some places they offered a transportation service.

A review of a large sample of the output suggests that it did much to support family day care in both its child caring and service aspects, on the one hand, and in its business and reporting requirements, on the other. The meal and feeding materials were substantively of high quality and the kits, manuals, aids, newsletters, and supplies attractive, readable, and often imaginative and ingenious.

In addition to all this, its organizational capacity gave Quality Child Care a base from which it could undertake other social welfare projects, less central to its basic program and therefore also debatable: administration of one of several experimental voucher systems in Massachusetts; a family day care program to support counseling in child abuse and neglect cases in Massachusetts; training and other support services for an overseas U.S. military child care program; small-scale participation in a program for teenage mothers in Illinois.

The success of the core food system program operated by Quality Child Care suggested the possibilities of bringing much of family day care up out of the underground with incentives in the form of food subsidies and assistance toward professionalization and small business success. Essential central services and supports were invented and successfully implemented. The entrepreneurial bent, which was in tune with much that is admired in business and promoted in the Reagan administration's privatization ideology, left some eyebrows raised in the social welfare field: Was this an exemplary program in family day care or a new breed of expansionist social welfare business? Was this a proper model for a nonprofit agency?

For present purposes we need only note the model: organizing a modern child care supply system and supporting it—if somebody else organizes demand. Quite different from the other patterns.

Summing Up Two "Tendencies"—Or Three?

In recent years, Save the Children in Atlanta, Georgia, has conducted a national workshop-conference for family day care providers each spring and attracted increasingly larger groups of providers and related professionals. Children's Foundation, a Washington-based advocacy group, has supported the growth of the National Association for Family Day Care, which has had two-similar meetings. Both have had attendance growing to the 500–800 range. Both groups note and relate to the existence of about 150 state or regional family day care associations throughout the country, variously serving their members with regard to the federal child care food program, liability and health insurance, training, books and supplies, mutual support, and state-level advocacy.

The August 1985 conference of the National Association of Family Day Care may serve to illustrate current tendencies. In addition to nationally known child care advocates and a federal legislature update, the participants heard talks and participated in workshops about the following:

- Business aspects of family day care.
- Administrative and delivery requirements and problems.
- Professional content and role.

Thus, for example, there were sessions on taxes, liability insurance, effective management, and use of computers. There were meetings about I&R, media visibility, legal issues, and developments in the food program. There were many sessions, as well, about "developmental activities for infants through age 5 in the family day care setting," "provider-parent-child teamwork," "a well-organized day," "your caregiving self," and "training providers." All of this is obviously a far departure from some public perception of family day care mothers as "babysitters."

As we met with groups of providers at this and similar meetings, we were impressed with the fact that while those who attend these national conferences and workshops tend to be leaders in state and regional day care associations and probably atypical providers, they do constitute an element that is changing the field. First, there are a group of women of limited educational background, many from deprived minority groups, who have come up through aide positions in Head Start or day care centers, or as family day care providers, but have taken courses and perhaps child development associate certification. They have assumed local and state association leadership and projected personal roles as semiprofessionals and professionals in this emerging field. Some are small-business entrepreneurs, and many are in nonprofit "systems."

Then there are college graduates, or, more often, graduates of two-year colleges who have taken course work in child development or child care. Theirs were not major universities, and they tend to reside in medium-sized cities or small towns. Some went to school before they had their babies and some after, but most left the labor market or delayed entry to stay home for some years with their children. They have assumed care of other children because of the need to earn some money and are adding to their training and contacts because they have decided to enter the field as a business-profession in the longer term. Several collaborate informally with friends and relatives, expanding to family group homes (6 to 12 children) and employing part-time staff assistance, often students. A few are talking of eventually setting up centers. Several are designing supplementary services for working parents (supermarket shopping service, for example).

These tend to be young married women. Tax advantages in converting part of their homes to business use are very visible to them. Their net incomes are quite low, and they often employ help despite this, with a view to the long-term. Most are regulated, licensed, and/or registered. A few, in high-income suburbs or in states that don't care, see such formal status as an unnecessary nuisance.

We are impressed with the fact that any long-term perspective on family day care cannot avoid considering the two alternative models that have evolved over the past two decades:

1. The semiprofessional provider who has had some educational background in child development and subsequent specialized course work is often oriented to a professional model of child care by participation in a "system" and its activities and relationships, conducts the home as a miniature preschool or center, often plans for or has at least part-time assistance, and may even grow beyond family day care size to a center or related service business. (To illustrate: Two cousins running group homes in Pennsylvania were planning a shopping service for the mothers and expansion to center size.)

2. The warm "mother" or "grandmother" who operates a day care home as an attractive family environment, as though her own or relative children were in care with her, who makes good use of the resources and help that a relationship with a sponsoring agency may offer, and continues to have a "per-

sonalized" rather then formal concept of program, program day, and relationships to children and their parents.

One could argue that these two "ideal-type" models, which are in reality points on a continuum between the fully "professional" and the completely "natural" family day care mother, represent the choices. However, recall that there is currently, at least, a third subgroup:

3. The young mother who takes some outside chidren on an informal basis to make her decision to stay at home with her own child financially possible. Unlike the first two categories, this is not a group that sees a future in child care. However, there is inevitable overlap. Some of these young women express themselves in terms similar to the other two; some, indeed, become members of the other categories.

One could make a case for the two, or three, types in a pluralistic system. Each corresponds to the preferences of some parents. However, as one looks ahead, there are differences in the public policy consequences of these models and one must predict some choices and differentiations.

Family Day Care in a Comprehensive Strategy

We have expressed the view elsewhere in the volume that group programs, both those based in school systems and those in the social welfare stream, are essential components of a full child care design. We would stress the need for family day care as another vital part of this developing system of social provision. Family day care, therefore, should have claim on possible public support and be held accountable by appropriate systems of regulation and inspection. It should be buttressed by appropriate training and delivery system resources as well. All of this requires explication.

One might, in a sense, project both a middle-term and long-term perspective. While the latter is somewhat elusive, some outlines may nonetheless be discerned. The middle-term perspective covers the transition over the next 5 to 10 years from a largely unregulated, underground resource of uncertain characteristics to a reliable component of community care for children.

The case for devoting energy and resources to this task has already been suggested. Many parents, perhaps most, prefer family day care for infants and toddlers. There is a major shortage of infant care in the United States. Few centers offer care to infants. Provision of such care at the desired quality levels is difficult and expensive in centers. There are still sufficient research uncertainties to represent a case against center care for infants, in the view of some professionals and agencies. Currently, family day care for infants and toddlers is expandable with very little capital cost; the human capital investments appear modest by comparison, and, thus far, a potential labor force appears to be at hand.

Family day care also serves school-aged children before and after school. Many families see it as accessible, and most like the home arrangements. This is likely to continue, as well, although many school-, church-, center-, and community-based group programs are also developing. It is for the urgent infant-toddler care tasks that family day care particularly appeals to those concerned with public policy.

In effect, many of these considerations are motivating some of the cities and states discussed in the earlier chapters. However, we would depart from several of them on one fundamental point: The investment in family day care and its expansion should not and need not take place at the expense of child protection and program quality. Given concern about ensuring wholesome child care environments, as the country places ever-larger proportions of its very young children in substitute care while their mothers work, it is self-defeating to have licensing systems that are hollow, lacking real monitoring or enforcement. The solution is not to go from licensing to registration "because that is more realistic," when registration often is no more than self-certification and leads to no public visits or verification prior to a series of complaints. One cannot understand such approaches so soon after the public clamor about alleged and reported abuse in child care programs. And absent scandal, how can one ignore what child development researchers and professionals have learned about the importance of a wholesome care situation? Can public policy legitimately assume that parents-consumers can take full monitoring responsibility with regard to a service that is not visible to most parents most of the time? Moreover, the young parent may feel the insecurity of inexperience vis à vis the experienced family day care provider to whom other parents also have entrusted their children

Therefore, while endorsing the efforts to expand family day care, we see the simultaneous need for, indeed the preconditon of, adequate public licensing and monitoring. Whereas voluntary "accreditation" under a professional association could perhaps work for group programs in some parts of the country, and is now being developed on a small scale by the National Association for the Education of Young Children, it is not an option for family day care.

In short, justifying continued acceptance of the large family day care underground is difficult. Locating family day care services and insisting that they be licensed would not be difficult, were the general public to decide that such regulation is essential and worth the cost. There is need for public education, publicity, and a public campaign to achieve this goal—once a state is convinced that the time has come to move. The motivation could be one reported outrage or another, and there unfortunately will be opportunities, given the large numbers of children now in unregulated care. We would prefer to see a more positive state argument, in terms of the well-being of children and the sense of security of parents about arrangements they have undertaken.

For the moment, absent federal standards, the initiative will need to flow from state governments. They, in turn, will require prodding from and consultation by national and state professional associations and advocacy groups. Eventually, one would hope that the federal government would do its part by reviewing the plan of regulation scuttled in late 1981, under which states could not spend federal funds for child care unless they enforced specified standards. The specific 1981 norms, while attractive, are, of course, subject to review. What is essential is a national minimum that protects children yet does not ignore pluralism and the possibilities of alternative care theories and models.

But such an initiative will take more than enforcement, more than a stick. Citizens would be better prepared to report illegal operators and providers would continue the current trend along the "continuum of visibility," to use Kappner's term, if public policy were to produce more attractive supports while publicizing the advantages of more formal affiliation with the care network.

The supports needed are known and valued by those who have experienced them: I&R networks that improve recruitment of children; training opportunities; low-cost or free loans for equipment or house renovation; respite services when one needs a break; access to book and toy libraries; the opportunity to join a child care food system; group or cooperative food and supply purchases; access to consultants who are expert in matters of child development, health, nutrition, social service referral, relationships with parents; assistance in obtaining reasonably priced medical care and liability insurance; advertising; clarification of the advantages of social security coverage; tax and bookkeeping consultation and guidance.

A significant, if small, portion of the family day care field has begun to move in these directions. State determination to bolster these components while strengthening enforcement could be valuable and effective. As seen, one instrument to assist in this effort is the family day care "system," the organized network of family day care homes. A small amount of state money and some publicity could accelerate what the federal child care food program has already begun. As family day care homes become part of sponsored networks, the supports listed are more readily provided and at less cost. Certification of providers by a responsible system (supplemented by health department or fire department inspection and "spot" checking by state staff) could be less onerous and even more effective than direct state licensing or registration—as found in a number of instances.

As the latter process proceeds, reexamining the relationship of the provider to the system will be necessary. We have identified many situations throughout the country in which agencies, trying to establish high-quality family day care networks, supply such essentials as equipment, training, some fringe benefits, vacations, guarantees, respite services, and other supports, undertake what is in fact supervision, but still define their family day care network members as independent entrepreneurs. There are two motivations: to avoid both costly fringe benefits tied to compensation and the minimum-wage rules and to have a degree of flexibility. Some providers also enjoy tax advantages, especially with regard to the use of their homes, and get tax-free payments (based on a much older fiction of foster care as volunteer service for which the agency reimburses only out-of-pocket costs!).

While we do not have final conclusions about this matter, we cannot but wonder whether a future family day care system might not more readily achieve the desired quality and accountability if caretakers, who in fact are staff members, were seen as employees, as they are in centers. If private entrepreneurship has advantages beyond those of filling a gap in a period of unregulated care, could such advantages be identified and exploited—perhaps in regard to recruitment to the work or provision of unique services in some way unusual and attractive to some parents? We do not reject the private, semiprofessional entrepreneur but do question not naming and treating employees as such and paying them adequately.

All of these proposed reforms and enrichments must add to costs and decrease some of the financial attractiveness of the family day care option, yet we see no alternative. It is not in the interests of children, parents, or providers to "solve" the child care problem through exploitation of its labor force and neglect of the children served. If despite poor pay and little societal support many providers currently display commitment and a spirit of sacrifice in caring for children, the society has been fortunate; this is more than can or should be expected of the many and over a long haul. It will certainly not occur on a sufficient scale should the expected tighter labor market develop over the next several years. Massachusetts began to show the way in 1985 by investing simultaneously in higher reimbursement to, or pay for, providers and more extensive licensing and inspection for family day care. Other jurisdictions will need to follow.

What is the response to the fact that all of this will inevitably make daily and weekly family day care fees more costly for all users and exceptionally difficult for the working-poor parent? In addition to the higher subsidies from federal social service, employment, and other funding sources, covering those eligible for completely publicly financed care, there will be need to raise thresholds for sliding fees, the "tapered" scales allowing supplementation for those who can partially pay their way but not meet full marketplace costs. As long as the minimum wage remains as low as it is and salaries are not geared to family responsibilities, it is in the public interest to supplement low wages in such fashion, permitting parents to work and avoid more extensive dependence upon public welfare programs. Nor is it in the public interest to relegate the children of the working poor to the inferior, often dangerous, black market care that their parental incomes could purchase. We have long since repudiated such public policy for education and medical care, as we have, in theory, for housing. As the significance of child care is similarly appreciated, the larger investment will be seen as inevitable. Parental employment and self-support, and a satisfactory child development environment, are no small return on such investments.

What, then, does all this imply for the family day care model? Will all this yield a system of what we called in our shorthand "the semiprofessional" or "the warm mother or grandmother"? What of the so-called third group, the mothers who do this work during a period of personal transition, as their own children grow out of infancy?

We doubt that there will be a clear pattern for a while, but see middle-term stability in an emphasis on the "natural," the parent-substitute whose main virtues are ability to provide a warm, protective, sensitive, nurturing environment that is safe and stimulating, where meals are nutritious, and where problems are noticed. Based in a system or network, such a family day care home could have access to social services as needed and to consultants responsive to special circumstances or problems. The short-term courses and workshops offered, the consultant suggestions made, and the materials provided would buttress this role.

The goal would be a good homelike environment, not a small preschool. Obviously, these homes, concentrating on infants and toddlers, would offer the cognitive stimulation, encouragement, and cues that parents provide for their own children—to the extent that there is successful recruitment, operation, and support.

Much attention has been directed of late toward strengthening and expanding the federally supported Child Development Associate assessment and competency-based credential program (currently administered by a subsidiary unit of the National Association for the Education of Young Children). An expansion of that effort is listed as an essential component of any effort to improve the quality of care currently available to many infants and toddlers.[23] A credential for family day care has now been developed, but rules for scholarships have not yet been announced. We agree with regard to group programs. CDA credentialing has been valuable for Head Start and many day care centers. There is continuing need to upgrade the formal qualifications of those child care aides who are assistants where fully qualified teachers are available and of others who are completely responsible for groups in many centers. However, we believe that the "warm mother or grandmother" model is different from that of the child development paraprofessional. It is an option that many parents prefer, strengthened by well-designed brief courses and workshops and the ongoing supports described, but altered if redefined in subprofessional terms. We see here the possibility of a stable occupation, adequately paid, less expensive than the child development graduates of two-year and four-year colleges, and the core respected and adequately paid work force for family day care.

What of the "semiprofessionals" who also are doing this work now and are visible at the national meetings and workshops, as in the leadership of state and regional family day care associations? During a transitional period, such providers are and will be part of the supply. We would expect a gradual evolution of their role, however.

Given the educational backgrounds and career expectations of such personnel, they cannot be the core family day work force. Neither the potential salary levels nor the status of the work could sustain them. We would expect some of them to serve as the administrators, supervisors, and consultants in the sponsored networks. Others are becoming or will become more specialized, operating family day care homes for children with special needs because of developmental problems or handicaps, or specialized sick-child and emergency facilities. Some will give leadership to family day care group homes in the 7- to 12-year-old range, which indeed might become more like preschools. These and other specialized facilities will inevitably be more costly than centers and preschools; they will be professionally specialized services without economies of scale. They will appeal to some high-income parents. They will be called upon by public authorities paying for publicly subsidized services for special children.

In the somewhat longer run, as the general upgrading continues, all of family day care could become as expensive or even considerably more expensive than center care. Recall that, apart from unregulated care, the centers were only a little more expensive than the family day care homes studied in the NDCHS in the late 1970s! As caregivers are better treated (even though not trained at the levels of center staffs), the economy of scale of the group programs could even cancel out advantages created by salary differentials. We found that this had occurred by the late 1970s in Sweden and France where tighter regulation, salaries closer to parity, and organization of family day care into systems had ended its "advantages" as the cheaper care mode. When the regulated, updated, future family day care system loses its substantial cost advantages, parents who pay and public authorities who subsidize will then use family day care only out of strong preferences or conviction that a particular child requires it. Then family day care is likely to be reserved for the ages in the interval between the parental leave and about age 2½—or for the special needs children mentioned. In the latter case it will be a therapeutic or special education program, in the former a short-term investment.

Whether school-age children would still come to family day care before and after school would depend on cost levels, as compared with alternative community- and school-based programs, on access, and on parental preference. In any case, the before- and after-school service is adequately offered by the "natural" mother or grandmother type and does not require a semiprofessional.

These, then, will be the central roles for family day care providers in the "warm mother" and "semiprofessional" and professional modes. The very informal, unaffiliated role of the young mother who adds some other children to her own will probably persist, serving as a transitional resource for the short-term. Increasingly, that mother will be the recent immigrant, helping with the children of others like herself during a period of transition, acculturation, and the gaining of access to the general system. If efforts to inform the public are successful and funding adequate, most parents will want their children in a better regulated and protected system, one of the two earlier models.

We see ahead a challenge to public departments and nonprofit social agencies to position themselves in support of such developments. There is need for a larger, more reliable, more visible, family day care supply, reached through I&R services, regulated, supported and upgraded—and ultimately differentiated into a basic, solid, service and a specialized resource. Federal and state initiatives will be required to ensure funds, research, training and regulation. But local organizational and operational inventiveness will need to begin where we are and to reshape a useful institution into an instrument for a new time.

Chapter 7 Appendix

State FY 1985 Provider Reimbursement Rates for Centers and Family Day Care (daily rates unless otherwise specified)

State	Family Day Care	Center-Based
Alabama	$95.00/month	$140–$155.00/month
Alaska	$14.00–$16.46	$14.00–$16.46
Arizona	$8.60	$8.60
Arkansas	$.50–$1.10/hr[b]	$.50–$1.10/hr[b]
California	$16.77	$16.77
Colorado	$8.00–$12.00[a]	$9.50–$15.00
Connecticut	$30.00/wk	$40–$60.00/wk
Delaware	$35.00/wk	$50–$52.00/wk
District of Columbia	$9.00	$13.00
Florida	$37.50/wk	$13.00
		$37.50
Georgia	$25.00–$30.00/wk[a]	$49.00/wk[a]
Hawaii	$1,079.00/annual	$1.079.00/annum
Idaho	$13.00	$13.00[b]
Illinois	$7.63	$11.72[b]
Indiana	—	$9.50
Iowa	$5.00–$9.00[a]	$12.25–$12.50[a]
Kansas	$6.05[a]	$7.55
Kentucky	$7.00	$7.00
Louisiana	$28.84/wk	$7.00
Maine	$55.00/wk[a]	$59.75/wk[a]
Maryland	$6.30	$9.75
Massachusetts	$13.46[a]	$13.50[a]
Michigan	$6.08	$7.74
Minnesota	------Counties set rates------	
Mississippi	$6.00	$7.00–$12.00
Missouri	$7.00–$8.00	$7.00–$8.00

Montana	$8.50	$8.50
Nebraska	$6.00[a]	$7.84[a]
Nevada	$12.00	$12.00
New Hampshire	$6.50[a]	$8.00
New Jersey	$1.00–$1.50/hr[b]	$8.93–$9.50
New Mexico	$6.50	$6.50
New York State	—	$55.00/wk
New York City	—	$82.50/wk
North Carolina	$150.00/month	$185.00/month
North Dakota	------Counties set rates------	
Ohio	—	$15.83
Oklahoma	$7.00	$8.00
Oregon	$200.00/month	$200.00
Pennsylvania	$9.64(b)	$13.68[b]
Rhode Island	$25.00/wk[a]	$44.00/wk[b]
South Carolina	$1.98/hr[b]	$1.20–$1.50/hr
South Dakota	$1.00/hr[b]	$1.00/hr[a]
Tennessee	$27.50/wk[a]	$30.00/wk
Texas	$6.40	$10.28
Utah	$6.35[a]	$7.60
Vermont	$1.06/hr[a]	$1.31/hr
Virginia	$5.56–$9.00[a]	$7.57
Washington	$8.61	$8.61
West Virginia	$4.00–$7.00[a]	$7.00
Wisconsin	------Counties set rates------	
Wyoming	$.70/hr	$1.00/hr

SOURCE: Helen Blank and Amy Wilkins, *Child Care: Whose Priority?* (Washington, D.C.: Children's Defense Fund, 1985), pp. 216–217, 222–223.
[a]average rate
[b]absolute rate

Endnotes

1. Department of Health and Human Services, *Final Report of the National Day Care Home Study* (8 vols. including the Executive Summary, 1980 and 1981). For a general overview see Vol. I, Steven Fosburg et al., *Family Day Care in the United States: Summary of Findings* (Washington, D.C.: U.S. Government Printing Office, 1981).
2. Diane Adams, "Summary of Findings: National Survey of Family Day Care Regulations" (Chapel Hill, N.C.: Bush Institute for Child and Family Policy, 1982, processed).
3. UNCO Inc., *National Child Care Consumer Study, 1975*, Vol. I (Washington, D.C.: U.S. Government Printing Office, 1978).

4. Sandra L. Hofferth and Deborah Phillips, "Working Mothers and the Care of Their Children" (publication pending, 1986). See especially Tables 9 and 10.

5. Fosburg, *Family Day Care in the United States*.

6. Sheila B. Kamerman and Alfred J. Kahn, *Child Care, Family Benefits, and Working Parents* (New York: Columbia University Press, 1981), pp. 134–140.

7. Patricia Maltz, at that time chief executive officer of Quality Child Care, Inc., Mounds, Minnesota, as presented to Hearing before the Select Committee on Children, Youth, and Families, House of Representatives, April 4, 1984, in *Child Care: Beginning a National Initiative* (Washington, D.C.: U.S. Government Printing Office, 1984), p. 103.

8. See note 1.

9. What follows is based on the National Day Care Home Study (NDCHS), especially Vol. 1 *(Summary)*, Vol. 2 *(Research Report)*, Vol. 3 *(Observational Report)*. See note 1.

10. Ibid., *Summary*, p. 93.

11. A.C. Emlen et al., *Child Care by Kith* (Portland, Oregon: Oregon State University, 1971; and Ester Wattenberg, "Family Day Care: Out of the Shadows and into the Spotlight," *Marriage and Family Review*, Vol. 3 (1980) 35–62; and Wattenberg, "Characteristics of Family Day Care Providers," *Child Welfare*, Vol. 56 (1977), 211–219.

12. Martha Abbott-Shim and Marsha Kaufman, "Characteristics of Family Day Care Providers," Georgia State University, processed draft, 1986.

13. M. Golden et al., *The New York City Day Care Study* (New York: Medical and Health Research Association, Inc., 1978). Also Moncrieff M. Cochran and Lars Gunnarsson, "A Follow-up Study of Group Day Care and Family-based Childrearing Patterns," *Journal of Marriage and the Family*, Vol. 47, No. 2 (May 1985), 297–309. Also, Betsy Squibb, "The Dynamics of Family Day Care: A Review of the Research" (1986) (publication pending).

14. As reported in a memorandum from the Children's Foundation, Washington, D.C., 1984.

15. U.S. Department of Health and Human Services, *Comparative Licensing Study*, 5 vols. (1982). See especially Vol. 5, *Profiles of State Day Care Licensing Requirements*. *Family Day Care Homes*.

16. Adams, "Summary of Findings."

17. Helen Blank and Amy Wilkins, *Child Care: Whose Priority?* (Washington, D.C.: Children's Defense Fund, 1985), pp. 194–198, for a full listing. The state-by-state reports in the volume also report state adult-child ratios required for public reimbursement, or for licensing/registration, or for both.

18. National Commission on Working Women, *Who Cares for Kids? A Report on Child Care Providers* (Washington, D.C.: 1986).

19. Augusta Kappner, *Factors Affecting Provider Movement Along A Continuum of Visibility*, Unpublished doctoral dissertation, Columbia University School of Social Work, 1984.

20. NDCHS "Summary," Vol. 1, Chapter 9; and also *Family Day Care Systems*, constituting Vol. 5.

21. A positive assessment of the child care food program, which contains a picture of operations, is contained in ABT Associates, Inc., "Evaluation of the

Child Care Food Program," contract No. 53–3198–40, submitted to the Food and Nutrition Service, U.S. Department of Agriculture, August 2, 1982.

22. On this, see ibid., "Executive Summary," p. 5. A new Abt study was commissioned late in 1986.

23. Ad Hoc Day Care Coalition, "The Crisis in Infant and Toddler Child Care" (Washington, D.C., 1985), p. 16.

Chapter 8

LEARNING WHILE DOING

In the first half of the 1980s, the demand for child care services continued to rise as work in the paid labor force became the usual lifestyle for most women, including those with very young children; and having a working mother became the common experience, even for very young children. At the same time many parents became convinced of the value of earlier exposure to educational and group socialization opportunities for their preschool-aged children who were growing up in ever-smaller families. The need for some kind of child care service for all or part of the day emerged as an increasingly universal need, not just for poor families but for almost all families. Indeed, participation in such programs was increasingly becoming normative.

Although relatives continued to provide care for many young children, nonrelative care became more prevalent generally. Family day care remained important, but group care emerged as even more significant, in particular for children aged 3 and older. Demographic and labor force projections suggested that nonrelative care would continue to grow in its share of the care picture.

Despite reduced direct financial support by the federal government, the supply of child care services expanded during these same years. Tax benefits to parents increased, and tax incentives to employers led to some modest additional child care support by them. Head Start grew modestly. Several states made up federal cuts or added to their funding for services, and some had their version of a child or dependent care tax credit. Of particular importance, concern with school reform as well as evidence that preschool programs subsequently paid off in reduced school problems led to growing—if thus far modest—state support of enhanced kindergarten, preschools for 4-year-olds, and some afterschool programs. In this evolution there was no significant federal leadership, encouragement, or aid.

The Reagan administration's income maintenance policies, coupled with changed lifestyles for women, also led a growing number of states to establish employment and training, AFDC diversion, and workfare projects. In several states child care emerged as an important component of new efforts designed to "move low-income women off welfare." To include women with children under age 6 (and, in some states, under age 3 if the mothers wish to participate), acceptable and affordable child care is essential. California, Massachusetts, and New York were among the states that highlighted this issue.

Nevertheless, the gap between exploding demand and modestly expanding supply continued. Access to many programs was limited to those who could afford market rates; subsidies for low-income users were curtailed; and shortages in the supply of infant and toddler care as well as school aged child care remained a major problem.

We have characterized the policies launched by the Reagan administration in 1981 as combining cutback, decentralization, deregulation and privatization. What has this yielded?

To summarize: First, the cutbacks led to a decline in subsidized center places for low-income children. Eligibility ceilings were lowered, and rules about employment and training as a qualification became more stringent. Publicly operated programs, except for those based in public education, have largely disappeared; nonprofit centers have a substantially smaller share of the market and have declined as a proportion of providers generally. Fewer low-income children are being served despite the increase in the numbers of income-eligible children and in the numbers of young children with working mothers. Poor children are increasingly "bumped and dumped" from subsidized care as income ceilings are lowered and small wage increases lead to loss of eligibility. More and more of these children may be entering unregulated, less costly family day care, not out of parental preference but out of lack of options. Many communities face the growing probability of seeing a two-tier system emerge: informal unregulated care for the poor and group care, often in proprietary nursery schools and day care centers, for the better off.

Second, the administration's policy of decentralization has succeeded completely, at least in one sense. A federal child care presence has largely disappeared, and a federal capacity for experimental programming, technical assistance, and data collection has been dismantled. Only Head Start remains as a federal child care program. Child care tax benefits are not monitored as to their use. Social Service Block Grant (SSBG) funds are provided to the states without any constraints, and reporting requirements are minimal. In effect, the United States has become a country with at least 50 different sets of child care policies, and maybe hundreds. Not only do states set their own policies, but often counties do also; thus policies may vary substantially even within the same state. Few states have anything resembling a coherent, statewide child care policy—or even statewide child care program initiatives. Political strategies and economic considerations guide contending interest groups, and policy making is ad hoc, remedial, incremental, often inconsistent, and frequently inadequate.

Third, the administration's policy of deregulation was successfully implemented. The SSBG eliminated the proposed minimum standards for federally subsidized programs, and many states subsequently reduced their standards and/or reduced their efforts at monitoring and enforcing the standards that did exist. Parent-consumer efforts at monitoring have not been shown to be an adequate substitute.

Fourth, the administration's policy of privatization has had a series of contradictory effects. Publicly operated programs (in any case, long in decline) have largely disappeared. Proprietary programs have increased in numbers and increased their market share substantially. More public dollars are going into family day care, mostly a private system of very small entrepreneurs. Vendor/voucher programs have been established in almost every state. At the same time, states have begun to establish or expand public preschool programs, and current trends in school reform and early childhood education as well as pressures from middle-class parents suggest that these efforts will increase. However, many proponents of such reform focus completely on formal education and do not plan adequately to simultaneously meet the child care need.

In the context of these developments, there were places where local child care agencies and advocates did what they could to restore funding, salvage services, respond to the growing needs, and improve the delivery systems. This may be described as decentralization and privatization at its best. We have reported on extraordinary energy, creativity, and advocacy in a limited number of places. Important lessons have been learned for the future child care delivery system. We have particularly noted expansion of information and referral (resource and referral) programs; experience with vendor/voucher arrangements; improved application of sliding fee scales, based on combining funds from several sources; the integration of family day care "systems" with the broader programs; parent and consumer education and library services; community education and advocacy.

Nonetheless, only a minority of jurisdictions enjoyed such expansion and innovation. School developments, where they have occurred, are haphazard. There is no case to be made that the local response is or will be enough—and that the state backup is sufficient.

Despite creative individual initiatives, what we have, basically, is a disorganized political and economic market. Responding to increased citizen and community pressures for more services, states follow a variety of strategies, helping providers at one time and consumers at another. The pressures from different child care interest groups—day care, early child development, schools, family day care—lead to shifts and disjunctures in policy and program, not to coherence or consensus. The results are inefficient and often ineffective. Nobody has an overall concern for and perspective on access, supply, finance, quality, and balance.

The time has come for the society—and thus state and federal governments—to acknowledge child care as a major need and participation in child care as normative. Child care services should evolve and become as much a part of the social infrastructure as schools, libraries, parks, highways, and transportation. With more than half the preschoolers in need of care because their mothers are working, with extensive knowledge about the value of these programs at least for children aged 2 or 3 and older, and with more than half the parents who can afford such programs preferring them for their 3- to 4-year-olds, it is time to plan for these as "essentials," not as offering some special "enrichment." As David Hamburg, president of the Carnegie Corporation, has stated, "It's a question of equity. Middle-class parents are already giving their children these benefits. It is in the interests of society to find some way of making them universal."

Child care needs to be seen as an entitlement, like schools. If family day care is to be the dominant mode for the very young children, it, too, needs to be developed so that it constitutes good quality for those who prefer such programs for their still younger children.

A few states also have already acknowledged the role child care can play as a strategy for economic development. North Carolina was among the first states to adopt this strategy and sell the state legislature on the importance of child care services as a drawing card for industry. With one of the highest rates of female labor force participation in the country, North Carolina officials recognized that many of the industries that were most important in the state employed large numbers of women. One way to attract new employers would be to assure them of a stable labor force. This could be done by expanding the supply and improving the quality of child care services for low-income women. North Carolina child care standards for nonsubsidized care are still low, but they are a lot higher than previously; and the supply of services has increased.

Massachusetts has gone still further. With a 3 percent unemployment rate, one of the lowest in the country, a growing base in high technology and a highly skilled labor force, Massachusetts government views child care as an essential device for attracting more related industries. Some employers, disenchanted with the media campaign urging employers to do "more," now are beginning to talk about the need for states and communities—if not the federal government—to be doing more. School systems, preschools, and all forms of child care are being viewed, increasingly, as what attracts industry to a state or region. They are an investment in human capital, in the quality of the future labor force.

Whether to attract and hold employers whose industries employ many mothers, or to attract industry in need of an ever more skilled labor force, or in recognition of the fact that out-of-home care is becoming the usual experience for young children, states will want and need to look ahead. The sometime, spasmodic attention to child care—occasionally focusing on early childhood education and at other times on social welfare child care programs, periodically being concerned about latchkey children, and then turning to child care tied to work training for "welfare" mothers—cannot be enough. Blue ribbon panels and commissions, appointed by governors or legislatures, do not solve the problem either unless they have the capacity for a long and broad view, going beyond the immediate budgetary compromise to a sense of direction and ongoing governmental structure. In short, the current marketplace has yielded important supports and initiatives in recent years but must be supplemented by some capacity for policy review, coordination, planning at the state level, buttressed as well by some essential federal support.

We do not wish to be misunderstood. Child care strategy is intertwined with a community and a state's cultural, ethnic, and demographic characteristics. There is no need for national uniformity or state rigidity. Diversity has been and remains an important value in this field. An argument for state-level foresight, policy development, coordination, and planning carries with it the view that all such activity can and should incorporate the value of diversity and protection of preferences. Moreover, participation in preschool programs should remain voluntary.

Laissez faire is not enough, but rigid planning is not the only alternative. Indeed, as we have shown, much is as yet unknown about delivery systems, program content, parental preferences, staffing, and much else. It is a time for experimentation, empirical approaches, flexibility—but also for constant efforts to learn, communicate learning, and make bold choices. We need large designs and a sense of direction, as well as room for diversity and preferences.

In the following sections we review some of the major choices now visible and suggest how they may be viewed.

Building a Delivery System

Inevitably, we discuss the specifics of the delivery system. The essential context, however, must be quality and responsiveness. American parents and children have the right to expect state-of-the art programs and experiences that can be enjoyed. A child's day should offer coherence and continuity.

Given a diversified delivery system, I&R services are a necessity. They are expanding throughout the country, aiding parents entering the system and helping to provide consumer education for those who are not sure how to assess existing options. Thus far only California has funded a statewide system, but Massachusetts has begun and other states are subsidizing modest operations. The I&R strategy can become the fulcrum for more general system development. But there are, as seen, important questions about the system's components.

Avoiding a Two-Tier System

Plans for child care delivery should attend to efficiency, quality, cultural and ethnic diversity, and economy. Nor can public policy ignore equity and equality concerns.

One obvious consequence of the decline in federally funded child care programs and the modest growth in consumer subsidies is the potential for developing a two-tier child care service system. All the data we have indicate that although affluent working parents may use in-home care for their infants and toddlers, they use preschool programs for at least a part of the day for their 3- and 4-year-olds (and for some of their 2-year-olds, too). Almost all 5-year-olds are in kindergarten or first grade, regardless of family income. In contrast, poor and working-class families use family day care, not only for their infants and toddlers but also for their 3- and 4-year-olds. It is the latter, who may also be in subsidized day care while middle class children are in nursery school, about whom we have concern. If the more advantaged children are exposed to the richer, more professionally led, developmentally oriented programs, while the more deprived children are placed with untrained family day care mothers (or in good, but segregated, centers reserved largely for children in single-parent families), the gap between the two will increase even more than now.

By the mid-1980s the only children who were assured of access to a subsidized place in care were children in need of protection against neglect and abuse. Indeed, in several states there was a basis for suspicion that this group had grown, in part, because some parents were prepared to label themselves neglectful or potentially abusive in order to qualify for decent affordable care.

In the mid-1980s most very young children of working parents were still cared for in private programs, and still paid for largely through parent fees. Only a minority were in public programs. About one million children of the approximately 10 million preschoolers with working mothers in 1986 were in some form of federally funded "center" program, about half in Head Start and half in Title XX funded care. In addition, more than one and a half million 5-year-olds with working mothers and the same number of 3- and 4-year-olds were in preschool programs. Five-year-olds are, overwhemingly, in public preschools (kindergartens). Four-year-olds enrolled in preschool programs are in private rather than public programs in a 3 to 2 ratio, while 3-year-olds are enrolled in private programs in a 2 to 1 ratio. Income and mother's education are by far the major differentiating factors in determining use of a school-based program rather than some other form of child care.

Many states reported "bumping" low-income 3- and 4-year-olds from center care because income eligibility standards were made more stringent when federal funds were cut back. Where the state had no sliding fee scale, the family and child lost eligibility as soon as wages went above the income ceiling. Although the Reagan administration stressed privatization as the strategy for assuring parents freedom of choice, the reality was that low-income parents had less choice because most could not afford to enter the market.

A few states are now beginning to establish prekindergarten programs for low-income or otherwise deprived 4-year-olds. These are still largely only part-day programs and do not cover the usual working day. Moreover, only a few states have statewide programs, and even then only for a minority of children.

Thus far, in addition to children in need of protection, we have begun to serve poor children and children defined as deprived or "at risk." There is some emerging consensus that this group should receive subsidized care. Some people are urging expansion of subsidies to cover all poor 3- and 4-year-olds, but to cover infants and toddlers only if there are special needs, on the assumption that poor single mothers with children under 3 will be at home, receiving AFDC. Some others are discussing making programs for the 4-year-olds universal, like kindergarten for the 5-year-olds, but limiting the 3-year-olds to those with special needs.

One argument for expanding preschool programs in the schools for 3- and 4-year-olds is that this seems to be the only possibility for a free, universal, nonstigmatized program. Programs for children under 3—and perhaps the after-school programs, too—could charge income-related fees, with public subsidies provided parents through a refundable tax credit or through a vendor/voucher program. If programs for the 3-year-olds and older are to be universally available, a substantial increase in public funding will be needed. If this is not forthcoming, however, a move toward a two-tier system will be inevitable.

Education, Social Welfare, and Child Development

Slowly a consensus has evolved. A variety of programs exist. Their names are distinct, but their "contents" overlap, and each may in its way meet the needs of children for care while parents work. From the point of view of function they are all child care. From approximately age 6, school systems provide coverage for whatever is the basic school day. The organized specific system of response, other than school care, now identifiable as child care (some prefer "child day care" or "child developmental care"), is concerned with infants, toddlers, preschoolers (ages 3 to 5), and with the after-school (and, sometimes, before-school) hours of those in nursery school, prekindergarten, kindergarten, and the elementary school grades.

As we have already seen, the major service systems available are institutionally located in either the educational or social service systems for whatever financing, standard-setting, or personnel preparation and certification is present. They are now known operationally as day care centers, family day care, Head Start, special classes, nursery schools, prekindergartens and kindergartens, and after-school programs. The auspices are schools, proprietary chains, individual private owners, private and public social welfare agencies, churches and other religious institutions, community centers, employers, hospitals, recreation departments, and others.

It is widely understood that if children are to be in out-of-home

care, the insights of child development knowledge should govern
their care, and the programs must attend to socioemotional development as well as to cognitive growth—whatever the setting is
called or the institutional auspice. Those who observe programs,
monitor developments, and carry out research on program effects
are agreed: These program features are well developed under a
diversity of auspices. They are found in public preschool programs,
day care centers, nursery schools, and Head Start.

As the labor force participation of mothers has expanded, both
the social welfare and educational systems have responded. Each
has experienced enormous growth. The society has invested increasingly in both. With competition has come some tendency to
dismiss one system as "only custodial care" and the other as
"bureaucratic and too preoccupied with the cognitive." Yet there is
perforce substantial system overlap, in particular as increased
knowledge about child development has begun to inform all
systems.

It therefore occasions no surprise that most of the I&R services
we have discussed refer to all these kinds of programs, that parents
talk about most of the group programs as "school," and that city and
state officials turn to all of them as they respond to constituents'
interest in improved provision. What we also have noted, however, is that with few exceptions the local child care organizations
that we have described are involved most heavily with the social
welfare components of the system. Their developmental and advocacy scope is largely center care and family day care, except insofar
as they call for increased voucher appropriations. As a result,
despite their creativity and valuable contributions, and their referral to educational settings in their I&R and voucher work, they
tend to be unrelated or peripherally involved in the education-
based system. Other advocacy groups and public officials are
considering the all-day kindergarten and public preschool questions. When the use of school buildings for after-school programs is
debated, day care advocates are often concerned only with the
question of whether these will be educator-operated programs or
social service and community groups gaining access to school
buildings.

At this level of issue the new local organizations, which we have
described very positively, are also special interests and partisans.
They are part of the debate, not the locus for its resolution or
reformulation. Somebody must ask which of these activities are
best located institutionally in social welfare and which in education. Or should they be pulled out and conceptualized as "child
care" or "child development," something new and apart? Perhaps a

case can and should be made instead for separate, parallel offerings—but then we need some definition of differences, a concept of
division of labor, guidance to parents as to how each of these
systems is best used.

Cities and states will need to decide something. Child care is a
sizable, costly, and growing program involving public commitments. Unrelated social welfare and educational system growth is
by now impossible. If the issue is ignored, there is competition and
confusion. There will need to be coordination, cooperation, mer-
ger, planning, cooptation—or something. We have found much
evidence of the need but no models for solution. If there is to be
child care policy, new combinations, overarching leadership, it
probably must come from the states.

What eventually occurs will determine the significance and
future roles of the local organizations we have described. To
illustrate with one possibility: Should public educational systems
undertake universal preschools, all-day kindergartens, and school-
age child care programming, the future I&R needs will be limited
to infant and toddler programs and special problem cases. The
vouchers and social service funding will become even more circumscribed. The child care–related family education and family
support services then would probably be shaped around needs of
specific "cases," not as a universal developmental service. On the
other hand, if there are to be better conceptualized and more
specialized but parallel child care offerings at the preschool level in
both educational and social welfare streams, the responsibilities of
access services will multiply beyond where they now are. I&R will
remain important but there will need to be a strengthened counseling service and a commitment to between-system neutrality
within these local agencies. (Several that also operate direct services would have clear conflicts of interest.) Parents will be making
major choices for their children and have a right to know what is
involved. We have chosen only two illustrations. There are still
other possible directions as well.

We have looked at school developments in some detail in
Chapter 5 and have concluded that if the United States is to have
enough child care in the future, the schools will need to play a very
large part. Child care should be universally available, and the
public education system is a universal one. Public education has a
more reliable funding base than does the social welfare system. An
education-based development will eliminate the trend toward a
two-tier child care system, with private nursery school or part-day
public preschool for the affluent and social welfare day care (largely
family day care) or Head Start or compensatory preschool for the
poor.

Skeptics doubt that rigid school bureaucracies can mount the types of sensitive, flexible preschool programs in which young children will thrive. Educators, willing to take on part-day prekindergartens, show little interest in the child care possibilities of the development, opponents note. Others doubt whether public school systems, which have been unsuccessful with large cohorts of minority children, should now be given this added responsibility. Given these doubts and the fact that despite the upsurge of interest state investment in preschool and school-age programs remains modest, one can at this time only propose a strong beginning based on state leadership and an exploratory approach. The following would be some of the key elements:

- Creation of separate state and local administrative structures to lead the preschool development and give it a character quite independent from the elementary school system.
- Experimentation with both public preschools operated completely by public education systems and various forms of Head Start, community day care, and proprietary agency alternatives, operating both within and outside of school buildings (as elaborated in Chapter 5).
- Assurance of adequate local school board and parental participation in the planning and implementation of these programs.
- Attention to standards, staff qualifications, and provision for monitoring.

There are significant state beginnings. We are convinced that a new child development institution can emerge, anchored in the schools, to offer services to most 3- to 5-year-olds (or 2½ to 5 eventually). Then, the family day care–center care systems for infants and toddlers will slowly evolve into a more adequate delivery system, anchored in I&R services and supported by parent fees (with tax help) and public subsidy for low-income families. While the prospect may unnerve the social welfare day care system initially, any assessment of the supply/demand picture and of costs and staffing implications suggests that the process will inevitably be gradual, that there will be enough to do, and that the public interest calls for better long-range institution building for child care.

The school-age child care issue is another matter. Before- and after-school programs could be successfully developed in school buildings, churches, community centers, parks, and elsewhere under a diversity of auspices, including school systems, nonprofit social agencies, community groups, religious organizations, youth groups, parent cooperatives, and others. What are needed are some start-up funds, protective standards that are different for different types of programs, and funds to help low-income children in jurisdictions that do not offer free services.

Organized Service Delivery or a Better Functioning Market?

Cross cutting the "education" or "social welfare" question is the issue of whether society, to the extent that it helps families with child care, will subsidize supply or subsidize demand, whether it will organize delivery systems or help consumers to find their way in a system that "just grows." What states do could make the difference.

Until relatively recently the formal public commitment was to provide services. School systems offered kindergartens; social welfare departments funded center care and family day care service and assigned eligible clients to them. Then, with federal aid, both systems operated Head Start, and school systems included programs for the very young among their remedial/compensatory program and special programs for the handicapped. However, during all of this, given the limited public provision or commitment, some parents also made their choices in the marketplace, deciding to spend their money for private nursery schools or child care centers, for in-home care, or for family day care. They paid for their children's participation in after-school educational, cultural, athletic, or other recreational groups. They still do.

The situation began to change when a federal child care tax credit was enacted. Government had elected to subsidize demand and had foregone the option of direct expenditure on specific programs that it had chosen. The process continued with legislation permitting employers to subsidize child care costs of employees, to build centers, and to create flexible spending accounts to be used by employees to meet dependent care costs. These and other tax expenditures are in some sense at least alternatives to direct government program development, and they decrease the need for planning and program choices. Government, of course, may enact regulations that affect how the resources thus freed may be used and may even do things that encourage some bidders for consumer business and discourage others. Government regulates only modestly, however, because the demand strategies are, in fact, intended to maximize consumer sovereignty and to rid government of program development and regulation responsibilities.

There also is a general movement to create extensive tuition tax credits and vouchers in lieu of traditional governmental operation of core educational services, but this is a controversial step and has not gone far.

On the other hand, the public "supply" subsidies for family day care and center care have been expanding as the various states or counties have enacted comprehensive, partial, or experimental vendor/voucher approaches. These approaches have begun to affect the availability of purchase-of-service contracts in some places. Many of the local community groups that we have described are committed to the vendor/voucher approach, and, indeed, several have been organized specifically so as to carry out such innovation. Nonetheless, a general public policy commitment has not been made. Most publicly subsidized child care is still offered under some form of purchase-of-service arrangement, whereby local departments contract with centers for a specific amount of space for children eligible for partial or complete public subsidy.

If the settling of the education–social welfare roles and relationships holds some of the keys to the future of child care, future balance of demand versus supply strategies probably holds the other. Governments do not generally make policy in such abstract terms, but the matter could be partially settled by a political decision responsive to public demand to expand direct, all-day prekindergarten and kindergarten services within the schools as a universal service. Such expansion of education, meant largely to improve learning but also to provide daytime "care," would move the demand-versus-supply policy issue to the field of infant and toddler care only—and perhaps to after-school programming. Then, schools might either operate free universal programs, charge fees, or open their buildings to private groups that would. On the other hand, a "Massachusetts" solution—creating options for the local school district—would result in a mixed system.

Or, if there is not to be a large move in education for the children under age 5, a universal publicly financed system, the issue of vouchers could come to a head. If some families are fully publicly subsidized for child care and some partially, if employers pay the fees of others as fringe benefits, if there are to be income-related sliding fee systems with government or private philanthropy picking up part of the cost, there will be a strong case to maximize the child care option open to all, to avoid a two-tier system separating the subsidized and the unsubsidized. The voucher or a vendor/voucher plan then becomes a very attractive community vehicle. It could share an access system (I&R) to all possible child care services with "full-fee" users who want information and referral (and whose costs may be partially subsidized through child care tax credits and similar demand subsidies, as well).

This kind of development would cast some of the organizations we have described in the role of pioneers and pilots for what would need to become a familiar and available local service. As indicated, a demand-subsidy strategy is premised on consumer sophistication, good information and referral systems, the monitoring and reporting of below-standard service, an alertness to unmet need, and its communication to potential providers. There is now technology, knowledge, philosophy, and practice competence to guide such work. What would be needed at the state level is a superstructure to create larger networks, sustain them, and consolidate what they can learn as windows on the operating system.

The issue to be highlighted might be put another way. Are we heading toward a development under which there will emerge a child care design, insofar as it involves expenditures of public resources and commitment of public power? If there is such a design, will it take the form of a series of defined responsibilities to deliver specific services, assigned to the educational system, and other responsibilities for the social welfare system? Then the issues would be program-specific in education and, probably (given past history), the degree of privatization within social welfare; that is, the question would be, What would government operate and what would it purchase from for-profit and nonprofit programs? Or will there be a continuation of the present semianarchy of competition, gaps, overlap, and unassigned responsibility for coverage? Since affluent consumers will then seek what they need and want in the marketplace, an argument can be made that others, too, should be helped at the demand side. Or perhaps the strategy would be some subsidy of demand and some service provision for deprived consumers, who need more protection, rather than a completely free marketplace.

These may not be the precise choices, and there are alternative scenarios. The point to be conveyed is that the cluster of issues should be faced by those who see some point to the application of analysis and organized intelligence to the choices. Despite the importance of federal tax policy as it shapes these matters, states do have choices to make about their own funds and expenditures of social service block grants. Even as they increase their planning, they may move more heavily toward demand or supply strategies, and these do yield different delivery systems. Absent some planning, they are left completely to the type of political and economic marketplace that now prevails. In such an environment, localities with some of the agencies we have described are indeed somewhat better off, but the situation could be a lot better!

The Future of Family Day Care

Facing the inevitable fact that in-home care by nonrelatives is beyond their financial capacities, and that there is not a satisfactory work force for this assignment in any case, some parents tend to prefer family day care for their infants and toddlers; others find "underground" unlicensed family day care to be more affordable than centers. This much-used type of service provides the vast majority of nonrelative infant-toddler care, as well as a significant amount of before- and after-school care for older children; yet it is largely invisible, said to be generally of poor quality and some-times scandalous, and may even endanger some children. The services need to be licensed or registered (there is debate about which), the homes made to conform to responsible health and safety requirements, and the caretakers examined for health and personal fitness and trained or prepared for their roles. They should have health insurance and liability coverage and be assisted in claiming their tax rights if their homes are used as places of business. Perhaps the providers should be employed and not be regarded as entrepreneurs (see Chapter 7). As we have noted, some of the "systems" organized to conform to the requirements of the federal child care food program have achieved some of these results, but many family day care homes are not eligible.

Some providers may be hiding welfare status, others do not understand legal requirements, and still others shun the bureau-cratic processes. Public strategies fluctuate between simplifying the "coming out" (registration through the mail and no visits unless trouble is reported) and recognizing that meaningless public regu-lation is irresponsible. We have argued the latter position. States will make little progress on the supply or quality issues unless they develop an approach to family day care. The specific issues have been explicated and possible actions outlined.

The Role of Employers

Here state policy makers may need to evolve a point of view and a level of expectations as much as a policy. Much of the encourage-ment to a business must come, as it has been coming, from the

federal level since tax benefits represent the major public leverage. We have concluded, as have many others, that at-the-work-
site child care will be a small part of the future response to need in
this field. The incentives for most employers to operate child care
are few, except in a very tight labor market, and the obstacles and
fears are considerable. Parent-workers resent taking children out
of their neighborhoods for care and subjecting them to the daily
unpleasantness of mass transportation or highway traffic. There are
obvious disadvantages as well to tying one's child care arrangements to one's job. Children get older and employees' needs for
care change over time, leaving employers with an unused facility.
Despite more than five years of federal promotion, encouragement, and even exaggeration, most on-site care is limited to
hospitals, where it has some real advantages, and to a very small
number of firms located near where their work force lives. On the
other hand, firms have found attractive the provision of I&R
services, some education about child care and parenting, and the
inclusion of child care among flexible benefits or other fringe
benefit arrangements.

The community groups we have described have explored the
corporate child care possibilities and counted on them, only to
discover that the above conclusions tend to hold except where
there is a company that wants particularly to make a point as a
community citizen, or where there are special labor market and
residential intertwinings. Beyond this, some corporations moving
into new areas of functioning as responsible citizens have contributed to planning or to a locality's capacity to create child care
resources for all residents.

Our exploration of employer sponsorship of child care suggests
that only major employers will undertake any significant child care
activities. Moreover, even among the most progressive large employers, a child care initiative is unlikely to involve delivering the
service (operating a program directly or contracting for it), nor will
it involve a significant subsidy to employees. Employers may pay
for I&R services, a useful aid in a diversified market but not a
strategy for adding in any significant way to existing supply. Some
employers may also continue to provide salary reduction accounts.
However, these accounts involve employees' money largely, plus a
modest subsidy provided by their tax-exempt status. Apart from
such help, employers are unlikely to do more. With fewer than 20
percent of the labor force as parents of young children (and still less
as employees of large organizations), and only half of these, at
most, interested in child care, employee pressure will be modest.
And given current trends to reduce fringe benefits costs, offering

more benefits seems unlikely. As employers become more sophisticated, however, what they may be more likely to do is to become stronger advocates for local, state, and even federal government services.

Federal and State Leadership

It is difficult to consider what has gone before and to believe that child care can be left completely to the individual family, church, voluntary association or business—despite all that these can and should do. We refer, first, to several clear-cut specifics and conclude with the larger issue of public responsibility.

Protecting Standards. A long effort to enact federal quality and safety standards to apply to child care paid for with federal funds ended in 1981 when the Social Service Block Grant replaced Title XX of the Social Security Act. Programs reverted to state licensing and registration requirements. Those not federally financed did not need to conform to anything but state rules, in any case, and the federal standard-making initiatives had little leverage with family day care in the pre-Reagan era. Some states also exempt some or all church-operated programs from licensing or registration requirements. Most have similar policies with regard to programs operated by education authorities. For the most part but not uniformly, state standards have followed successive federal leads since the 1960s, and most now require less than what years of research and hearings produced by way of new—and never enforced—federal standards in 1981. With federal social service funding cutbacks and the end of federal standards, some states have decreased their own capacities to visit, inspect, and act if standards are violated. In addition, particularly in the family day care field, there has been some tendency deliberately to ease requirements so as to increase supply. Or rules are eased in the face of the state's lack of enforcement capacity (registration to replace licensing, the elimination of home inspections, assigning the certification task to community agencies).

The public decision to place infants, toddlers, and prekindergarteners in the care of others is not easily made. A society that inspects and monitors food, drugs, water, and the environment—and for good reason—surely is obligated to tell parents whether programs operating in a given locale conform to certain standards defined by professional expertise and community preferences. There is an available knowledge base, and it is not beyond the capacity of any state to select and publicize requirements and to enforce them. We would expect this item to be of concern even in states that do not undertake more comprehensive policy planning.

In the interim, a promising system of voluntary center accreditation, developed and tested over several years under the auspices of a professional association, the National Association for the Education of Young Children (NAEYC), has become operational and is attracting many applications. A first group of centers has been accredited. This is not an option for family day care that needs state licensing and inspection. A responsible society would not let this matter be by-passed.

A Database.   Where are the children? State planning has been hampered by lack of data about children, whether they are or are not in care, how it is paid for, what kind of care is used by whom, what is being sought, and so forth. No single state has coped with this problem adequately. Some initiatives and creativity will be needed in those states that take on the serious policy and planning challenge. They cannot manage otherwise.

Some cities, counties, and even subareas have done enough to serve immediate limited purposes; often the data are presented only to argue a case for one action or another, and are quite flimsy at that. A standard state database would serve local planning purposes as well, while making area comparisons possible for state officials who are called upon to allocate scarce resources.

For still other purposes and also to enable states to see themselves in national comparative perspective, it is important that national statistical reporting continue to be improved in this field. Until about a decade ago national data reflected the separation of "educational" from "custodial" or social welfare programs, suffered from definitional confusion, or were not accessible to essential disaggregation. Gradually, Bureau of the Census and Center for Statistics (Department of Education) reporting systems have been improved and brought more in line with one another. The possibilities of other regular surveys and data sets have been recognized; further, and much needed, enrichment and improvement are proposed, but funds are not yet assigned. Backing from the states and interested national professional and academic associations could contribute to the process.

A Work Force.   No discussion of future child care services would be complete without mention of the inadequate salaries now paid caregivers; in addition, there is the discrepancy between the salaries of school "teachers" and center and home "caregivers."[1] Child care typically is a minimum wage job. As a consequence, few who are well trained enter, or remain, in the field. Turnover rates of staff average over 50 percent a year. Obviously, unless salaries and benefits are improved for staff, there will be problems with the quality of the care provided. And yet if salaries are improved, there will be problems with differential access to adequate care or with the costs of care.

This problem can be solved only slowly and with federal and state cooperation. There will need to be training opportunities, licensing requirements, as well as transitional plans which gradually will regard school-based and social welfare-based child care staffs as part of one work force. Anything else distorts planning and administration. The family day care providers, as we indicated in Chapter 7, will be of two types: line workers and better-educated specialists. The former need not be qualified at the level of school-based or center-based personnel but cannot be expected to create and run a reliable system of care if exploited at below minimum wage salaries.

Leadership. For reasons discernible only by students of ideology, the federal government arrived at the mid-1980s without any staff concerned with national child care trends, without capacity for technical assistance to states and localities, without funds to encourage development and dissemination of new knowledge, without evidence of genuine concern for what was occurring. Faced with data about labor force participation of mothers of young children, social service officials said that employers and voluntary efforts could meet the needs. They ignored the numbers and the experience. Small developments were exaggerated. Officials allocated funds for helpful demonstrations, but they approved only proposals that reflected their ideological positions and provided no authentic research opportunities to test alternative and competing theories and models or to disseminate real findings. There were modest sums to train and certify paraprofessional child care staffs ("child development associates"). Only Head Start, favored by the Congress, had federal staffing! Only the Census Bureau and the National Center for Statistics in the Department of Education provided some helpful data, but they lacked funds to follow through with their plans.

One cannot identify any arena in national life with such large ramifications and so little responsible, helpful federal presence. The answer is not "federalism." No matter how wedded one may be to a major state role in service arenas, where a case for variability and diversity can certainly be made, a full retreat of national government from this field is difficult to accept. Washington was better-staffed, more expert, better informed in 1950, 1960, 1970, and 1980 than it is in 1987—yet the need has exploded.

One could list hundreds of areas with far less serious ramifications and fewer citizens concerned, where it is recognized that the market alone or the states, each separately, cannot meet the needs of their citizens. We merely list a few topics, discussed in earlier parts of the volume:

- Subsidy for low-earner families who need child care coverage if they are to work—and who get no or inadequate help from the (federal) tax credit and no fringe benefit consideration.
- Determining and defining minimum standards for child care facilities that are to enjoy federal subsidy or tax considerations.
- Investment in research, demonstrations, innovation to improve content and methods in child care programming and delivery, and the dissemination of findings.
- Start-up funds to help low-income regions or states develop essential delivery system components (I&R, prekindergartens for the 3- and 4-year-olds, licensing systems, after-school care, and so forth).
- Provision of scholarship or training funds to ensure the preparation of a work force for this low-salary field. Exploration and development of ways to upgrade salaries and work conditions of the lowest paid center and family day care personnel.
- Maintenance of a capacity for technical assistance and exchange to assist states and localities ready to do their part.

We stress that we see child care as essentially a decentralized and diversified delivery system and note that we have underlined the urgency of developing state capacity for policy development, leadership, and administration. This process will thrive only if the federal government gives it support and backing, doing as well those things that states have a right to expect from Washington.

Nor should citizens and their children accept any less. Child care is neither a luxury nor a sometime thing for a few problem families. It is a central component of family and community life in a modern society. Government, too, has a role in facilitating its sound development.

Accelerating the Action

We see the policy perspective here outlined as covering perhaps a half-decade of new initiatives followed by an equal period for implementation. For those who are involved in state and federal action, we list the following priority recommendations, addressed to circumstances that prevail as this book goes to press:

A Major Expansion of Public Preschools for the 3- and 4-Year-Olds, Based on State Initiative, with Possible Federal Funding Support. As indicated, this is the most promising vehicle for rapid expansion of child care for preschoolers, universal like public elementary school, and funded in the same way as local public education. Our rationale has been spelled out. There should be separate administrative control of these programs to ensure that operationally they look like the best of current day care, private nurseries, and public preschools. Some states have begun. New York City has. The National Conference of Governors has moved toward the concept in its resolutions, but as yet committed itself only to compensatory and part-day programs. If "education" is traditionally a state/local responsibility, the federal government has historically committed itself to supporting child care that enables parents to work—thus the rationale for joint federal/state financing. A federal 50 percent matching block grant, based on some core quality and access standards, is a reasonable goal.

In the meantime there is good reason for the states to experiment, build, develop capacity, and move as state and local funding permits. It is urgent that ways be found to engage the support of education, social welfare day care, and Head Start professionals and advocates. We have reported on the Massachusetts, California, and New York discussions and provisions.

State Action on School-Age Child Care. Both politically and from a cost perspective, this is an important initiative; a modest investment will affect large numbers of children because per capita costs are low. Many nursery school and kindergarten classes are part-day. Many 6- to 10-year-olds lack care before and after school and on school holidays and need it whatever the debates about self-care for those age 11 and over. There is an enormous public investment in school buildings that are not used afternoons, evenings, holidays, weekends, and summers. Token federal start-up funds were made available in 1986. A few states have made good beginnings on their own. Dozens of local communities offer exemplary programs. There can be experimentation with many forms of programming and administrative sponsorship (schools, community groups, day care centers, parent cooperatives, social agencies, and so forth). This clearly is an area for immediate state action, and the expenditure could be modest. If poor children are to be served, states will need to vote more than start-up funds.

Adequate Federal and State Financial Support for Child Care for Low-Income Families and the Poor. If single mothers or two parents are to work, children need good care. Parents cannot manage full costs except at very high income levels. There is a middle level at which tax credits similar to those now in place offer adequate help. At a lower income level, "tapered" or "sliding" fees are essential. (There is need for a commission to set these amounts and for them to be legislatively indexed.) All this will be feasible for the states only if more adequate federal funds (social services block grant, employment programs, refugee programs, child welfare, and so forth) become available—preferably restoring earlier state-match requirements.

In short, if school-based programs become free and universal, the supplementary after-school programs, as well as infant and toddler services, can and should expect parent cost-sharing by those who can afford it and complete or tapered public participation where parent incomes are low. (This principle should hold for preschoolers, too, until universal and free programs are accepted as public policy.) Immediate action to establish a reliable funding stream is an extremely important part of any child care agenda. Both federal and state governments have a stake in services that support labor market, welfare, and protective policies, and they have traditionally contributed toward social service funds for these purposes.

State Action to Define Standards and Protections in Family Day Care and Center Child Care and, Where Needed, the Development of Capacity to Implement Such Standards and Protections. This recommendation need not be elaborated. We do not believe that the society should increase out-of-home care without assuring itself and the parents involved that children are exposed to wholesome experiences and reasonably protected. Marketplace dynamics and parent-consumer education are not sufficient. Federal and state money should not be spent where there are no protections. The federal government should offer both technical assistance and research support, but any state could act at once.

Federal or State Actions to Ensure Paid, Job-Protected Disability and Parenting Leaves. Too many newborn infants enter into out-of-home care before they and their parents have had a good start together. Too many parents are unable to remain home for a while after child birth, for lack of income or job protection. Only 40 percent of women in the labor force currently have even modest coverage from disability insurance allowing six to eight to ten weeks of partial income replacement. As a result, the United States requires and uses too much out-of-home care for very young infants.

Any national infant care policy must take note of the half of all married mothers who are in the workforce by the time their baby is one year old. A consensus is emerging that one essential component of an infant care policy must be provision of a paid, job-protected disability and parenting leave to cover at least 4 months (and preferably 6 months) at the time of childbirth or adoption. More than 100 countries around the world, including many among the developing countries, provide a paid, job-protected maternity leave. Working women in the European countries typically are entitled to a 5- to 6-month paid leave and an additional one year unpaid but job-protected *parental* leave. Fathers are increasingly entitled to some part of the paid leave in many of these countries as well as sharing the right to an unpaid leave in most. This is an essential policy if we are concerned about good child development and about protecting the economic security of families with children. Such a policy could be established by federal law; but if none is forthcoming, as a beginning, states could follow the lead of the five states now providing temporary disability insurance (TDI). Under the federal Pregnancy Discrimination Act (1978), this leave must cover what is called "maternity disability." All states, including those that now have TDI programs, could add to this a law requiring job and benefit protection while out on disability leaves, also.[2]

As the reader will recognize, we have suggested much more in this final chapter. These items, however, offer focus and state some priorities.

Endnotes

1. This is a large subject which we have not explored in detail in this volume. For an illustration of salary discrepancies, see Caroline Zinssner, *A Study of New York Day Care Worker Salaries and Benefits* (New York: Center for Public Advocacy Research, 1986). Specific recommendations appear in Caroline Zinssner, *Day Care's Unfair Burden* (New York: Center for Public Advocacy Research, 1986).
2. For background, see Sheila B. Kamerman, Alfred J. Kahn, and Paul Kingston, *Maternity Policies and Working Women* (New York: Columbia University Press, 1983). There were congressional hearings in 1986. Legislation was proposed, but not passed, in the House.

INDEX